VITAL
CHRISTIAN LIVING
ISSUES

THE VITAL ISSUES SERIES

VITAL ISSUES SERIES

VITAL CHRISTIAN LIVING ISSUES

*Examining Crucial Concerns
in the Spiritual Life*

ROY B. ZUCK
GENERAL EDITOR

kregel
RESOURCES

Grand Rapids, MI 49501

Vital Christian Living Issues: Examining Crucial Concerns in the Spiritual Life by Roy B. Zuck, general editor

Copyright © 1997 by Dallas Theological Seminary

Published by Kregel Resources, an imprint of Kregel Publications, P.O. Box 2607, Grand Rapids, MI 49501. Kregel Resources provides timely and relevant resources for Christian life and service. Your comments and suggestions are valued.

For more information about Kregel Publications, visit our web site at http://www.kregel.com.

Cover design: Sarah Slattery
Book design: Alan G. Hartman

Library of Congress Cataloging-in-Publication Data
Roy B. Zuck.
Vital Christian living issues: examining crucial concerns in the spiritual life / Roy B. Zuck, gen. ed.
    p.   cm. (Vital Issues Series; v. 9)
1. Christian life. I. Zuck, Roy B. II. Bibliotheca sacra. III. Series.
BV4501.2.V554   1997   248—dc21   97-7364
                                  CIP

ISBN 0-8254-4097-1

Printed in the United States of America

1 2 3 / 03 02 01 00 99 98 97

Contents

Contributors

Lewis Sperry Chafer
Late Founder, President, and Professor of Systematic Theology, Dallas Theological Seminary, Dallas, Texas

Kenneth O. Gangel
Vice-president for Academic Affairs, Academic Dean, and Distinguished Professor of Christian Education, Dallas Theological Seminary, Dallas, Texas

Michael P. Green
Associate Professor, Moody Graduate School, Chicago, Illinois

John D. Hannah
Chairman and Professor of Historical Theology, Dallas Theological Seminary, Dallas, Texas

D. Edmond Hiebert
Late Professor Emeritus of New Testament, Mennonite Brethren Biblical Seminary, Fresno, California

Zane C. Hodges
Partner and Editorial Director, Redençion Viva Publishers, Dallas, Texas

H. Wayne House
Academic Dean and Professor of Theology, Michigan Theological Seminary, Ann Arbor, Michigan

S. Lewis Johnson Jr.
Professor Emeritus of New Testament Studies, Dallas Theological Seminary, Dallas, Texas

Allen P. Ross
Professor of Old Testament Studies, Trinity Episcopal School for Ministry, Ambridge, Pennsylvania

Charles C. Ryrie
  Professor of Systematic Theology, Emeritus, Dallas
  Theological Seminary, Dallas, Texas

Robert L. Saucy
  Distinguished Professor of Systematic Theology, Talbot
  School of Theology, La Mirada, California

James R. Slaughter
  Professor of Christian Education, Dallas Theological
  Seminary, Dallas, Texas

Richard L. Strauss
  Late Senior Pastor, Emmanuel Faith Community Church,
  Escondido, California

John F. Walvoord
  Chancellor, Minister-at-Large, and Professor of Systematic
  Theology, Emeritus, Dallas Theological Seminary, Dallas,
  Texas

Kenneth S. Wuest
  Late Faculty Member, Moody Bible Institute, Chicago,
  Illinois

Preface

lost	saved
enslaved	redeemed
ungodly	justified
enemies of God	children of God
dead	regenerated
in sin	in Christ
under God's wrath	under God's grace
condemned	freed
eternal death	eternal life

These contrasts between non-Christians and Christians highlight some of the many stunning changes wrought by the Holy Spirit the moment a person trusts Christ as his or her Savior.

But then what? How does a newborn live the Christian life? What does God expect of His children? Though forgiven of their sins, how can Christians deal with and overcome the temptations of the world, the sin nature, and the Devil?

This volume addresses these and many related questions—questions faced by every believer who sincerely desires to please God and to be more Christlike.

The Bible's many epithets for Christians point out the multifaceted nature of living for Christ. Saints, soldiers, vine branches, laborers, ambassadors, learners, servants, heirs, and builders—each figure comprises a significant aspect of the spiritual life.

In walking with Christ, God's children are to be prayers, worshipers, and crossbearers. They are to exercise spiritual gifts to the benefit of others. They are to obey the Lord's commands, while living in anticipation of the Lord's return at any time.

May this volume's articles, chosen from past issues of *Bibliotheca Sacra,* help guide you in your Christian walk as you seek to "please him in every way" (Col. 1:10 NIV).

ROY B. ZUCK

9

About *Bibliotheca Sacra*

A flood is rampant—an engulfing deluge of literature far beyond any one person's ability to read it all. Presses continue to churn out thousands of journals and magazines like a roiling, raging river.

Among these numberless publications, one stands tall and singular—*Bibliotheca Sacra*—a strange name (meaning "Sacred Library") but a journal familiar to many pastors, teachers, and Bible students.

How is *Bibliotheca Sacra* unique in the world of publishing? By being the oldest continuously published journal in the Western Hemisphere—1993 marked its 150th anniversary—and by being published by one school for more than six decades—1994 marked the diamond anniversary of its release by Dallas Seminary.

Bib Sac, to use its shortened sobriquet, was founded in New York City in 1843 and was purchased by Dallas Theological Seminary in 1934, ten years after the school's founding. The quarterly's 153-year history boasts only nine editors. Through those years it has maintained a vibrant stance of biblical conservatism and a strong commitment to the Scriptures as God's infallible Word.

Each volume in the Kregel *Vital Issues Series* includes carefully selected articles from the 1930s to the present—articles of enduring quality, articles by leading evangelicals whose topics are as relevant today as when they were first produced. The chapters have been edited slightly to provide conformity of style. We trust these anthologies will enrich the spiritual lives and Christian ministries of many more readers.

ROY B. ZUCK, EDITOR
Bibliotheca Sacra

For *Bibliotheca Sacra* subscription information, call Dallas Seminary, 1-800-992-0998.

CHAPTER 1

What Is Spirituality?

Charles C. Ryrie

Oddly enough, the concept of spirituality, though the subject of much preaching, writing, and discussion, is seldom defined. Usually anything that approaches a definition will be in the nature of a description of the characteristics of spirituality, but one searches in vain in literature for a concise definition of the concept itself. The reason for this is that the concept includes several factors, and it is not easy to weave these together into a balanced definition. Too, the only verse in the Bible that approaches a definition is rather difficult to interpret: "But he who is spiritual appraises all things" (1 Cor. 2:15). So it is avoided. Nevertheless it is important to try to formulate a definition, for this is like a cornerstone that determines the shape of an entire building.

The Concept of Spirituality

Genuine spirituality involves three factors. The first is regeneration. No one can be spiritual in the biblical sense without having first experienced the new life that is freely given to all who believe in the Lord Jesus Christ as their personal Savior.

Second, the Holy Spirit is preeminently involved in producing spirituality. This is not to say that the other persons of the Godhead do not have their particular work in this, or that the believer has no personal responsibility, or that there are not other means of grace, but it is to affirm His major role in spirituality. The ministries of the Spirit involve teaching (John 16:12–15), guiding (Rom. 8:14), assuring (Rom. 8:16), praying (Rom. 8:26), the exercise of spiritual gifts (1 Cor. 12:7), and warring against the flesh (Gal. 5:17)—and all these depend on the filling of the Spirit for their full manifestation (Eph. 5:18).

To be filled with the Spirit means to be controlled by the Spirit. The clue to this definition is found in Ephesians 5:18, which contrasts and compares drunkenness and Spirit-filling. The comparison gives the clue, for just as a drunk person is controlled by the liquor consumed, so a Spirit-filled Christian is controlled by the Spirit. This causes him to act in ways that are unnatural to him. This is not to imply that such ways will be erratic or abnormal, but that they will not be the ways of the old life. Control by the Spirit is a necessary part of spirituality.

The third factor involved in spirituality is time. If the spiritual person appraises (i.e., judges, examines, or discerns) all things (1 Cor. 2:15), this must involve time to gain knowledge and acquire experience for such discerning. The Amplified Bible elaborates on the verse this way: "He can read the meaning of everything, but no one can properly discern or appraise or get an insight into him." This could not be accomplished overnight; it is true only of a mature Christian.

The word *maturity* gives the key to the concept of spirituality, for Christian maturity is the growth the Holy Spirit produces over a period of time in the believer. The same amount of time is not required for each individual, but some time is necessary for all. The time itself does not determine maturity; rather the progress made and growth achieved is what is important. Maturity may be acquired in a shorter time if the rate of growth is accelerated. And it will be accelerated as the believer is controlled not by self but by the Holy Spirit.

Here is a proposed definition of spirituality that is concise and at the same time keeps these factors in mind: *Spirituality is a mature and maturing relationship to the Holy Spirit.* While this may simply be another way of saying that spirituality is Christian maturity, this definition seeks to recognize the element of Spirit-control over a period of time. Certainly the definition satisfies the requirements of the description of a spiritual person in 1 Corinthians 2:15, for one who is experiencing a grown-up relationship to the Holy Spirit will be able to discern all things (i.e., have spiritual insight) and at the same time may not be understood by others.

Certain ramifications of this concept need to be considered.

A new Christian cannot be called spiritual. He has not had sufficient time to grow and develop in Christian knowledge and experience. A new believer can be Spirit-controlled, but the area of control is subject to expansion in the normal process of Christian growth. A young Christian has not yet been confronted with many areas within the general sphere of Christian conduct; for instance, while he may be completely willing to let the Spirit control his life and actions, he has not yet gained the experience and maturity that comes from having faced those problems and having made Spirit-controlled decisions about them. When he is first saved, he may not even know there is such a person as a "weaker brother," and, although he may not be unwilling to curb his liberty for the sake of that individual, he has not yet faced the doing of it, to say nothing of having guided others into right decisions about such matters. Spirit-control may be total over the new Christian's life insofar as he has knowledge of that life in his newborn state, but as his knowledge increases and his growth progresses, new vistas of life break on him that must also be consciously yielded to God's direction. Time to gain maturity is needed for genuine spirituality.

A Christian of longer standing, however, is not necessarily spiritual. This is because he has not allowed the Holy Spirit to control him. Whereas the new Christian may lack the time required to become spiritual, the believer of longer standing may be deficient in yieldedness. And without complete and continued control by the Spirit he cannot be spiritual. This, of course, was the burden of the writer of the Epistle to the Hebrews, for his readers were in this exact condition.

A Christian may backslide in certain areas of his life without losing all the ground he has gained during his Christian lifetime. The flesh may control his actions during a period of backsliding, but when he comes back to the Lord he does not necessarily have to start the process of growth all over again. For example, a believer may backslide with regard to personal Bible study, but when he comes back to it he will not have forgotten everything he formerly knew. However, this principle does not apply in every area of life, for there are some aspects of living, such as fidelity in marriage, which if violated can never be fully redeemed. The sin can be forgiven and fellowship restored, but the ground lost cannot be recovered.

Stages of growth occur within the area of maturity. This is like physical and emotional growth; even in adulthood the individual continues to grow, develop, and mature. The believer who is experiencing a grown-up relationship to the Holy Spirit is not stagnant in his Christian life, for he also has a growing relationship in his walk with the Lord. Christians never arrive at perfection in this life; it is also true that they never ascend to a plateau above and beyond which there is no further ground to gain. Spirituality, then, is a mature and growing relationship to the Spirit.

The state of babyhood need not last long. No one should seek to take refuge in a fraudulent kind of piety that demeans or ignores the processes of growth that have advanced him to a state of maturity. False humility is sometimes the reason for such lack of recognition of maturity that has actually been achieved. After all, when Paul wrote 1 Corinthians those believers were about four or five years old in the faith, and he expected them to be spiritual by that time. He made it clear that, although when he was with them he could not speak to them as spiritual people (for they were then babes in Christ), he fully anticipated that by the time he wrote this letter to them they would have matured to the point where he could address them as spiritual believers (1 Cor. 3:1–2). With the passing of only a few years, babyhood should also disappear.

The Characteristics of Spirituality

Spirituality is more easily characterized than defined. And these biblical characteristics of spirituality are tests by which one may determine whether one is spiritual.

SPIRITUALITY WILL BE SEEN IN ONE'S CHARACTER

Because spirituality involves control by the Spirit (Eph. 5:18) and because the Spirit has come to glorify Christ (John 16:14), a spiritual person will manifest Christ in his character and actions. "To glorify" is to show, display, or manifest. The evidence that the Holy Spirit is in control of a life is not found in manifestations of the Spirit but in the display of Christ. The fruit of the Spirit (Gal. 5:22–23) is a perfect description of the character of Christ; thus the Christian who is spiritual will display love, joy, peace, long-suffering, gentleness, goodness, faithfulness, meekness, and self-control. These are the traits that will describe his character.

In his conduct a spiritual believer will imitate Christ. Some victorious-life teachings wrongly demean this aspect of the truth. Believers are told not to imitate Christ since this involves striving, which is a work of the flesh; rather, believers are told simply to allow Christ to live out His life through them. Actually it is not a question of one view or the other; both ideas are scriptural. Christ lives in each believer, and the life each believer lives is by faith in the Son of God (Gal. 2:20), but each believer is also exhorted to "follow in His steps" (1 Peter 2:21) and to walk as He walked

(1 John 2:6). Obviously if the Holy Spirit is allowed to produce the character of Christ in an individual, the life he lives will imitate Christ. One of the most rewarding studies in the Gospels is to note the qualities of Jesus' life that His followers would do well to imitate.

SPIRITUALITY WILL BE SEEN IN ONE'S KNOWLEDGE

The strong meat of the Word of God belongs to mature Christians (Heb. 5:14), and Paul expected the Corinthians after four or five years of Christian experience to be able to understand strong meat of the Word. Because the milk of the Word is for spiritual babies, Paul did not scold the Corinthians for feeding on milk when they were first converted. But when their diet continued to consist only of milk, he, like the writer of the Epistle to the Hebrews, denounced them as defective Christians. What is "meat" truth? Of course, the Bible does not label passages *milk* or *meat* so it is not easy to answer that question. However, one subject is clearly designated meat, and that is the subject that reminded the writer to the Hebrews of his readers' inability to understand what he was writing about. And that subject is the truth about Melchizedek and his priesthood (Heb. 5:10–11). Here is an example from the Bible itself of the meat of the Word, and it may rightly be used as a test of one's spirituality.

SPIRITUALITY WILL BE SEEN IN ONE'S ATTITUDES

A spiritual Christian will exhibit at least two attitudes throughout life. The first is thankfulness. Paul's words, "Always giving thanks for all things in the name of our Lord Jesus Christ to God, even the Father" (Eph. 5:20), follow the command to be filled with the Spirit (Eph. 5:18) and is thereby one of the characteristics of a Spirit-filled life. It is to be an all-inclusive attitude in the life of the believer. It should apply at all times ("always") and in all situations ("for all things"). No time and no circumstance is excepted. This means that grumbling, carping criticism, discontentment will not characterize a spiritual Christian. This does not mean one can never be discontent in the proper exercise of godly ambition nor that one should never criticize in the sense of exercising discernment (Phil. 1:9–10). But the kind of attitude that blames God for what one does not like or that is disturbed with His dealings with the believer is not a characteristic of genuine spirituality.

The other attitude that characterizes the spiritual Christian is that of "being diligent to preserve the unity of the Spirit in the bond of peace" (Eph. 4:3). This is not entirely a positional matter; that is, it relates to more than the unity within the body of Christ that the Holy Spirit has brought about by baptizing every believer into that body (1 Cor. 12:13). It is true that Christians could never make such unity, but they are exhorted to seek to keep it. The very fact that the word "preserve" is used shows that the unity has been made by the Spirit, but the fact that there is also an exhortation shows that one must not disrupt that unity. Obviously there is no problem in keeping unity with members of the body of Christ who have predeceased a believer, nor is there any difficulty in maintaining unity with Christians whom one does not know or with whom one has no contact. Therefore the only sphere in which this exhortation has any relevance is the group of believers with whom one is in contact. And of course there are many practical problems in trying to keep the unity of the Spirit among believers one knows. But, difficult as this may be, it is a requirement of spirituality.

The lack of this attitude called forth Paul's scathing denunciation of the Corinthians (1 Cor. 3:1–7; cf. 1:12–13). Disunity had developed among believers who should have been worshiping together. Actually, there were four groups in Corinth (1:12). The Paul Party was perhaps a large group in the church who had been converted under Paul and who continued to follow him. But as is often the case, they seemed disposed to be more Pauline than Paul was and to disparage other gifted people, which resulted in their detracting from the glory of Christ. The Apollos Party (Acts 18:24–28) also contained some personal converts as well as those who had been won over by Apollos's genial manner and eloquent preaching. Some may have followed him because they considered his teaching more advanced than Paul's plain Gospel preaching or they were attracted to his more cultured manner. The Peter Party would undoubtedly have been composed of conservative Jewish believers who rallied to the hero of Pentecost. The Christ Party was perhaps the most difficult to get along with, for those in this group prided themselves on being His followers, not any mere human's disciples. They were Gnostics before Gnosticism, and they unquestionably strutted their supposed spiritual superiority before all.

This is the kind of situation, attitude, and activity Paul

unhesitatingly labeled "fleshly" (1 Cor. 3:3; carnal, KJV), for it broke the unity of the Spirit.

However, this is an area in which there needs to be carefully balanced thinking, for all division is not necessarily wrong, and all unions as such are not right. In the same epistle (11:19) Paul said, "For there must also be factions [heresies, KJV] among you, in order that those who are approved may have become evident among you." The noun *heretic* is used one time in the New Testament (Titus 3:10), but the adjective is used twice (here and Gal. 5:20 where the action is condemned as a work of the flesh). The word means a willful choosing for oneself, which results in division. Even though heresy is a work of the flesh often performed by a carnal Christian, it may be used for good so that those who are not involved in heresy will stand out in the churches. But heresy seems to involve the espousal of error that in turn causes the division. In such instances the heretic is to be admonished twice, then ignored (Titus 3:11), while the part of the divided group that did not follow the error goes on demonstrating its purity of doctrine by abounding in the work of the Lord. Putting 1 Corinthians 3:1–5 and 11:19 together, one may say that divisions involving heresy may be good and necessary, but divisions over personalities are carnal.

Thankfulness at all times and in all circumstances and the maintenance of unity in that part of the body of Christ of which each believer is a part are two basic attitudes of life that must characterize genuine biblical spirituality.

SPIRITUALITY WILL BE SEEN IN ONE'S CONDUCT

Spirituality is also demonstrated by proper conduct, which results from the correct, discerning, and mature use of knowledge (Heb. 5:13–14). As already noted, knowledge of the Word including meat truth is a prerequisite for spirituality, but such knowledge must be used properly in order for a believer to be spiritual. The readers of the Epistle to the Hebrews were unskillful in the word of righteousness (Heb. 5:13), that is, the word concerning uprightness in both doctrine and practice. As a result, they were unable to discern between good and evil (5:14). This should not be limited to things morally good or evil; it includes things superior versus things inferior, things better versus those that are best. A spiritual Christian will be able to tread the way carefully through the complexities of Christian living so as to not only do what is right but also what is useful and for the good of others.

The matter of time in maturity or spirituality is also noted in this passage. These people had had time to use and to exercise their spiritual senses but they had not done so. Time is required to reach this state and achieve the ability to use God's Word skillfully.

SPIRITUALITY WILL BE SEEN IN ONE'S HOME

The easiest place in which to be spiritual is in public, the most difficult is at home. The relationships of the home are intimate and continuous, while activities and impressions made in public are intermittent and casual. This axiomatic reminder is especially necessary for Christian workers, who too often make a show of professional spirituality in public ministry while living a carnal life at home.

Again the Ephesian passage concerning the filling of the Spirit (Eph. 5:18–21) provides the biblical basis for this characteristic of spirituality. The command to be filled with the Spirit (5:18) is followed by four coordinate phrases, each of which begins with a participle. Together they constitute results or characteristics of the Spirit-filled life. The four participles are speaking, singing (5:19), giving thanks (5:20), and submitting (5:21 KJV), and the last (submitting) is not only the conclusion to verses 18–21 but it also introduces what follows beginning in verse 22. In other words, submission, an evidence of the filling of the Spirit, will be seen most vividly in the relationships in one's home.

The word *submit* means to place oneself in a subordinate rank. This means distinctive things for the husband and for the wife in the home, but both are to be submissive to one another (not just the wife to the husband, as is commonly taught). For the husband, at least three things are involved. First, he is to lead, for he is the head of the wife (Eph. 5:23). This makes him not a dictator but a responsible leader of the family. Second, he is to love his wife (5:25). A man needs this reminder, for he may be prone to be less demonstrative if not less loving than a woman. Third, he is to nurture his wife (5:29). The word translated "nourishes" means "to bring to maturity" and is used in the New Testament in this verse and in Ephesians 6:4 only. The word *cherishes* means "to warm" and in the New Testament it is used only here and in 1 Thessalonians 2:7. The point is simply that the husband is ultimately responsible for helping bring his wife and family to spiritual maturity. Unfortunately the opposite is often the case. Too often the wife is the one who is spiritually astute and who is forced, so to speak, to pull her husband along. Both should be spiritually keen, and it is the husband's responsibility to take the leadership in this most important matter.

The spiritual wife will be subject to the leadership of her husband (Eph. 5:22, 24). In other words she will not work at cross-purposes with her husband's leadership in the family. This does not mean she has no voice, for the husband is a presiding officer over the members of the family (1 Tim. 3:4).

SPIRITUALITY WILL BE SEEN IN ONE'S CHURCH

The other principal area in which personal spirituality will be demonstrated is the church. As already noted, a spiritual person will seek to keep the unity of the Spirit in the sphere with which he is chiefly concerned—his own local church.

The positive contribution a spiritual Christian brings to the church is through the exercise of his spiritual gifts. The immature Christian promotes division; the mature one, unity through the use of his gifts (1 Cor. 12:25). Obviously a church member who is always creating problems and who constantly demands being catered to is not a genuinely spiritual person. But the one who is serving the Lord by promoting the welfare of his local church is evidencing a mature spiritual life. Accusing the believers is the work of the Devil (Rev. 12:10); caring for the believers is the work of the Lord through His mature children.

Genuine and wholesome spirituality, then, reflects a mature and maturing relationship to the Holy Spirit, which is demonstrated in one's personal life. This is biblical spirituality.

CHAPTER 2

The Specific Character of the Christian's Sin

Lewis Sperry Chafer

No aspect of the biblical doctrine of sin is more extensive or vitally important than that which contemplates the Christian's sin; yet systematic theology, as set forth in its written standard works and as taught in seminaries generally, often does not recognize this feature of the doctrine. The loss to the theological student is beyond calculation, for when graduated and ordained to the ministry of God's Word he is at once constituted a doctor of souls and the majority of those to whom he ministers will be Christians who are suffering from some spiritual injury that sin has inflicted on them. Indeed, what Christian, waging, as all Christians do, a simultaneous battle on three fronts—the world, the flesh, and the Devil—is not often, if not almost constantly, in a state of spiritual injury?

The soul doctor himself does not escape this conflict, and sad indeed is his plight if he is so ignorant of the essential truths regarding the Christian's sin and its divinely provided cure that he cannot diagnose even his own case or apply the healing to his own stricken heart! Though the pastor is a doctor of souls, his first responsibility to others is so to teach the members of his flock with regard to the whole subject of sin as related to the Christian that they may themselves be able to diagnose their own troubles and apply the divine cure intelligently to their own hearts. The Bible proposes no intermeddling human priest or Romish confessional for the child of God. It does propose an instructed pastor and teacher and a worthy ministry on his part in that field of truth that concerns the spiritual progress, power, prayer, and potency of those of God's redeemed ones who are committed to his spiritual care. The blight of sin on Christian experience and service is tragic, but how much more so when pastor and people alike are ignorant of the most elementary features of the well-defined and divinely revealed steps to be taken in its cure by the Christians who are injured by sin.

The Christian's Sin

Because of its unlikeness to God, sin is always equally sinful and condemnable whether it is committed by the saved or the unsaved, nor is anything provided in either case for its cure other than the all-sufficient blood of Christ. Unregenerate people "have redemption" through the blood of Christ; that is, the blood has been shed and its saving, transforming application awaits faith's appropriation. Over against this, Christians are told that "if we walk in the light, as He Himself is in the light, we have fellowship with one another, and the blood of Jesus His Son cleanses us from all sin" (1 John 1:7). Most significant is the use here of the present tense. It is while the Christian is walking in the light that he has both fellowship (fellowship that is with the Father and His Son, v. 3) and perpetual cleansing by the blood of Christ. The cleansing, it is evident, depends on the fellowship rather than on the holy walk, being wrought by Jesus' blood itself as the actual objective cause, once for all, of the believer's purification. However, while sin is always exceedingly sinful and its cure is by the blood of Christ alone, the divine reckoning and consequent method of remedial dealing with the Christian's sin, because of his relationship to God, is far different from the divine reckoning and remedial dealing with the sin of unregenerate persons who sustain no such relationship to God.

The divine forgiveness of sin for the unregenerate is available only as it is included in the sum total of all that enters into their salvation. At least thirty-three divine undertakings are wrought simultaneously and instantaneously at the moment an individual is saved, and this marvelous achievement represents the measureless difference between those who are saved and those who are not. Deeply in error and dishonoring to God are those current definitions that represent the Christian as different merely in his ideals, his manner or life, or his outward relationships, when in reality he is a new creation in Christ Jesus. His new headship-standing being in Christ, every change that is needed has been wrought to conform him to his new positions and possessions. Forgiveness, then, in its positional aspect (Col. 2:13), is final and complete, and of the Christian thus forgiven it may be said, "There is therefore now no condemnation for those who are in Christ Jesus" (Rom. 8:1); however, this is but a part of all that God accomplished in his salvation. Unregenerate individuals are not encouraged to seek the forgiveness of sin alone or any other individual feature of saving grace. If they secure forgiveness, it must come to them as a part of and included in the whole divine undertaking. *Forgiveness of sin* and *salvation* are not synonymous terms. On the other hand, when sin has entered into the life of a Christian, the sin question alone is involved. The remaining features of his salvation are unchanged. Thus the terms of cure that are divinely imposed respectively on these two groups must be different, as indeed they are.

The difference between the divine method of dealing with the sins of the regenerate in contrast to the divine method of dealing with the sins of unsaved members of the human family is a major distinction in doctrine, which if confused cannot result in anything short of spiritual tragedy for all concerned. The preaching of the Arminian notion that, having sinned, the Christian must be saved again, has wrought untold injury to uncounted millions, but an even greater disaster has been wrought by the careless and misguided preaching to unregenerate people of repentance as a divine requirement separate from believing, confession of sin as an essential to salvation, and reformation of the daily life as the ground on which a right relationship to God may be secured.

The Scriptures distinguish with great clarity the divine method of dealing with the sins of these two classes of individuals. First John 2:2 reads, "And He Himself is the propitiation for our sins; and not for ours only, but also for those of the whole world." Without question, the passage sets up a vital contrast between "our sins," which could not refer to those of the mass of unregenerate human beings, and "the sins of the whole world," which classification certainly includes more than the sins of the regenerate portion of humanity, unless language is strained beyond measure in the interests of a theory. This passage is a great revelation to the unregenerate. Because of Christ's death, God is now propitious toward them. But who can measure the comfort to the crushed and bleeding heart of a Christian when he discovers that already the very sin so much deplored has been borne by Christ and that, on the most righteous basis, the Father is now propitious toward the suffering saint—a propitiation so real and true that the Father's arms are outstretched to welcome the returning Christian who, like the prodigal son, makes unreserved confession of his sin? It will be remembered that, according to the infinite accuracy of the Scriptures, the prodigal was kissed by the father even before any confession was made. Thus it is disclosed that the

Father is propitious toward His sinning child even before that child can be supposed to have merited anything either by repentance, restitution, or confession. How persistent is the false notion that God's heart must be softened by one's tears! And yet how marvelous is the assurance that He is already the propitiation for the sins of the one who believes and is regenerated by the Spirit of God.

The first five chapters of the epistle to the Romans present the fact of the unregenerate world's position before God and set forth the ground of the Gospel of God's saving grace. Chapters 6 through 8 are addressed to believers and have to do with the problem of a holy walk and the divine provisions for it. The sin problem as it concerns the believer is not in view in the first five chapters of Romans, nor is any phase of salvation as it concerns unbelievers to be found in Romans 6–8. Similarly, the hortatory portions of all the epistles are addressed to those who are saved. They could not be addressed to the unsaved since the issue between God and them is not one of an improved manner of life; it is rather the reception of the gift of eternal life, which gift is conditioned not on any manner of works or human merit but on saving faith in Christ alone.

Similarly the deeper meaning of 1 John 3:4–10 is properly understood only when a distinction between the sins of the regenerate and the unregenerate is kept in mind. Possibly no other passage of Scripture contributes more to the present theme than this. Also few portions of Scripture have been subject to more varied interpretations. The passage sets up a distinction between sin, with its source in Satan, and righteousness (in conduct—not conduct that generates righteousness as a ground of standing before God but conduct that is prompted to deeds of rectitude because of the perfect standing in the divine righteousness imputed to all who believe), with its source in God.

Probably the key statement in this context is "sin is lawlessness" (v. 4) in which the force of "is" amounts to "is equivalent to." Sin began with Satan in heaven; he thus became the father or originator of it, and sin, in its essential character, is a lawless departure from the purpose and will of God. The passage under present consideration is in accord with the most distinctive characteristic of sin, namely, lawlessness. The apostle John included here all sin, not some sin. If the interpretation were permitted that only some sins were in view, there would be provided a supposed explanation of the strong statements that follow in the context. Roman Catholic theology distinguishes here between mortal and venial sins. Augustine, Luther, and Bede, in harmony with the tenor of the epistle, sought to restrict this form of sin to sin against brotherly love. Others have restricted it to deadly sin. However, the passage is clear in its declaration. It most evidently refers to all sin, and the passage clearly asserts that the essential character of sin (as the Greek ἁμαρτία implies) is lawlessness—lawlessness, indeed, that is foreign to the Christian's redemption, new birth by the Spirit, and present position in Christ. In verse 5, "And you know that He appeared in order to take away sins; and in Him there is no sin," the apostle referred parenthetically to the ground of all saving grace. The unqualified declaration of verse 6, "No one who abides in Him sins; no one who sins has seen Him or knows Him," need not be softened by any modifications. When abiding in Him, lawless sinning is excluded. Over against this, the lawless sinner neither sees Christ nor knows Christ. Some have introduced here the notion that the Christian's vision and understanding is dulled by the practice of sin, which truth could not be denied by any believer who knows from personal experience the effect of sin on his own heart. To be observed, however, is the fact that the contrast in this passage is not between spiritual and unspiritual Christians but between the children of God and the children of Satan. The statement of verse 7, addressed to the "little children" of God, is exceedingly forceful and vital: "Little children, let no one deceive you; the one who practices righteousness is righteous, just as He is righteous." This verse declares that the only one who practices righteousness is by his new birth a partaker of the imputed righteousness of God. He not only does righteousness, but is righteous according to his eternal standing in Christ. Conversely, he who practices lawlessness is of the Devil (v. 8).

At this point it may clarify what follows in this context if citation is first made of the culminative statement in verse 10: "By this [the freedom to practice sin lawlessly] the children of God and the children of the devil are obvious." Verse 9 reads as follows: "No one who is born of God practices sin, because His seed abides in him; and he cannot sin, because he is born of God." Whatever specific qualities are in view in the concept of not practicing sin are predicated of all who are "born of God." No portion of this context has been more distorted by torturing exposition than verse 9, yet the truth disclosed here is simply the logical conclusion of what was stated before concerning lawless sinning. There is no basis in this passage for the doctrine of sinless perfection. It will be remembered that the apostle had warned against all such conclusions (1:8, 10). Nor does the Bible teach here or elsewhere that Christians do not sin. It does teach, however, that the Christian retains his Adamic, carnal nature until the day of his death, and, apart from the enabling power of the Spirit, there will be sin in the Christian's life. An important difference exists between the two phrases "not able to sin" and "able not to sin." The latter alone is within the divine provisions. The Bible also teaches that the Christian, being indwelt by the Holy Spirit, is possessed with a new standard as to what is good or bad. His conduct either grieves or does not grieve the Holy Spirit. There is limitless suffering of heart in the path of the child of God who sins lawlessly. The Scriptures abound with illustrations of this suffering in the lives of saints whose history it records. David likened this heart suffering at the time of his lawless sinning to the waxing old of his bones through his roaring all day long, asserting that the heavy hand of God was on him and that his moisture was turned into the drought of summer (Ps. 32:3–4). Paul, because of his failure to reach his spiritual ideals, testified that he was a "wretched man" (Rom. 7:24). It is to be concluded, then, that the true child of God cannot sin lawlessly without great suffering and that suffering is due to the presence of the divine seed or nature in him. This reaction of the divine nature against sin in the Christian, which could never be experienced by unregenerate people, for they do not have the Spirit (Jude 19), constitutes a ground for distinction between those who are the children of God and those who are not. Many other statements in the Word of God serve to emphasize the specific character of the Christian's sin. Some of these will be discussed in what follows.

The Nature of the Conflict

The Christian's conflict is threefold: against the world, against the flesh, and against the Devil. A Christian's solicitation to evil arises from any or all of these three sources. It is of supreme importance, then, that the child of God be intelligently aware of the scope and power of each of these mighty influences. Only the most restricted treatment of these forces can be undertaken here.

THE WORLD

Of the three Greek words that are translated by the English word *world,* only one—χόσμος—presents the thought of a sphere of conflict, and though this word occurs almost two hundred times in the New Testament, only a limited portion of these occurrences are related to the sphere of conflict. The scope of the meaning of this word may be seen by comparing its use in John 3:16, where the Father is said to love the world, with 1 John 2:15, where it is stated that to love the world is to be unlike God (cf. James 4:4). The context alone must guide as to when χόσμος refers to order and arrangement and when it refers to a world system—orderly indeed, but not of God, being under the authority of "the god of this world," by the evident permission and authority of the Lord (Rom. 13:1). The word χόσμος, when referring to a sphere of conflict, might be translated "the satanic system" for the following reasons:

1. Satan is its governing head (John 12:31; 14:30; 16:11; 2 Cor. 4:4; Eph. 6:12; cf. Luke 4:5–17; Eph. 2:2; 1 John 4:4; 5:19).
2. Satan's system, or order, is wholly evil in its character (John 14:30; James 1:27; 4:4; 1 John 4:3; 5:4; cf. Rom. 12:2; Gal. 1:4; Col. 1:13).
3. Satan is permitted the exercise of great power in the satanic system (Job 1:9–12; Isa. 14:12–17; Luke 13:16; 22:31–32; Acts 10:38; 2 Cor. 12:7).
4. Satan's works are defined (John 18:36; 1 John 2:16).
5. Earthly goods are of the satanic system, and these the Christian may use but must not abuse (1 Cor. 7:29–31; 1 John 3:17; cf. Mark 4:19).
6. The satanic system is opposed to Christ, and its members will hate Christ and His witnesses (John 15:18–19; 17:14–16; 1 John 3:13; 4:5).
7. The satanic system is limited (1 John 2:17; 3:1; 4:4; cf. 1 Cor. 2:14–15; 2 Peter 3:10).

The world system is based on greed and is defended by armament. It offers its entertainment, culture, and attraction with surpassing allurement to the children of God. It is indeed true that believers are in the world but not of it. Taken out of the world system by the new-creation relationship, they are no longer any more a part of the world than is Christ, but Christ has sent them into the world, even as the Father sent Him into the world, not to be conformed to it but to be witnesses in it (John 17:18).

One, and only one, plan is provided as a means of victory over the world. It is stated in 1 John 5:4, "And this is the victory that has overcome the world—our faith." Reference here is not to a present vacillating faith; the past tense is used, looking back to that faith that identified the believer with Christ. Thus the apostle added, "Who is the one who overcomes the world, but he who believes that Jesus is the Son of God?" (5:5). Though there is need for victory in the believer's present experience, the victory is *Christ,* and all *in Christ* are already equipped to be more than conquerors.

THE FLESH

Among the believer's enemies is the σάρξ, the fallen nature. In this connection, attention is called to the threefold division of the human family as disclosed by the Spirit through the apostle Paul. While the distinctions between these classes are far-reaching, involving almost every phase of human life and experience, the central passage (1 Cor. 2:9–3:4) distinguishes these groups on the basis of their attitudes toward the written Word of God. The ψυχικός, or unregenerate man, cannot receive the things of God; they are foolishness to him (2:14). The πνευματικός, or spiritual man, discerns all things (2:15). The σαρκικός person, though a "babe in Christ" and addressed as a brother in the Lord, is, because of carnality, able to receive only the milk of the Word. As has been seen, there is a wide difference between the unregenerate and the regenerate, but the present point of discussion is of the difference that exists between the carnal Christian and the spiritual Christian. Too much emphasis could not be given to the fact that they are both perfectly saved and safe for all eternity, being in Christ Jesus. The issue is one of daily life, which issue is never related to salvation by grace but does look on to the judgment seat of Christ where and when the children of God must appear and their works be judged. There is divine acknowledgment and reward promised at that judgment seat, quite apart from the issues of saving grace, to all who have been well-pleasing to the One who sits on that throne.

The word σάρξ, "flesh," is frequently used to indicate the human body (1 John 4:2) and thus becomes, to a limited extent, a synonym for σῶμα, "body," but in the majority of instances the word *flesh* is a reference to the fallen, degenerate nature, which is the only possession of unregenerate men and which regenerate persons continue to possess along with the divine nature throughout their earthly lives. The New Testament presents the Christian as in a conflict between the flesh and the Spirit, which conflict is still experienced by those who reach the most advanced spiritual state. No experience in true spirituality could ever surpass that described in Galatians 5:16–24, yet that experience is there declared to be due to a domination the Spirit of God exercises over the flesh and not to any supposed eradication of the flesh.

That the flesh is incurably and hopelessly bad and only bad is the testimony of the Scriptures. Of the flesh the apostle Paul declared, "nothing good dwells in me, that is, in my flesh" (Rom. 7:18); and again "the flesh sets its desire against the Spirit, and the Spirit against the flesh; for these are in opposition to one another" (Gal. 5:17). Then follows in the context of Galatians 5:16–24 a list of the "deeds of the flesh," which deeds are only evil. But over against this is the "fruit of the Spirit" tabulated under nine divine graces, indivisible as to the total they form, which appear in the believer's life only as they are wrought by the Spirit who indwells him.

Two extended passages bear on the conflict that continues in every believer between the flesh and the Spirit, and therein is presented the only way of deliverance. In the first of these passages (Rom. 7:15–8:4), the apostle testified, first, of his own complete failure and, second, of his victory. The failure was complete in spite of the fact that he had made his greatest possible effort to succeed. In Romans 7:15–25 the conflict is between the regenerate man (hypothetically contemplated as acting independently, or apart from the indwelling Spirit) and his flesh. It is not between the Holy Spirit and the flesh. Probably there is no more subtle delusion common among believers than the supposition that the saved person, if he tries hard enough, can, on the basis of the fact that he is regenerate, overcome the flesh. The result of this struggle on the part of the apostle was defeat to the extent that he became a "wretched man," but out of this experience he learned a most vital and important lesson, namely, that there are two mighty tendencies always in the child of God, one aspiring to what is good and the other demanding what is evil. This is the meaning of the new conflict between "I," the old nature, and "I," the new nature, and there could be no more conclusive verdict rendered at the end of this impotent effort than the apostle set forth in verse 25: "So then, . . . I myself with my mind am serving the law of God, but . . . with my flesh [I serve] the law of sin."

The apostle's testimony then reports the discovery of a new principle of procedure and a new and sufficient available power. The "Spirit of life in Christ Jesus," quite apart from his own regenerate self that had so ignominiously failed, makes him free from the law or power of sin and death (8:2). He testified further that "the righteousness of the law"—meaning here vastly more than any written code, including, as it does, all the will of God as to every detail in every moment of the believer's life—is fulfilled in him but never fulfilled by him. This marvelous experience, the apostle stated, is granted only to those "who do not walk according to the flesh, but according to the Spirit" (8:4). Thus he prepared for the truth set forth in the second major passage (Gal. 5:16–24) where the conflict is not between the regenerate person and his flesh with its inevitable defeat but between the indwelling Holy Spirit and the flesh. "But I say, walk by [or by dependence on] the Spirit, and you will not carry out the desire of the flesh" (5:16). No greater promise of victory over the flesh could be extended to the child of God than this. Such victory is not by self-crucifixion of the flesh nor by a supposed second work of grace by which the flesh is eradicated, but by the overcoming power of the Spirit. The believer must learn the life of faith in which he depends on the power of God. Apart from this faith there is only defeat, but with this faith there is deliverance from the flesh and its lusts or desires.

THE DEVIL

The Christian's three enemies—the world, the flesh, and the Devil—are closely related. Especially related are the world, or the satanic system, and Satan who is the god and prince of that system. However, the world and the flesh are impersonal influences, while Satan, the wisest of all created beings, is personal. He exercises μεθοδεία—"circumvention of deceits, wiles, or artifices"—against the children of God. There is no conflict between the unregenerate and Satan; they are energized by him (Eph. 2:2). On the other hand, the Christian is in the center of the most terrible, supernatural warfare. Paul described it in Ephesians as a *wrestling*. The word implies the closest life-and-death struggle, a hand-to-hand tug-of-war. Nor is the uttermost device and power of Satan inspired by any enmity against regenerate people as such. His enmity is against God, as it has been since Satan's fall in the unknown ages past, and against believers only on the ground that they have partaken of the divine nature. To possess the priceless indwelling presence of the divine nature is to become so identified with God that His enemy also becomes that of believers.

Solemn, indeed, is the divine revelation that the wisest of all created beings, and the most powerful, never ceases studying the strategy by which he may snare the child of God and, were it in his power, to bring that one to destruction. How unconcerned, unconscious, and ignorant Christians are! How ungrateful they are, because of their limited understanding, for the divine deliverance wrought on their behalf every hour of every day! Yet, how much of defeat, especially in the spiritual realm, is suffered by all who are saved because of their failure to wage their warfare in "the strength of His might," who alone can give victory, and to "put on the full armor of God"! No more vital injunction was ever addressed to the Christian than that he must "be strong in the Lord, and in the strength of His might." He must "put on the full armor of God that [he] may be able to stand firm against the schemes of the devil" (Eph. 6:10–11; on the meaning of "schemes" see Eph. 4:14). Faith, it has been seen, is the only way of victory over the world and the flesh, but it is equally certain according to the Word of God that faith is the only way of victory over the power of Satan. How assuring is the truth, "Greater is He who is in you than he who is in the world" (1 John 4:4). Even Michael the archangel, when contending with Satan, did not in his own strength bring a "railing judgment" against him but said, "The Lord rebuke you" (Jude 9). True, James stated, "Resist the devil and he will flee from you," but that is a word of admonition to those who have first submitted themselves to God (James 4:7). Likewise Peter declared in reference to Satan, "resist him, firm in your faith" (1 Peter 5:8–9; cf. John 15:5; 2 Cor. 10:3–5; Phil. 2:13; 4:13).

Quite apart from human opinion or experience that is of a contrary nature, it must be concluded that in his threefold conflict there is nothing but defeat and failure for the Christian if he does not pursue the way of faith or dependence on the Spirit of God. The child of God must fight "the good fight" of faith (2 Tim. 4:7). His responsibility is not to war with his enemies in his own strength but rather to maintain the ever-triumphant attitude of faith.

The Threefold Provision

In recognition of the believer's conflict while in the world, God in His marvelous grace has provided a threefold prevention against the Christian's sin. If a Christian sins, it will be in spite of these provisions. These great requisites are revealed in the Old Testament as well as in the New Testament.

THE WORD OF GOD

The psalmist wrote, "Thy word have I treasured in my heart, that I may not sin against Thee" (Ps. 119:11), and in 2 Timothy 3:16–17 Paul declared, "All Scripture is inspired by God and profitable for teaching, for reproof, for correction, for training in righteousness; that the man of God may be adequate, equipped for every good work." As His Word abides in the believer, the believer is in the place of spiritual achievement (John 15:7). There is little hope for victory in daily life on the part of those believers who, being ignorant of the Word of God, do not know the nature of their conflict or the deliverance God has provided. Over against this, there is no estimating the sanctifying power of the Word of God. Jesus prayed, "Sanctify them in the truth; Thy word is truth" (John 17:17).

THE INTERCEDING CHRIST

Again the psalmist recorded, "The LORD is my shepherd, I shall not want" (Ps. 23:1), and the New Testament revelation of the interceding Christ is also broad enough to include His shepherding care. Little did Peter know of the testing that was before him or of his own pitiful weakness, but Christ had anticipated it all. He could say in assurance to Peter, "I have prayed for you" (Luke 22:32), as, in fact, He prays for all whom He has saved. Probably His high-priestly prayer recorded in John 17 is only the beginning of His prayer for "all whom Thou hast given Him" (v. 2), which prayer is now continued without ceasing by Him in heaven. On the ground of this unceasing intercession, the believer is assured of his security forever. Romans 8:34 states that there is none to condemn since, among other efficacious forces, Christ "intercedes for us." Similarly the writer to the Hebrews disclosed the truth that Christ as Priest, in contrast to the death-doomed priests of the old order, will never again be subject to death. He therefore has an unchangeable or unending priesthood, and because He abides forever as a sufficient priest He is able to save eternally those who come to God by Him, since He ever lives to make intercession for them (Heb. 7:23–25). This guarantee of abiding endurance, based as it is on the absolute efficacy of the interceding Christ, is final and complete. But, as has been seen, the intercession of Christ is a preventive against failure as well as a source of security for the children of God.

THE INDWELLING SPIRIT

The saints of the old order were reminded that it is "'not by might nor by power, but by My Spirit,' says the Lord of hosts" (Zech. 4:6). So, as has been indicated before, every defense and protection as well as every victory for the Christian depends on the power of the indwelling Spirit.

Two Spheres of Effect of the Christian's Sin

As to its effect, the Christian's sin reaches into at least two spheres, namely, the effect on himself and the effect on God. There could be no question as to the relative importance of these two results of the Christian's sin.

THE EFFECT OF THE CHRISTIAN'S SIN ON HIMSELF

Because of his new birth by the Spirit, his new positions and possessions, and his heaven-high responsibility in daily life and service, the Christian is a supernatural person. Normally he should experience unceasing miracles in every department of his life: his victory over the world, the flesh, and the Devil; his empowerment for God-honoring character and service—which is nothing short of the showing forth of the virtues of Him who called him from darkness into His marvelous light (1 Peter 2:9) and the realization of the apostle Paul's ideal expressed in the phrase, "for to me, to live is Christ"—his knowledge of God's Word; and his prevailing power in prayer. All these realities and much more are not only supernatural, but are wrought in and through the child of God by the energizing power of the indwelling Spirit. God is reasonable in calling on every regenerate person for this holy, heavenly manner of life on the ground of the fact that the sufficient resource—the indwelling Spirit—is given to all who are saved. Of surpassing importance, however, is the added revelation that directs the Christian in the divinely arranged plan whereby he may experience these supernatural realities.

Sin in a Christian's life causes the grieving of the indwelling Spirit, and, when He is grieved, He turns from His normal ministry through the Christian to a ministry of pleading with the Christian. When a Christian sins, the manifestation of those things in his life that are supernaturally wrought of God either become greatly lessened or cease altogether until the required adjustment is made and he is again restored to fellowship with God.

The effect then of the Christian's sin on himself is the loss of all supernatural realities in the sphere of his daily life and experience. He ceases to manifest the divine virtues, he no longer knows the surpassing blessedness of fellowship with the Father and His Son, his witness for Christ becomes ineffective, and the measureless ministry of prayer is paralyzed. It is tragic indeed that any regenerate person should enter into the realm of darkness for one hour, but it is even more tragic when multitudes of Christians abide in this darkness (1 John 1:6) because of their ignorance of the divinely provided and revealed way of escape and cure!

THE EFFECT OF THE CHRISTIAN'S SIN ON GOD

It is far beyond the range of the finite mind to comprehend what sin means to God, and, as has been stated, sin is as sinful when committed by the saved as it is when committed by the unsaved. God could never deal with any aspect of sin on the basis of mere generosity, big-heartedness, or mercy. Could this have been possible, there would have been no need for Christ to die that death by which He bore in humankind's place the unavoidable penalty a holy God must impose on every creature that departs from conformity to His holiness. The gospel message to the unsaved does not mean that God will be good and gracious if only they persuade Him to be thus. God has been good and He is gracious to the extent that He has provided in Christ all a sinner will ever need, and this is available on no condition other than that the sinner believe. Likewise the child of God is not now a favorite with God and free to indulge in sin without thought of divine holiness being thereby outraged. In itself the least sin committed by the Christian, because of its unlikeness to the character of God, would have power to hurl that one from the presence of God forever and to dissolve every relationship grace has formed. And indeed the Christian's sin would thus work the Christian's eternal ruin were it not for the efficacious blood of Christ that is at once both the ground of salvation and of security—salvation through the application of that blood when the sinner believes and security through the present advocacy of Christ in heaven.

CHAPTER 3

"Sinners" Who Are Forgiven or "Saints" Who Sin?

Robert L. Saucy

The question of the true identity of the Christian has been the topic of discussion for some time. Although not directly framed as a question of identity, the issues of self-love, self-esteem, and self-worth all relate in some way to the question, "Who am I?" This question has been posed more sharply in the alternatives, "Am I as a Christian basically a sinner who is forgiven or a saint who sins?"

The first of these alternatives may be associated with what Warfield favorably termed "miserable-sinner Christianity."[1] He referred to it this way because similar terminology runs through Protestant confessional formulas and catechisms.[2] Luther's Short Catechism, for example, teaches the believer to say, "I, miserable sinner, confess myself before God guilty of all manner of sins." A Lutheran confession of sin reads:

> I, poor sinful man, confess to God, the Almighty, my Creator and Redeemer, that I not only have sinned in thoughts, words and deeds, but also was conceived and born in sin, and so all my nature and being is deserving of punishment and condemnation before His righteousness. Therefore I flee to His gratuitous mercy and seek and beseech His grace. Lord, be merciful to me, miserable sinner.

A similar expression is found in the prayers of the Church of England. After acknowledging sinfulness and declaring that "there is no health in us," the prayer closes with the petition, "But thou, O Lord, have mercy upon us, miserable offenders." One of the most rhetorical expressions of the concept of miserable-sinner Christianity is given by the Scottish minister Alexander Whyte, in his work *Bunyan Characters.*

> Our guilt is so great that we dare not think of it. . . . It crushes our minds with a perfect stupor of horror, when for a moment we try to imagine a day of judgment when we shall be judged for all the deeds that we have

done in the body. Heart-beat after heart-beat, breath after breath, hour after hour, day after day, year after year, and all full of sin; all nothing but sin from our mother's womb to our grave.[3]

It would be wrong to take such a statement as necessarily signifying miserable Christianity rather than miserable-sinner Christianity. Many of those who confessed their situation in this way knew how to flee to the grace of God and find the joy of forgiveness. But such statements would also seem to color the self-understanding of believers as to their basic nature.

An example of the alternative understanding of Christian identity as saints who sin is a statement by Neil Anderson in one of his popular books.

Many Christians refer to themselves as sinners saved by grace. But are you really a sinner? Is that your scriptural identity? Not at all. God doesn't call you a sinner; He calls you a saint—a holy one. . . . Why not identity yourself for who you really are: a saint who occasionally sins.[4]

If the word "occasionally" is excluded from Anderson's statement (Anderson has indicated to this writer in personal conversation that it was not his intention to include this word), there is truth in both alternatives of the question. Believers are sinners in that they continue to sin, but Scripture also refers to them as saints. Believers, therefore, are sinners who by God's grace are forgiven, and they are saints who sin.

Thus in a sense Christians have a kind of double identity. But this does not mean they are schizophrenic or multiple persons. Each believer is one person, one ego or "I." The apostle Paul wrote, "I have been crucified with Christ; and it is no longer I who live, but Christ lives in me; and the life which I now live in the flesh I live by faith in the Son of God" (Gal. 2:20). There was only one "I" and one Paul throughout this transition. The question of the believer's identity is therefore the question of the identity of that ego or "I." And it would seem that that identity must be related to the actual nature and behavior of that ego. If the nature and activity of the person is primarily sinful, then it is difficult not to see his core identity as a sinner. On the other hand if the believer's nature and activity is primarily holy, then that person's real identity is that of a saint.

The Believer's Positive Identity

Consideration of the scriptural description of the believer and his activity obviously reveals a mixture of sin and holiness. But when the focus is on the actual description of the person's identity, the picture is decidedly positive. Even in the Old Testament, believers are described as living with hearts of integrity, soundness, and uprightness (e.g., 1 Kings 8:61; 9:4; Pss. 78:72; 119:7). This of course does not mean that they were sinless or were unaware of their sin. But they had hearts and lives that were fundamentally devoted to God. Turning to the New Testament, Christians are frequently addressed as "saints" (e.g., Acts 9:32; Eph. 1:1; Col. 1:2). This surely has reference to their status in Christ, but other descriptions reveal that it also denotes something about the believer's nature. Believers in the Lord are "sons" and "children of God," which, along with speaking of position or status, also depicts something of the nature of the believer who is now oriented toward righteousness (1 John 2:29–3:2). Those in Christ are also called "light" (Eph. 5:8) and "sons of light" (1 Thess. 5:5), which means "they are characterized by light" as a result of the "transformation that takes place when anyone believes."[5]

The believer is part of the new creation (2 Cor. 5:17). He has put off the "old man" and put on the "new man" (Col. 3:9–10; cf. Rom. 6:6). This transition refers to the believer's transference from the old corporate humanity under the headship of Adam to the new humanity with Christ as Head. But it also has reference to a change in the individual.[6] Pointing to the imagery used of putting off and putting on clothing, Lincoln rightly explains that this "change of clothing imagery signifies an exchange of identities, and the concepts of the old and the new persons reinforce this."[7] Since the appellation "new man" also has reference to the individual, the descriptions of it as "created in righteousness and holiness of the truth" (Eph. 4:24) and "being renewed . . . according to the image of the One who created him" (Col. 3:10) both have reference to the individual believer. Thus Bruce says, "The new man who is created is the new personality that each believer becomes when he is reborn as a member of the new creation whose source of life is Christ."[8] Putting off the old man and putting on the new are related to the teaching of the believer's death and resurrection with Christ (Rom. 6:4–6).[9] In codeath and coresurrection the individual's identity is radically changed. The old "I" dies and the new "I" rises in newness of life (Gal. 2:20).

These descriptions of the Christian clearly indicate a positive identity and refer not only to status but also to the nature of the believer. This conclusion is borne out by the fact that the apostolic exhortation to new ethical behavior is made directly on the basis of the believer's new identity. The apostles were not grounding their hope for a new behavior simply on a new position or status, but on a new nature that can produce new actions. True, these actions are due to the life of God in the believer and are called "the fruit of the Spirit." But at the same time they are the product of the believer even as the fruit of the vine is the fruit of the branches (John 15:2–5, 16). The exhortations to new ethical life are based on the principle Jesus taught that "good fruit" is borne by "good trees" (Matt. 7:17). The nature as well as the identity of the believer is therefore seen as primarily "good."

These descriptions of the believer point in the direction of the root identity of the Christian as a saint who sins, rather than a sinner who is saved. But that is not the whole of the matter. Practical experience as well as biblical teaching still relate the believer to sin. Consideration of the identity of the believer therefore cannot avoid discussion of his relationship to sin.

The Believer's Relation to Sin

THE BELIEVER STILL SINS

It is not difficult to convince most believers from Scripture as well as from experience that sin is still a part of their existence. They sometimes act carnally (1 Cor. 3:1–3). The promise of continual cleansing of sin as they walk in the light (1 John 1:7) as well as the present tense used for the confession of sins (1:9) suggest that sin is continually present with believers. To say "we have no sin," John wrote, is self-deception and impossible for believers (1:8). Although the personal identity of the believer is in Christ, and thus in the new man that is being transformed into His image, the manner of life of the old man remains a part of the believer's experience. This is why Paul directed believers to put off the practices of the old man (Eph. 4:22; Col. 3:8–9).

Calvin's statement of what Christians ought to be should convince any believer that he has not attained sinlessness. "Since all the capacities of our soul ought to be so filled with the love of God," he said, "it is certain that this precept [to love God with all our heart, soul, and mind] is not fulfilled by those who can either retain in the heart a slight inclination or admit to the mind any thought at all that would lead them away from the love of God into vanity."[10] "There remains in a regenerate man a moldering cinder of evil, from which desires continually leap forth to allure and spur him to commit sin."[11]

Does this true but rather bleak perspective make the identity of the believer a "sinner" as well as a "saint" so that he is actually both? Interestingly, although the New Testament gives extensive evidence that believers sin, it never clearly identifies believers as "sinners." Paul's reference to himself in which he declared, "I am foremost" of sinners is often raised to the contrary (1 Tim. 1:15). Guthrie's comment on Paul's assertion is illustrative of a common understanding of Paul's statement and what should be true of all believers. "Paul never got away from the fact that Christian salvation was intended for *sinners,* and the more he increased his grasp of the magnitude of God's grace, the more he deepened the consciousness of his own naturally sinful state, until he could write *of whom I am chief (prō tos)*."[12]

Despite the use of the present tense by the apostle, several things make it preferable to see his description of himself as the foremost of sinners as a reference to his preconversion activity as an opponent of the Gospel. First, the reference to himself as "sinner" is in support of the statement that "Christ Jesus came into the world to save sinners" (v. 15). The reference to "the ungodly and sinners" a few verses earlier (v. 9) along with the other New Testament uses of the term *sinners* for those who are outside of salvation[13] shows that he was referring to sinners whom Christ came to save rather than believers who yet sinned.

Second, Paul's reference to himself as a sinner is followed by the statement, "And yet . . . I found [past tense] mercy" (v. 16), clearly pointing to the past occasion of his conversion. Paul was grateful for God's mercy toward him, the foremost of sinners. A similar present evaluation of himself based on the past is seen when the apostle wrote, "I am [present tense] the least of the apostles, who am not fit to be called an apostle, because I persecuted the church of God" (1 Cor. 15:9). Because of his past action, Paul considered himself unworthy of what he presently was by God's grace and mercy, an apostle who was "not in the least inferior to the most eminent apostles" (2 Cor. 11:5; cf. 12:11).

Declaring that he was the foremost of sinners, the apostle also declared that Christ had strengthened him for the ministry, having considered him "faithful" or "trustworthy" for it, to which He had called him (1 Tim. 1:12). As Knight concludes, "Paul regards this classification of himself as 'foremost of sinners' as still valid (εἰμι, present tense); though he is fully forgiven, regarded as faithful, and put into service, he is still the notorious opponent who is so received."[14] Thus the apostle was not applying the appellation "sinner" to himself as a believer, but rather in remembrance of what he was before Christ took hold of him.

James's reference to turning "a sinner" from the error of his ways is also best seen as bringing someone into salvation rather than as restoring a genuine believer to repentance (James 5:19–20). Though the erring one is described as one "among you," the resultant outcome of saving the soul of the turned "sinner" from "death," which is most likely spiritual death, suggests that the person was not a Christian.[15] Scripture surely teaches that unbelievers can be "among" the saints (cf. 1 John 2:19).

This is not to say that in the Scriptures believers did not see themselves as sinful. Confrontation with the righteousness and holiness of God frequently brought deep acknowledgment of an individual's own sinful condition. Peter's recognition of himself before the Lord as a "sinful man" is not uncommon among the saints (Luke 5:8; cf. Gen. 18:27; Job 42:6; Isa. 6:5; Dan. 9:4–20). The believer is sinful, but Scripture does not seem to define his identity as a "sinner."

THE BELIEVER IS OPPOSED TO SIN

Instead of being identified as a sinner, the real person or "I" of the believer is opposed to sin. Before salvation the "I" or the ego of the believer, like the "I" of all sinners, was in radical rebellion against the true God. Now the "I" of the believer is on God's side seeking to mortify the rebellion that is still present in the believer. Several truths combine to teach this new identity of the believer and his change of nature.

First, death and resurrection with Christ severed the believer from sin. The believer's participation in Christ's death and resurrection is a way in which Paul expressed the change that takes place when one becomes a Christian. According to the most extensive explanation of this truth in Romans 6, the primary significance of this transaction is the change of dominions over the believer. Christ's death and resurrection signify (a) death to the old age of sin and its dominion and (b) resurrection to a new sphere ruled by God. These objective realities take place in Christ as the Head of the new humanity, much like His actions as the Head of the corporate "new man."[16] But also like the transfer from the "old" to the "new" man, Christ's death and resurrection apply subjectively to the believer.

> In Rom. 6 Paul is not simply concerned with the two dominions, but with the decisive transfer of the believer from the one dominion to the other. The believers were enslaved to sin, but now they stand under a new master. This change has taken place through dying with Christ. . . . Dying with Christ means dying to the powers of the old aeon and entry into a new life under a new power.[17]

The believers' union with Christ in His death and resurrection transforms them not just legally but also personally. As the person's "I" previously had a nature that willingly chose to serve sin, now he is a new "I" who willingly chooses God. Paul's testimony was that having been crucified with Christ, he now lived in such union with Him that his "I" could hardly be separated, not just legally but morally. Paul's "I" was willingly united with Christ, who continually and willingly obeyed the Father's will. As Bonar said, "The cross, then, makes us *decided* men. It brings both our *hearts* and our *wills* to the side of God."[18]

Second, the transformation of the believer in the change of dominions over him through dying and rising with Christ is further seen in the biblical concept of having a "new heart." As Jewett explains, "A characteristic of the heart as the center of man is its inherent openness to outside impulses, its directionality, its propensity to give itself to a master and to live towards some desired goal."[19] This characteristic stems from the fact that Christians as finite persons can live only in "radical dependence on otherness."[20]

Most significantly, as Jewett noted, what the heart takes in becomes its master, stamping the heart with its character. What truly determines the heart and consequently the person is therefore the nature of the desire of the heart. After defining the heart as "our center, our prefunctional root," Kreeft adds, "at this center we decide the meaning of our lives, for our deepest desires constitute ourselves, decide our identity."[21]

According to Scripture the deepest desire of the believer has been changed. This truth is seen in the apostle's words to the Galatians: "And because you are sons, God has sent forth the Spirit of His Son into our hearts, crying, 'Abba! Father!'" (4:6). The cry, "Abba! Father!" is typical of a son and represents the believer's most basic relationship with God. This cry is determined by the presence of the Spirit who brings Christ the Son into the center of the believer's personality to live within his heart. "The center of man is thus his heart; the heart's intentionality [or desire] is determined by the power which rules it. In the case of Christian[s], the direction of the heart's intentionality is determined by Christ's Spirit."[22]

The desire or intentionality of the human heart is in reality its love. As Augustine noted, love is what moves an individual. A person goes where his love moves him. His identity is determined by his love. The identity of the believer is thus a person who basically loves God rather than sin.

The presence of sin in the life of the believer indicates that remnants of the old disordered love of self remain. But those remnants now stand at the periphery of the real core of the person who is redeemed, God-oriented, and thus bent toward righteousness in his nature. "God begins his good work in us, therefore, by arousing love and desire and zeal for righteousness in our hearts; or, to speak more correctly, by bending, forming, and directing, our hearts to righteousness."[23]

This core of the new person is often not evident in conscious life, but it is nevertheless the dominating aspect of being. As Delitzsch notes, there is a kind of will of nature that is basically self-consciously unreflected. This deep will of nature precedes the conscious actions of the person. The will of the believer has been changed through regeneration despite the fact that remnants of the old life still remain and continue to express themselves. The action of regeneration is directed not so much to "our occasional will, as to the substance of our will, i.e. to the nature and essence of our spiritual being."[24]

Thus the regenerate individual in the depth of his heart is changed; he has a nature oriented toward God. Although the person can still sin, this sin is related to a more surface level of his being that can still act contrary to the real person of the heart. But these surface actions do not change the real nature of the heart and thus the person's identity. The relationship of the real core nature of the human heart to its more surface activities is seen in Pedersen's discussion of the "soul" or what is perhaps better termed the *heart*.

> It [the soul] is partly an entirety in itself and partly forms an entirety with others. What entireties it is merged in, depends upon the constant interchange of life.
>
> Every time the soul merges into a new entirety, new centres of action are formed in it; but they are created by temporary situations, only lie on

the surface and quickly disappear. There are other entireties to which the soul belongs, and which live in it with quite a different depth and firmness, because they make the very nucleus of the soul. Thus there may be a difference between the momentary and the stable points of gravity in the soul. But none of the momentary centres of action can ever annul or counteract those which lie deeper.

The deepest-lying contents of the soul are, it is true, always there, but they do not always make themselves equally felt.[25]

This understanding of the human heart helps explain the practice of sin in the believer's life as well as the "good" in the life of the unbelieving sinner. The true nature of the person does not always express itself fully in actual life. But the basic identity of the individual is still there, and in the case of the believer it is positive.

Third, this same truth is seen in the positive nature of the ego or "I" of Romans 7:14–25. Paul's description of the "I" in this passage suggests that it refers to someone who has experienced the regenerative grace of God. Also this person is viewed in relation to the law of God apart from the empowerment of the Spirit of God. It could thus have reference to a Christian living according to the flesh in his own strength[26] or, more probably, to the experience of the pious Jew living under the Mosaic Law viewed from a Christian perspective.[27]

Of interest in this passage is the description of the "I" that is solidly on God's side. If what is said of this "I," or ego, could refer to a pious Jew living under the old covenant, how much more would it be fitting for the believer of the new covenant as part of the new creation through union with Christ. Considering the actions of the "I," all three dimensions normally seen as constituting personhood, that is, thought, emotion, and will, are all oriented toward God and His righteous law. Regarding the element of thought, the apostle wrote in 7:15, "For that which I am doing, I do not understand," or perhaps better with Cranfield, "I do not acknowledge" or "approve."[28] In other words, his thinking was opposed to his action of sin. This is also seen in verse 25: "I myself with my mind am serving the law of God, but . . . with my flesh the law of sin."

His emotion is likewise seen to be on God's side in opposition to sin. "I am doing the very thing I hate" (v. 15). As Dunn puts it, "he wholly detests and abhors what he does."[29] If hatred is the opposite of love, then his love is directed toward righteousness. A further expression of emotion is indicated in verse 22: "I joyfully concur with the law of God in the inner man."

Also his will or volition is for God and against sin. "What I want [or, will, θέλω] to do," Paul wrote, "I do not do. . . . I have the desire [θέλειν] to do what is good" (vv. 15, 18 NIV). The verb θέλειν is used seven times in the passage, the last when he described himself as "the one who wishes to do good" (v. 21).

These descriptions of the personal attributes of the "I" clearly define it as one with a positive nature. But more than this, the apostle went so far as to absolve, as it were, the "I" from sinning: "if I do the very thing I do not wish to do . . . no longer am I the one doing it, but sin which indwells me" (vv. 16–17; cf. the same thought in v. 20).

Since the same passage clearly shows the "I" as the subject of sinful actions as well as being opposed to sin, the apostle was not trying to evade the personal responsibility of the "I" in sin. But when the "I" is related to sin, it is never described in terms of the functions of personhood. There are no equal statements of thought, emotion, and will on the side of sin. Paul did not say, "I want to do the will of God, but I also want to sin." Nor did he say, "I love the law of God, but I also love sin." Thus the "I" that is positively oriented toward God is the person in the deepest sense of his personhood or identity. He is the "I" of the "inner man" (v. 22), the "I" that is the subject of the "mind" (v. 25).

The assertion that it is no longer "I" but sin that actually does the sinning is similar to other apparently contradictory statements of the apostle when he was referring to the dominating power that mastered him: "it is no longer I who live, but Christ lives in me; and the life which I now live . . ." (Gal. 2:20); "I labored even more than all of them, yet not I, but the grace of God with me" (1 Cor. 15:10; cf. Matt. 10:20). In these statements Paul was not intending to disavow responsibility but to affirm the existence in himself of a power that exercised a dominating influence on him. The real person of the believer willingly assents to this dominating power, but in the case of sin as in Romans 7 the real "I" opposes it and can thus be set against it. Here the ego, or real "I," in the believer is viewed as so opposed to sin that they can be isolated from each other. And the actual committing of sin, instead of being the action of the ego, can be regarded as the action of the sin that enslaves the ego contrary to its will. As Delitzsch says, "the Ego is no longer one with sin—it is free from it; sin resides in such a man still, only as a foreign power."[30]

Romans 7 thus presents the real person of the believer as

positive. To be sure, he commits sin both in thought and act but he also does righteousness. Sin and righteousness, however, do not characterize the real person of the believer in the same way. The believer is capable of experiencing a double servitude expressed in the apostle's words, "on the one hand I myself with my mind am serving the law of God, but on the other, with my flesh the law of sin" (v. 25).[31] But as this statement, along with the entire passage, indicates, the real person of the believer willingly serves God.

The description of the believer in Romans 7 thus fits the same picture of the believer seen in the teaching of his death and resurrection with Christ and his new heart. The Christian has been radically changed in his relationship to sin and righteousness from what he was before salvation. And this change is more than simply positional or judicial consisting in the forgiveness of sin and the imputation of righteousness. It includes a radical change of nature. The Christian is a new person. He has a new heart which is the real identity of the person.

Conclusion

The full picture of the believer's relationship to sin and righteousness is obviously beyond the scope of this study. But when the question of his identity is posed—is the Christian a saved sinner or a saint who sins?—the Scriptures seem to point to the latter.

There is truth in the following explanation of so-called miserable-sinner Christianity expressed by Luther:

> A Christian is at the same time a sinner and a saint; he is at once bad and good. For in our own person we are in sin, and in our own name we are sinners. But Christ brings us another name in which there is forgiveness of sin, so that for His sake our sin is forgiven and done away. Both then are true. There are sins . . . and yet there are no sins. . . . thou standest there for God not in thy name but in Christ's name; thou dost adorn thyself with grace and righteousness although in thine own eyes and in thine own person, thou art a miserable sinner.[32]

Christians are sinners who are forgiven. But there is more to it than that. They are regenerated persons whose root core has been changed. They are forgiven, but also the heart—the spring of the life and the true identity—is new.

To confess as present-day Anglicans do[33] that "there is no health in us" or that "all my nature and being is deserving of punishment," as also stated in the old German Lutheran confession, is contrary to the biblical picture of the believer.

All the apostles' ethical imperatives are addressed to believers on the premise that their natures are now on God's side and have a new ability to obey God. The very assumption that Christians should grow demonstrates a belief that the positive dominates over the negative in their beings. For a Christian to grow, there must be a stronger inclination toward God than toward sin.

Although the terminology "miserable sinner" does not adequately define the true identity of the believer, several truths at the heart of so-called miserable-sinner Christianity must be retained even when viewing the believer as a saint who sins.

First, despite the truth that the believer's heart and thus his identity has been transformed to an orientation toward God and His righteousness, his acceptance before God is only on the basis of Christ's righteousness. One's salvation is complete in Christ's righteousness alone.

Second, the believer who sins must experience misery over sin. If a person's affections have truly been changed so that he is now on God's side, then that person must hate sin and experience a godly sorrow over what grieves and wounds the One who loves believers deeply. Fisher's description of sorrow over sin should be the experience of all believers.

> When faith hath bathed a man's heart in the blood of Christ, it is so mollified that it generally dissolves into tears of godly sorrow; so that if Christ turn and look upon him, O then, with Peter he goes out and weeps bitterly. And this is true gospel mourning; this is right evangelical repenting.[34]

Third, even though God in His grace has created in believers the germ of a new nature that gives them a new identity, their focus in life must be not on themselves but on Christ. Dying and rising with Christ means the end of self-trust. Therefore, even though they are new persons, their source of life and growth is not in their own identity but in Christ. Their focus must be on Him and not on their own new identity. In Him they are new creatures (2 Cor. 5:17).

CHAPTER 4

Prayer and the Sovereignty of God

John D. Hannah

Ff God is sovereign, why should Christians pray? This is one
of the perennial questions inquiring Christian minds
reflect on or are naggingly troubled with. If God is sovereign,
is not prayer a superfluous activity or at best an exercise in
meditation or some form of inspiring soliloquy? The question of
the tension between solicitations to prayer and the presupposition
of absolute sovereignty is but a harbinger of numerous other
difficulties with the doctrine of prayer. Does prayer limit
sovereignty? Does God change His mind? Is it possible that
one's will can prevail over God's will? Is God obligated to
answer prayer?

Prayer is so repeatedly commanded in the Scriptures that its
necessity is unquestioned (e.g., 1 Tim. 2:8); its necessity is as
manifestly evident as that of divine sovereignty. The initial step in
resolving the apparent conflict is to define prayer. In the Reformed
tradition prayer is viewed as an act of spiritual fellowship of the
creature with the Creator. According to Dabney, the brilliant
Southern Presbyterian theologian, prayer is "the natural homage
due from the creature to his heavenly Father."[1] Charles Hodge
states that prayer is "the converse of the soul with God."[2] He
further argues, "It is not therefore prayer as the mere uttering of
words, nor prayer as the uttering of natural desires of affection, as
when one prays for his own life or the life of those dear to him; but
it is prayer as the real intercourse of the soul with God, by the
Holy Ghost, that is, the Holy Ghost revealing truth, exciting
feeling, and giving appropriate utterance."[3] John Calvin's
discussion of prayer is located in an unusual place in his systematic
theology; he prefaces the treatment of election and predestination
with a lengthy treatment of the nature and significance of prayer.
To Calvin prayer is the vehicle of spiritual exercise whereby the
promises of blessing and comfort seen faintingly by the eye of
faith are actualized in sight.

> To prayer, then, are we indebted for penetrating to those riches which are treasured up for us with our heavenly Father. For there is a kind of intercourse between God and men, by which, having entered the upper sanctuary, they appear before Him and appeal to His promises, that when necessity requires, they may learn by experience, that what they believed merely of the authority of His word was not in vain. Accordingly, we see that nothing is set before us as an object of expectation from the Lord which we are not enjoined to ask of Him in prayer, so true it is that prayer digs up those treasures which the Gospel of our Lord discovers to the eye of faith.[4]

Prayer can be delineated as an act of faith and worship whereby the precious promises of God are brought home to the mind of the believer. In a formal definition the Westminster Shorter Catechism states: "Prayer is an offering up of our desires unto God, for things agreeable to His will, in the name of Christ, with confession of our sins, and thankful acknowledgement of His mercies."[5] Hodge defines the action of prayer as that wherein "we manifest or express to him our reverence, and love for his divine perfection, our gratitude for all his mercies, our penitence for our sins, our hope in his forgiving love, our submission to his authority, our confidence in his care, our desires of his favour, and for the providential and spiritual blessings needed for ourselves and others."[6] Elsewhere Hodge discussed the meaning of prayer in this way:

> It is not simply petition, but converse with God, including therefore, 1. The expression of our feelings in view of his greatness and glory, i.e., adoration. 2. The expression of our feelings in view of His goodness, i.e., thanksgiving. 3. The expression of our feelings in view of our sins and sinfulness, i.e., confession. 4. The expression of our feelings in view of our wants i.e., supplication.[7]

As the Calvinist approaches the knotty problem of prayer and sovereignty, he does not conceive of them as opposites. Indeed, prayer is valid only when it is foundationed on the sovereignty of God. Prayer is primarily, though not exclusively, an act of communication through worship whereby the "treasures" of God's promises come to the believer. Prayer is not so much the vehicle of benevolent acquisition as that of worship.

The Function of Prayer

While prayer is the subjective response of the rational creature to the benevolent deity, the question must be asked, What is the purpose for which God instituted it? Believers are to pray because

He ordered them in His infinite wisdom to do so, thus making prayer a wise human function, but for what purpose did He leave these instructions? In the Reformed tradition prayer is conceived under the rubric of the "means of grace," which are "those means which God has ordained for the end of communicating the life-giving and sanctifying influences of the Spirit to the souls of men."[8] By this means, as well as the Word of God and the ordinances, the saint is drawn to God and matured in spiritual experience. Prayer is a means of the self-disclosure of the great condescending God whereby His creatures are permitted to gain insight and understanding of His ways. A. A. Hodge views prayer as an educational vehicle.

> The great design of God in this relation is to effect our education and government as rational and spiritual beings. He accomplishes these ends by revealing to us His perfections, by training our intellects to follow the great lines of thought developed in His plans and revealed in His works, and by training us to action in the exercise of all our faculties as coworkers with each other and with Him in the execution of His plans.[9]

This prayer has been ordained of God as a means of "man's receiving His spiritual influences."[10] In what sense then is prayer a means of conveying God's gracious influences to the soul? The answer is twofold: first, by changing the saint inwardly without changing the saint's immediate circumstances, and second, by changing external circumstances.

Before delineating the two foci of prayer as a means of grace to the believer, a secondary yet important question should be raised regarding prayer. Does the believer obligate God to answer his requests if he sincerely, honestly, and selflessly pleads? If believers subscribe to the biblical conditions for answered prayer, are God's promises that He will answer to be considered absolute? Charles Hodge answers this question rather bluntly.

> A false doctrine has been deduced from these passages, viz: that every specific request made with the assurance of its being granted, shall be granted. This cannot be true.
> 1. Because it would be to submit the divine government to the erring wisdom of men.
> 2. Because it would lead to undesirable or disastrous consequences. Men might pray for things which would be their own ruin and the ruin of others.
> 3. It is contrary to all experience.
> 4. It is contrary to the desire of every pious heart, as every Christian would rather that God's will than his own should be done.[11]

Hodge concluded by affirming that the great promises of God do not apply to every case, but "assert the general course of providence. And this is enough for encouragement and direction."[12]

PRAYER AND THE BELIEVER

Prayer, as a means of sanctifying grace, results in the alteration of the saint, that is, it effects his spiritual maturity. Calvin is eloquent in arguing that prayer changes the one who prays.

> The necessity and utility of this exercise of prayer no words can sufficiently express. Assuredly it is not without cause our heavenly Father declares that our only safety is in calling upon his name, since by it we invoke the presence of his providence to watch over our interests, of his power to sustain us when weak and almost fainting, of his goodness to receive us into favor, though miserably loaded with sin, in fine, call upon him to manifest himself to us in all his perfections. Hence, admirable peace and tranquillity are given to our consciences; for the straits by which we were pressed being laid before the Lord, we rest fully satisfied with the assurance that none of our evils are unknown to him, and that he is able and willing to make the best provisions for us.[13]

Dabney simply writes, "Prayer is not intended to produce a change in God, but in us."[14] Calvin continues: "It was not so much for His sake as for ours. He wills indeed, as is just, that due honour be paid Him by acknowledging that all which men desire or feel to be useful, and pray to obtain, is derived from Him. But even the benefit of the homage which we thus pay Him redounds to ourselves."[15] To argue that prayer changes the one who prays is most likely not contested ground. It is readily apparent that people change as they spend time with God. But what about the thorny question about the kind of prayer designated as supplication or intercession?

PRAYER AND CIRCUMSTANCES

A second facet of prayer as a means of grace whereby the knowledge and worth of God is brought safely home to the saint's experience is that of the providential alterations of circumstance. These, like the confronting of the believer's soul and mind in the context of sorrow or humiliation, function to cause the believer to experience the reality of faith's profession. In brief, the Calvinist would reply that God changes not only the invisible and internal, but also He most certainly changes the visible and external. As A. A. Hodge acknowledges,

The Scriptures assure us, and all Christians believe, that prayer for material as well as for spiritual good is as real a means effecting the end sought as is sowing seed a means of getting a crop, or as is studying a means of getting learning, or as are praying and reading the Bible a means of sanctification. But it is a moral, not a physical, cause. Its efficiency consists in its power of affecting the mind of God and disposing Him to do for us what He would not do if we did not pray.[16]

The Reformed tradition argues strongly for the God of history, who sovereignly directs the course of all events. Similarly it is understood that the New Testament finds no conflict between the sovereignty of God and the effectual power of supplication by His people.

This Supreme Power is roused into action by prayer, in a way analogous to that in which the energies of a man are called into action by the entreaties of his fellow men. This is the doctrine of the Bible; it is perfectly consistent with reason, and is confirmed by the whole history of the world, and specially the Church. Moses by his prayer saved the Israelites from destruction; at the prayer of Samuel the army of the Philistines was dispersed. . . . This of course supposes that prayer is a power. Queen Mary of Scotland was not beside herself, when she said she found the prayers of John Knox more than an army.[17]

Thus Calvin's conclusion at this point is entirely appropriate: "It is very absurd, therefore, to dissuade men from prayer, by pretending that Divine Providence, which is always watching over the government of the universe, is in vain importuned by our supplications, when, on the contrary, the Lord Himself declares, that He is 'nigh unto all that call upon Him, to all that call upon Him in truth' (Ps. CXLV. 18)."[18]

While the Calvinists extol, even celebrate, the power of prayer, it must not be conceived that the power of prayer is unlimited. It is not correct to say that Christians can do or receive anything by simply praying. To bring the problem into a sharper focus, this question may be posed: Does prayer change God's mind? Sproul writes, "When we are talking about God's sovereignty, do we think for a moment that if there is a conflict of interests between the will of God and my will, that my will could possibly prevail?"[19] Prayer then functions as a moral not a physical stimulus to God; it is limited by the will of God, which always takes precedence over the will of His creatures. Sproul concludes, "You cannot manipulate God. You cannot manipulate Him by incantations, repetition, public utterances, or your own predictions. God is sovereign. So when you bring your requests to God He may say yes, and He may say no."[20]

Thus prayer is viewed as an action of man wherein God has ordained to reveal Himself by internal and external comfort with the result that the one who prays is encouraged to deepen his walk with God. Prayer, like the Word of God and the ordinances, is a means of grace, that is, a vehicle by which God so condescends to the mind of the believer as to reveal His person; God's intent in prayer is ultimately the strengthening of the saint and the extension thereby of His will on the earth.

The Tensions in Prayer

While it might safely be argued that prayer is a means of the believer's sanctification, that it changes both the believer and the believer's circumstances, the doctrine of prayer is not without difficulties related to the character of God. It may be granted that "He commands it because He has seen fit to ordain it as the appointed means for reception of His blessings";[21] yet the finite mind is perplexed to answer some of the issues that can be raised. One argument emerges from the infinitude of God: it would appear inconsistent with His dignity to suppose that He concerns Himself with the trifling affairs of humans. "It assumes that his knowledge, power, or presence is limited; that he would be distracted if his attention were directed to all the minute changes constantly occurring throughout the universe. This supposes that God is a creature like ourselves, that bounds can be set to his intelligence or efficiency."[22]

Does infinitude dispense with prayer? No; instead infinitude establishes prayer. Another argument of the same type deals with the relationship of God's omniscience to prayer. If God is all-knowing, then why should believers inform Him? Calvin argues that Christians pray because it is a commanded means of grace.

> But someone will say, Does He not know without a monitor both what our difficulties are, and what is meet for our interest, so that it seems in some measure superfluous to solicit Him by our prayers, as if He were winking, or even sleeping, until aroused by the sound of our voice. Those who argue thus attend not to the end for which the Lord taught us to pray. It was not so much for His sake as for ours.[23]

Thus these objections to pray are not so difficult that an immediate reply cannot be marshaled. But what about the problem theologians call *concurrence,* the relationship between the ultimate providence of God and human desires and activities? While it can and should be argued that prayer is a wonderfully powerful instrument, that it changes outward circumstances and inward turmoil, what is the relationship of the prayers of the saints to the determinate counsel of God? What is the fundamental relationship between secondary and primary causality?

PRAYER AND THE FIXITY OF NATURAL LAW

To approach an intelligent consideration of the relationship of secondary cause (i.e., prayer) to primary actualization, it must be understood that God has sovereignly, and without conflict or incongruity, established both. A. A. Hodge writes:

> In order to accomplish both these ends at once, the education of our thought and the training of our faculty by active exercise, God has established a comprehensive and unchangeable system of laws, of second causes working uniformly, of fixed consequences and established methods, by which he works, and by which he can train us to understand his working and to work with him. This careful adherence to the use of means, to the slow and circuitous operational second causes and established laws, is surely not for God's sake. It cannot be necessary to him. It is ordained and rigidly adhered to only for our sake.[24]

The argument has been raised that if God has constructed a machine that is so perfect and so completely His, then to modify that perfect machine (i.e., the natural laws) would be to break it. Therefore prayer cannot be a even secondary cause for natural change because God's creation cannot be altered even by God Himself. To so argue would imply that God established such laws as to exclude Himself and His own purposes. Dabney is more specific when he writes:

> Now only postulate that desire, prayer, and the answers to prayer are among these general laws, which as a complex whole, have been assigned to regulate nature, and the uniformity of nature only confirms the hoped answers to prayers. Has the philosopher explored all the ties of natural causation made by God? He does not pretend so. Then it may be that among the unexplored ties are some subtle and unexplained bonds which connect prayer with their answers as natural causes and effects.[25]

Does natural law govern the universe? Does God govern it by natural law? The answer to these questions must be that people are wrong in thinking that law is a power, for it is simply the method of power.[26]

> This great permanent framework of second causes and natural laws is, of course, incomparably more flexible in the hands of God than it can be in the hands of man. We know these laws partially and imperfectly: God acts upon them internally. We act upon them at a few isolated points:

> God acts upon every point of the infinite system at the same time. Surely, therefore, while God can act through nature in a supernatural manner, He can also, like us, only infinitely more perfectly, act through nature and in accordance with natural law in accomplishing His purposes.[27]

Thus with regard to the accomplishment of God's purpose through the agency of natural law, He not only wills an end but also the proper secondary causes productive of that effect. God does not violate natural law but natural law is not an immutable god; God alone, not His creation, is God. To effect an end God also ordains the proper arrangement of secondary causes (i.e., prayer).

PRAYER AND THE DOCTRINE OF SOVEREIGNTY

The relationship between divine sovereignty as primary cause and prayer as a secondary cause raises the tempo of the question of the relationship of causes. While one might agree that prayer is a divinely given constituent of natural law, it may be more difficult to conceive the direct relationship of absolute sovereignty to human petitioning. If God has absolutely decreed all that can and will come to pass to the smallest detail in the lives of every human being, does prayer change things? Or do believers pray because God has yet to determine His will for them? To state the issue theologically in the words of Francis Turretin, seventeenth-century professor of theology at the Academy of Geneva, "How can the concourse of God be reconciled with the contingency and liberty of second causes?"[28] Turretin discusses the difficulty of this question.

> The providence of God concurs with all second causes and especially with the human will, and yet its own contingency and liberty remain unimpaired. But how these two things can consist with each other no mortal can in this life perfectly understand. Nor should it seem wonderful since He has a thousand ways, to us incomprehensible, of concurring with our will, insinuating Himself into us, and turning our hearts, so that by acting freely what we will, we still do nothing besides the will and determination of God.[29]

One Calvinist who has most recently raised the issue of primary and secondary causality concludes with the answer, "I do not know! I have not a clue."[30] While this answer is blunt, it does speak to the inadequacy of finitude when confronted by infinitude. Dabney, however, adds these comments:

> The familiar old answer applies here, that God's decree embraces the means as much as the end. Whenever it was His eternal purpose that

anyone should receive certain graces, it was His purpose equally that he should ask. In a word, these objections are just the same with those of the vulgar fatalists, who object that "what is to be will be," therefore it is of no use to make any effort. . . . To be consistent, these rationalists who refuse to pray should also refuse to plow, to sow, to cultivate, to take medicine when sick, to watch against danger, etc.[31]

A. A. Hodge speaks to the same point.

Prayer is only one means appointed by God for attaining our ends. In order to educate us, he demands that we should use the means, or go without the ends which depend upon them. There are plenty of fools who make the transcendental nature of eternity and of the relation of the eternal life to God to the tome-life of man an excuse for neglecting prayer. But of all the many fools in the United States, there is not one absurd enough to make the same eternal decree an excuse for not chewing his food or for not voluntarily inflating his lungs.[32]

The Calvinist would argue for the truly effectual character of both primary and secondary causation, yet the exact relationship of the causative agencies is blurred in the complexities of conceiving infinitude from the vantage point of finiteness.

God so concurs with second causes that although He previously moves and predetermines them by a motion, not general only, but also special, still He moves them according to their own nature, and does not take away from them their own proper mode of operating. The reason is because the decree of God is occupied not only about the determination of things which ought to be done, but also the means according to which they are to be, relatively to the nature and condition of each; so actual Providence, which is the execution of this decree, not only secures the infallible futurition of the thing decreed, but also its taking place in the very manner decreed, to wit, consentaneously with the nature of each, that is, necessary things take place necessarily, free and contingent things, however, freely and contingently.[33]

Conclusion

Thus prayer is understood as primarily a means of grace, a vehicle of progressive sanctification. Prayer is essentially an act of worship wherein homage is given to God alone through praise, adoration, confession, or request. The purpose of prayer, while it points alone to God as the source of all benevolences, is a help for the saint to strengthen Christian experience. Calvin argues that the action of prayer is a Christian necessity.

Wherefore, although it is true that while we are listless or insensible to our wretchedness, he wakes and watches for us, and sometimes even assists us unasked; it is very much for our interest to be constantly supplicating him: first, that our heart may always be inflamed with a serious and ardent desire of seeking, loving, and serving him, while we accustom ourselves to have recourse to him as a sacred anchor in every necessity; secondly, that no desire, no longing whatever, of which we are ashamed to make him the witness, may enter our minds, and thus pour out our heart before him; and, lastly, that we may be prepared to receive all his benefits with true gratitude and thanksgiving, while our prayers remind us that they proceed from his hand. Moreover, having obtained what we ask, being persuaded that he has answered our prayers, we are led to long more earnestly for his favour, and at the same time have greater pleasure in welcoming the blessings which we perceive to have been obtained by our prayers.[34]

Prayer then is not so much asking favors as it is a worshipful experience that includes request. The fruit of answered prayer is most importantly the deepening of one's spiritual life. This is accomplished as God graciously quiets the turbulent saint without altering external circumstances or as He changes the course of history or as He does both. The end of prayer is not so much tangible answers as a deepening life of dependency and love that can come to the saint only through this means of grace. The call to prayer is a call primarily to love, submission, and obedience; it is a call to God who entreats the believer to a life of adoration.

While prayer has paradoxes, it should not drive the believer to uncertainty. It is because God is absolutely sovereign that the believer for his own sake must heed God's invitation to bring his petitions and praises to Him. Not only does God invite the child of God to His presence in prayer, He also has provided a Mediator who constantly carries the believer's weak, stuttering petitions to His throne of grace (Heb. 7:25). Furthermore, with the invitation comes the assistance of God's Spirit, who knows the secret counsels of the Father and who aids the saint in prayer (Rom. 8:26–27). While the relationship of prayer to the sovereignty of God cannot be fully comprehended by the finite mind, prayer can assuredly be enjoyed by believers as the avenue of sweet, intimate, and intense fellowship of the soul with the infinite Creator.

CHAPTER 5

The Meaning of Crossbearing

Michael P. Green

T he issue of crossbearing is relevant to all Christians who are sincere in their devotion to their Lord, for He Himself said, "If anyone wishes to come after Me, let him deny himself, and take up his cross, and follow Me" (Mark 8:34). But what is involved in taking up one's cross? Is it literal or figurative, active or passive, once-for-all or ongoing, required for all believers or optional for only the more mature? What are its prerequisites, and what are its consequences? In light of the many and diverse interpretations that have been proposed to explain this phrase and because of the stress laid on this concept by various Christian groups, especially those suffering or undergoing persecution, and because of its relationship to personal discipleship, it is important that the meaning of crossbearing be clearly understood by the church.

Various Interpretations of Crossbearing

An overview of the many proposed interpretations of crossbearing evidences the confusion that exists over what Jesus actually meant. The following views of Mark 8:34—more than a dozen of them—are grouped on the basis of their starting points. Often differing starting points yield views with similar interpretations.[1]

LITERAL VIEWS (MARTYRDOM)

The fully literal view. Proponents of this view argue that since Jesus' cross was unquestionably literal, so the cross for His followers should be.[2]

The theoretical-literal view. This view recognizes that not every believer will be crucified or even martyred. Thus it substitutes "willingness," "readiness," or "preparedness" for martyrdom (in place of actual martyrdom).[3]

FIGURATIVE VIEWS

The vast majority of Bible students hold that crossbearing is to be understood figuratively rather than literally. They approach the subject from one of four starting points: (1) the image of crucifixion, (2) the text, (3) a religious tradition, and (4) theology.

Those starting with the image of crucifixion. (a) The self-denial view. This interpretation is usually stated as "a vivid metaphor for self-denial"[4] or "the total death of the self-life."[5] (b) The suffering view. By far the most commonly offered interpretation of the disciple's cross is the view that it is a figure for suffering, pain, persecution, shame, humiliation, or rejection.[6]

Those starting with the text. (a) The lexical meaning of σταυρός as palisade view. This view sees the key to interpreting crossbearing in the lexical meaning of σταυρός as "a stake" or "a palisade." Thus crossbearing is understood as "a call to follow Jesus as the commander who has prepared a new life for His men behind the bulwark set up by Him."[7] (b) The proverbial expression view. According to this view, based on Plutarch (*Moralia* 554A), to carry one's cross is merely a proverb. Johnson, who holds this view, offers no interpretation of the phrase.[8] (c) The lifelong crossbearing view. Carrying one's cross "suggests a beginning of discipleship which then becomes a lasting state: the disciple of Christ is a crossbearer, and he remains this his whole life."[9] Crossbearing is thus a lifelong process culminating in one's death.

Those starting with a religious tradition. (a) Those starting with Jewish tradition. Three views on the meaning of crossbearing look to Jewish tradition for their starting point. One is the Zealot-expression view. This view sees the statement on crossbearing as an adaptation by Jesus of an expression used by Zealots. Crossbearing is thought to be "a profane popular expression,"[10] "which perhaps arose among the Zealots and was then applied to the discipleship of Jesus."[11] Another view pertaining to Jewish tradition is the cultic-marking view. Based on the precedence of signs or markings for possession, protection, and confession, this view explains crossbearing as a mark or seal of possession. Crossbearing is understood to mean "marking the forehead with a Tau; it is confession that one belongs to Jesus."[12] Another variation is the Abrahamic parallel view. This is developed from the *Midrash Rabbah* on Genesis 56:3, which reads, "and Abraham took the wood of the burnt offering (22.6)—like one who carries his stake on his shoulder." A footnote to this comment reads that the stake he carries is the one "on which he is executed."[13]

(b) Those starting with Christian tradition. One view from this vantage point is the yoke-equivalent view. Bonhoeffer has written, "The yoke and the burden of Christ are his cross."[14] This view argues that after the death of Jesus the saying in Matthew 11:29, "Take My yoke upon you," became the basis for "Let him . . . take up his cross" in Matthew 16:24; Mark 8:34; and Luke 9:23.[15] Another approach is the Pauline theology equivalent view, in which statements in the Gospels about crossbearing are understood to be the synoptic equivalent of Paul's theology of the cross and dying to self.[16]

Those starting with theology. Four views have their starting points in theology. (a) One is the requirement-for-salvation view. In his invaluable work *The Training of the Twelve,* Bruce says, "It is as if above the door of the school in which the mystery of redemption was to be taught, He had inscribed the legend: Let no man who is unwilling to deny Himself, and take up His cross, enter here."[17] Weber states, "In the face of the coming judgement there is, however, one way to salvation—to follow Christ." This is done when a disciple takes "seriously Jesus' word about taking up his Cross (Lk. 9.23)."[18]

(b) Another view may be called the proclamation-of-salvation view. This view finds a basis for understanding the crossbearing sayings in the proclamation of the Gospel. Morris, who holds to the suffering view, sees in the Christian's sufferings "the means of setting forward the purpose Christ achieved in His atoning death" which is "the taking of the gospel to those for whom it is intended," and this "is to tread the path of the cross."[19]

(c) Another view is the pacifist-kingdom view. Griffiths relates the saying to the "Messianic purpose" with Israel, which will "in its final acme . . . be realized in a spiritual destiny." In the "new house of Israel," the "new ἐκκλησία θεοῦ," the "Messianic aim of freedom from Rome's oppression" is not to be obtained by "armed rebellion" but by "the way of voluntary suffering."[20] This view could also be classified as a variant of the suffering view, but its eschatological orientation warrants seeing this as a separate view.

(d) Still another view is what may be called the body-of-Christ view. Morris, who supports several other views, has suggested that the crossbearing concept contains "the thought that in some sense Christ and His people are one."[21]

A Proposed Interpretation: Submission

It is this writer's position that the phrase "take up his cross" is a figure of speech derived from the Roman custom requiring a man convicted of rebellion against Rome's sovereign rule to carry the crossbeam *(patibulum)* to his place of execution. Thus the proper starting point is the historical basis for the phrase. This starting point, as will be shown, leads to an interpretation that crossbearing means to submit to the authority or rule one formerly rebelled against, or to obey God's will.

CONTEXTUAL EVIDENCE

All three Synoptic Gospels refer to taking up one's cross. Matthew 16:24; Mark 8:34; and Luke 9:23 place it after Peter's confession that Jesus is the Messiah and after Jesus' first intimation of His coming Passion. Matthew 10:38 and Luke 14:27 place it in a series of statements concerning discipleship.

A full development of the contextual argument for each of the five occurrences of the crossbearing sayings would require more space than is possible here. However, a few thoughts can be presented for the reader's further consideration. In Matthew 16:24 and Mark 8:34 the crossbearing statement follows Peter's rebuke of Jesus concerning His messianic role as One who must suffer many things. Then Peter was himself rebuked by Jesus (a) for not following ("Get behind Me," an echo of Jesus' response to Satan in the temptation [Matt. 4:10]), (b) for being an agent of Satan, and (c) for setting his mind on or expounding human interests, not God's. Jesus had explained what God's will is, and anyone who would dissuade Him from obeying God's will must be rebuked. For Jesus, obedience to God's plan for Him to be the suffering Messiah was imperative. Peter therefore needed to see that Jesus must always submit to the Father's will[22] and so must those who would follow Christ.[23] Thus the issue of submission to God, or obedience, was the occasion for the teaching on crossbearing in these two passages.

Though parallel to Matthew 16 and Mark 8, Luke 9 omits Jesus' rebuke of Peter. However, in verse 23 Luke records a significant variation: "take up his cross daily." This indicates that salvation is not in view here and also that the order of denying oneself, taking up one's cross, and following Christ is a logical order and not a chronological order.[24]

The two other occurrences of the crossbearing sayings are in Matthew 10:38 and Luke 14:27. In both verses the Passion context is absent. In Matthew 10, Jesus gave instructions to the Twelve before they were sent out to the lost sheep of Israel. In Luke 14, Jesus urged the multitudes to count the cost of being His disciples. Both chapters include a series of short exhortations to obedience and submission to God and His Son.

Jesus' call to crossbearing in Mark 8:34 was given to the multitudes, τὸν ὄχλον (the crowd). This indicates that these conditions for following Jesus apply to all, not just to a special class of believers. Jesus called them to "come after Me" (ὀπίσω μου ἐλθεῖν). The words "come after" have a Hebrew background meaning "to follow, to be obedient to."[25] The word translated "follow" means "to follow someone as a disciple."[26] The person who follows Jesus (as His disciple) must meet several requirements.

First, a disciple is to "deny himself." Was Jesus asking a disciple to "give up his personality"? No, because God has given each person a unique personality. Yet this idea is suggested by Arndt and Gingrich.[27] What is so inherent in "self" that it (rather than sin or greed or false gods) should be denied? The answer is simple; "self" is in rebellion against the King. One cannot follow Christ if he is in rebellion to Him.

To deny self is to begin to deal with one's inherent sin nature that results in his being hostile to God and His will (cf. Mark 7:15).[28] Self is what caused Peter to set his mind on human interests rather than God's (Mark 8:33). That same spirit of rebellion caused the elders, chief priests, and scribes to reject the King (Mark 8:31). One cannot follow Jesus if he is going the opposite way. But to deny oneself is incomplete. At best it leaves one in a neutral state, whereas *following* is active and positive. This calls for a second requirement.

Second, a disciple is to "take up his cross." This is the positive action needed after one has denied "himself." It is the active submission of the disciple, who formerly had been a rebel, to the authority of the King. To deny oneself is to cease rebelling against the King's rule and to take up one's cross is to submit to His rule. A disciple's cross, then, is not Jesus' cross, nor is it crucifixion. This distinction is crucial for a proper interpretation.[29]

In summary, the contexts of the crossbearing statements in the Synoptic Gospels lead one to expect the figure to mean obedience or submission. The phrases "come after," "follow Me," and "deny himself" all direct the reader to expect a command to obey and submit.

THEOLOGICAL EVIDENCE

Theologically Jesus' work on the cross was associated with obedience or submission. This has direct implications for disciples' crossbearing.

Morris wrote, "it is integral to the very nature of [Jesus'] sacrifice that it was . . . wrought in obedience."[30] Morgan has observed that "the cross was the supreme demonstration of Christ's absolute conformity to the will of God."[31] According to Murray, the atoning work of Christ is set forth in the Scriptures under four categories: sacrifice, propitiation, reconciliation, and redemption. But he includes them all under obedience.

> But we may properly ask if there is not some more inclusive rubric under which these more specific categories may be comprehended. The Scripture regards the work of Christ as one of obedience and uses this term, or the concept that it designates, with sufficient frequency to warrant the conclusion that obedience is generic and therefore embracive enough to be viewed as the unifying factor or integrating principle.[32]

In another place Murray provides an insightful summary of the role of obedience in Christ's atoning work as seen in the Old Testament.

> No passage in Scripture provides more instruction on our topic than Isa. 52:13–53:12. It is in the capacity as Servant that the person in view is introduced and it is in the same capacity He executes His expiatory function (Isa. 52:13, 15; 53:11). The title "Servant" derives its meaning from the fact that He is the Lord's Servant, not the Servant of men (cf. Isa. 42:1, 19; 52:13). He is the Father's Servant and this implies subjection to and fulfillment of the Father's will. *Servant* defines His commitment, and *obedience* the execution.[33]

According to the New Testament, Christ's atoning work is not to be thought of simply in terms of suffering, pain, grief, or even death, but in terms of a servant's obedience. It is not this author's desire to minimize the terrible agony of the Savior's sufferings nor their soteriological importance but rather to point out, as do the Scriptures, that their underlying value is found in their being the outworking of His obedience.

In Gethsemane Jesus prayed, "My Father, if it is possible, let this cup pass from Me; yet not as I will, but as Thou wilt" (Matt. 26:39), and "My Father, if this cannot pass away unless I drink it,

Thy will be done" (Matt. 26:42; cf. Mark 14:36; Luke 22:42). Jesus wrestled that night with His willingness to do the Father's will. He clearly saw the events before Him as requiring submission to the Father's will. In a similar way John 17 could be analyzed to demonstrate the theme of submission to the Father's will. "In obedience to God's will He accomplished the work of redemption."[34]

Paul also stated that Christ's atoning work should be understood in terms of obedience. "For as through one man's disobedience the many were made sinners, even so through the obedience of the One the many will be made righteous" (Rom. 5:19). Paul did not write that a person is made righteous because Christ *suffered,* but rather that one is made righteous because He *obeyed.* Philippians 2:6–11 is a classic passage on the nature of Jesus' incarnation.[35] Verse 8 is the climax, in which Paul explained the work of Christ as "becoming obedient." In extent His obedience was "to the point of death," and in manner it was "even death on a cross." For Paul the central issue in Christ's death was that it was an act of obedience; all else flows from this.

The writer of the Epistle to the Hebrews, referring to Jesus' prayer at Gethsemane, wrote, "Although He was a Son, He learned obedience from the things which He suffered" (Heb. 5:8). Westcott has commented that "sufferings in this sense may be said to teach obedience as they confirm it and call it out actively."[36] Thus the New Testament provides abundant evidence that Murray is correct when he says that the entire atoning work of Christ can be understood best under the rubric of "obedience." Calvin wrote that "our Lord had no need to undertake the bearing of the cross except to attest and prove his obedience to the Father."[37]

By advancing the interpretation of crossbearing as obedience/ submission and thereby excluding suffering from its meaning, some readers might be led to assume that this view excludes suffering from the believer's life as inevitable. On the contrary, this author believes that, assuming a believer lives long enough, every believer will somehow suffer, in view of his identification with Christ. Mark 4:17 seems to indicate this, as do Mark 13:9, 13. In addition, one could note Romans 8:17–25, 35–39, as well as 1 Peter 2:20–25; 3:14–4:2; and 4:12–13.

In summary, even if an interpreter desired to explain the figure of the disciples' crossbearing on the basis of a parallel to the Savior's cross rather than as a figure from Roman custom, he should still conclude that the figure represents obedience or submission to God's will. While this author emphasizes that the believer's cross is not Christ's, there is a strong and clear evidence from theology that for Christ the cross was in its essence an act of obedience or submission to the Father's will. If there is any sense in which the disciple is to imitate Christ in taking up his cross, it is this.

HISTORICAL EVIDENCE

The Roman penal system required a condemned man to carry his cross to the place of his execution. The phrase "take up his cross" is a reference to this practice. But why did the Romans require a condemned man to carry his cross through the city to the place of his execution?

Non-Roman references to crucifixion. Crucifixion was used by the ancient Persians, as well as by the Indians, Assyrians, Scythians, Taurians, and Celts. Later the Germani and Britanni adopted it.[38] The Numidians employed crucifixion and the Carthaginians especially used it. Hengel suggests that Rome adopted this practice from Carthage.[39] In Greece "it was never even considered for free Greeks,"[40] and in the pre-Roman Hellenistic period "crucifixion was not unknown as a punishment for state criminals."[41] Crucifixion was generally associated with crimes against the state, whereas other forms of capital punishment were used for other crimes.

Two helpful references to crossbearing occur in Greek writings from the Roman period. Plutarch, in describing the relationship of wickedness to punishment, cites several examples, one of which is that "every criminal who goes to execution must carry his own cross on his back."[42] Though Plutarch does not here explain the significance of crossbearing, his use of "every" (ἕκαστος) is significant because most ancient references to crucifixion do not mention crossbearing. Thus Plutarch's reference to crossbearing as apparently normative provides substantial evidence for assuming that the common people would be familiar with this practice.

The second Greek reference to crossbearing is by Chariton of Aphrodisias. He lived in Asia Minor and wrote in the first or second century A.D. Sixteen escaped slaves, having been captured, were led to their execution in chains, each carrying his own cross. Chariton comments, "The executioners supplemented the necessary death penalty by other wretched practices such as were *effective as an example* to the rest [of the slaves]."[43] Hengel comments that "the whole proceedings were designed above all as a deterrent."[44] Thus crossbearing and other practices associated with crucifixion had as their purpose not a more horrible death, as is usually assumed, but rather the fulfillment of an exemplary function. They were intended to be observed and understood.

Roman references to crucifixion. In the Roman Empire crucifixion was reserved for the most serious of capital crimes.[45] Bruce notes that crucifixion was "customary for seditious provincials."[46] Hengel concludes that it was "as a rule reserved for hardened criminals, rebellious slaves and rebels against the Roman state."[47] And "crucifixion was practised above all on . . . groups whose development had to be suppressed by all possible means to safeguard law and order in the state."[48] Tacitus wrote that the crucifixion of slaves was to prevent rebellion, to maintain the slaves in submission to Roman rule.[49] In a province, the local governor could impose the penalty of crucifixion as he willed "based on his *imperium* and the right of *coercitio* to maintain peace and order."[50] "Governors imposed this servile punishment especially on freedom fighters who tried to break away from Roman rule."[51] The imposition of crucifixion on those "who rose up against the empire"[52] and resisted its authority[53] "was seen as a disciplinary measure for the maintenance of existing authority, intended more as a deterrent than as a means of retribution."[54] Crucifixion was therefore done in a public place. Hengel refers to this deterrent function as "the chief reason for its use."[55] Again and again the literature on crucifixion stresses the themes of the sovereignty of the state, its rule and power, and the nature of those crucified as "rebellious." It is in this historical context that crossbearing occurred, and it is in this context that the purpose of crossbearing and thus its meaning will be found.

Crossbearing was only one part of the crucifixion process. Normally, in the Roman era, the process began with flogging until the criminal's blood flowed. Next the victim carried the transverse bar *(patibulum)* of his cross to the place of execution. The crossbearing journey was through public areas, and "crucifixion took place publicly on streets or elevated places."[56] The vertical stake of the cross was a permanent fixture, installed beforehand at the execution site. "On the way to execution a tablet was hung around the offender stating the *causa poenae,* and this was affixed to the cross after execution so that all could see."[57] Once at the execution site, the offender was fastened to the beam with ropes or nails and the crossbeam and body were lifted into place on the vertical stake.[58] There were many variations of cross structures and methods of affixing the offender to the cross.[59]

Judaism and crucifixion. God placed a curse on anyone who hung on a tree (Deut. 21:23). The Jews also applied this curse to anyone crucified.[60] "In the Hellenistic Hasmonean period crucifixion was practiced as the form of death penalty applied in cases of high treason."[61] Herod, however, broke with the Hasmonean practice, and in light of the excessive use of crucifixion in pacifying Judea, he abandoned it. By the time of Jesus, the death penalty and thus crucifixion was entirely a matter of Roman jurisdiction.[62] Thus the meaning of crossbearing to a Jew of Jesus' day would be derived from the Roman use of it.[63]

Crucifixion was well known to the Jews of Jesus' time. The best known example is the crucifixion of two thousand Jewish rebels in 4 B.C. (According to Hoehner's chronology Jesus was born in the winter of 5/4 B.C.,[64] thus placing this event in His lifetime.) Nazareth was a small village about four miles southeast of Sepphoris, the capital of Western Galilee.[65] After Herod's death in March/April 4 B.C., a revolt under Judas the Galilean broke out and the rebels raided the palace and armory at Sepphoris. The Roman commander Publius Quintilius, governor of Syria, put down the revolt, which had spread across the countryside, and crucified two thousand of the rebels.[66] Thus there is abundant evidence that even in the countryside the common Jew would have had enough experience with Rome to know what crossbearing meant. Hengel notes that "the cross never became the symbol of Jewish suffering."[67] The primary purpose of crucifixion was not to maximize the pain of death, though it certainly was painful. In support of this, "according to Talmudic tradition (bSanh., 43a; Str.-B., I, 1037) high-placed ladies in Jerusalem used to give an intoxicating drink to the condemned before execution in order to make them insensitive to pain."[68] If the purpose of crucifixion was to maximize suffering this would not have been allowed; yet it was done with the full knowledge of the Romans.[69] If, however, crucifixion was to be a public example that every rebel ultimately must submit to Rome's rule, then the authorities could allow the practice.

It is this author's opinion that the historical evidence best supports a submission view of crossbearing. In the provinces, Roman rule was held together by the popular perception that any challenge to Rome's authority was doomed. It was thus imperative that any serious challenge to Rome's rule be met not only victoriously, but also turned into a public demonstration that in the end the rebel had submitted. Having condemned a person to die for his rebellion, Rome required him, as his last act, to display submission publicly to the authority against which he previously had rebelled. This was done by having him carry the instrument of his judgment through the city to a public place while wearing a sign that said that he had been a rebel. But as all could see, he was now submissive. To "take up his cross" was thus a figure of speech easily understood by anyone in the Roman Empire to mean "to submit to the authority against which one had previously rebelled."

Conclusion

The requirement that a disciple "take up his cross" means "to submit to the rule against which he was formerly in rebellion." Evidence for this meaning of "obedience" or "submission" was developed from the biblical passages and their contexts, theology, and history. To "deny" self means to cease rebelling against the King and His rule—to cease being hostile to God, to stop being disobedient. To "take up his cross" means to submit actively to the King and His reign—to obey God and do His will. The one who does this is thus following Jesus.

CHAPTER 6

Encountering God at Bethel

Allen P. Ross

T he clear revelation of God's gracious dealings with humans can transform a worldly individual into a worshiper. It is a drama that has been repeated again and again throughout the history of the faith. Perhaps no story in Scripture illustrates this so vividly as Jacob's dream at Bethel, recorded in Genesis 28:10–22. Before this experience Jacob was a fugitive from the results of his sin, a troubled son in search of his place in life, a shrewd shepherd setting out to find a wife. But after this encounter with God he was a partner with Him as a recipient of God's covenant promises and a true worshiper. The transformation is due to God's intrusion into the course of his life.

The Narrative

The story unfolds quickly and dramatically.[1] Being *persona non grata* in Canaan after deceiving Isaac and receiving the blessing, Jacob went on his way to Haran until things settled down. At sundown he stopped at a "place" and took "one of the stones of the place" to prepare for the night. But in a dream that night God appeared to him from the top of an angel-filled stairway and confirmed that the blessing was indeed his. When Jacob awoke he was afraid because he realized that the Lord was in that place; at dawn he set up the stone as a memorial, named the place Bethel, "the house of God," and vowed to worship there when he returned to his father's house in peace.

The Narrative's Literary Features

The literary devices in the passage are designed to show that the vision inspired the manner of Jacob's worship and gave new meaning to the place of his vision. The repetition of key terms throughout the narrative ties the whole account together and explains the significance of Jacob's response.[2] In his dream Jacob saw a stairway standing (מֻצָּב) on the earth, and the Lord standing

(נִצָּב) above or by it. This repetition suggests that the stairway functioned to point to the Lord. Then in view of what he saw Jacob took the stone he had used and set it up as a מַצֵּבָה (pillar), this word recalling the previous two. By setting up the stone in this way Jacob apparently wanted to establish forever that he had seen the Lord standing over the stairway. The wordplays then focus the reader's attention on Jacob's vision of the Lord—the standing stairway pointing to it and the standing stone being a reminder of it.

The repetition of the word רֹאשׁ also confirms this connection between the two parts. Jacob had seen the stairway with its top (רֹאשׁוֹ) in the heavens, and so he anointed the top (עַל־רֹאשָׁהּ) of the stone that he set up in commemoration, a stone he had used for the place of his head (מְרַאֲשֹׁתָיו).

Moreover, the key words in verses 11–12, the last part of the vision, are reversed in their order in the first part of the response. Jacob saw the stairway reaching to *heaven,* in it the angels of *God,* and above it *the Lord.* That the central focus is on the Lord is clear from the inversion; what came last in the vision is the first thing Jacob was concerned with. He exclaimed, *"The LORD is in this place. . . . This is . . . the house of God, and this is the gate of heaven!"* (vv. 16–17, italics added).

The story deliberately emphasized the place's insignificance, which leads up to its naming in verse 19. The word "place" is used six times in the story. Verse 11 reports that Jacob came upon a place to spend the night, took one of the stones from the place, and lay down in that place. But in the second half of the narrative, after the theophany, Jacob said, "Surely the LORD is in this place," and "How awesome is this place!" Then he named that place "Bethel," though it was formerly called Luz (v. 19). It was not an anonymous place after all: there was a city nearby called Luz. But for the sake of this story it was just a "place" until it became Bethel.

The literary features, then, strengthen the development of the motifs of the narrative to show how a place became a shrine, a stone became an altar, and a fugitive became a pilgrim—God in His grace revealed Himself to Jacob in that place.

The Function of the Narrative

The two most significant events in the life of Jacob were nocturnal theophanies. The first was this dream at Bethel when he was fleeing from the land of Canaan, which, ironically, was his by virtue of the blessing. The other was his fight at Peniel when he was attempting to return to the land. Each divine encounter was a life-changing event.

But the location of these episodes in the Jacob stories is strategic. The Bethel story forms the transition from the Jacob-Esau cycle to the Jacob-Laban cycle, and the Peniel story forms the connection back to the Esau story. In each of the encounters with God there is instilled in the patriarch great expectation for the uncertain future. In this incident at Bethel, Jacob's vow expresses his anticipation for the future. God would now be with him and help him, even though he might be slow to realize it. The promise of God's presence and protection would bring continued encouragement during the twenty years with Laban.

The parallels between this story and the beginning of Genesis 32 are striking, showing that the story of Jacob's sojourn in Aram is deliberately bracketed with supernatural visions.[3] In this story Jacob saw the angels of God (מַלְאֲכֵי אֱלֹהִים) on the stairway, but in 32:1 the angels of God (מַלְאֲכֵי אֱלֹהִים) met him.[4] These are the only two places in the book of Genesis where reference is made to the "angels of God." In addition, in both passages (28:11; 32:1) the construction of the verb "encountered, met" is the same, a preterite form of פָּגַע with the preposition בְּ and the object. In 28:16–17 זֶה is used four times, the last two being in the statement, "This is the House of God, this is the gate of heaven"; and in 32:2 it reappears in the clause "this is the camp of God." Also in both accounts Jacob names the spot, using the same formula for each: "and he named that place (הַהוּא וַיִּקְרָא אֶת־שֵׁם־הַמָּקוֹם)." And finally, "go" and "the way" (הוֹלֵךְ and דֶּרֶךְ) in 28:20 KJV are reflected in 32:2.

The stories about Jacob's encounters with God or His angels also form an interesting contrast with the other Jacob stories. Jacob is usually working against another individual in the narratives, first Esau in the Jacob-Esau cycle of chapters 25–27, and then Laban in the Jacob-Laban cycle of chapters 29–31, and then Esau again in 33. The account in chapter 34 of the defilement of Dinah also shows a crisis, though Simeon and Levi figure more prominently in that narrative. But in the encounter passages (28:10–22 at Bethel; 32:2–3 at Mahanaim; 32:23–33 at Peniel; and 35:1–7, 14–15 at Bethel again, the latter forming a conscious liturgical conclusion to the whole complex[5]) Jacob alone is

mentioned. Neither Esau nor Laban were with him. In fact Esau
never experienced any divine appearance, and Laban received
only a warning dream. But when Jacob had these appearances he
participated in liturgical acts. The narratives, then, heighten
what the Bethel story declares, namely, that Jacob's life
functioned on two levels: his conflicts with individuals and his
encounters with God. The encounters assured Jacob that he
would prevail in the conflicts.

This liturgical motif forms the climax in the Bethel story. In
fact Westermann calls the whole story a sanctuary foundation
narrative.[6] It explains how Bethel came to be such an important
center for the worship of the Lord. Because God actually met the
patriarch on this spot, it was holy ground. Here then was a place
where worship was appropriate.

The Setting

The story begins with Jacob's departure from Beersheba for
Haran. The preceding narrative in Genesis explains the reason for
this trip—Esau was threatening to kill him for stealing the blessing.
So it was, as Kidner says, that Jacob was thrust from the nest he
was feathering.[7]

To be sure, Jacob had obtained the blessing by deception at
first but then had it confirmed by the shaken Isaac (28:1–4) who,
realizing what had happened, was powerless to change it (27:37).
But were the promises actually his? If he truly was the heir, why
must he flee from the land? Would God's blessing be his as it had
been Abraham's and Isaac's before him? Nothing less than a sure
word from God would ease his doubts and give him confidence
for the future.[8]

The narrative unfolds in a disarmingly casual manner. Jacob
came upon[9] a place where he would stay for the night, for the sun
had set. The only detail that is mentioned is that he took "one of
the stones" at random to lay by his head while he slept.[10] But this
casual finding of an anonymous place and taking one of the stones
in the darkness of night begins to build suspense.

The Vision

With an abrupt change of style that brings the vision into the
present experience, the narrative introduces the dream. Up to this
point the narrative sequence has employed preterites (וַיֵּלֶךְ, וַיֵּצֵא,
וַיִּפְגַּע, וַיָּלֶן, וַיִּקַּח, וַיָּשֶׂם, וַיִּשְׁכַּב, and וַיַּחֲלֹם), but this is now broken off

abruptly by means of the repetition of הִנֵּה followed by participles. Jacob was surprised by what he dreamed, and the reader is vividly made aware of this. Fokkelman points out that the particle הִנֵּה functions with a deictic force; it is pre- or paralingual. It goes with a lifted arm, an open mouth: "—there, a ladder! oh, angels! and look, the Lord Himself!"[11]

The arrangement of the clauses also narrows the focus to the central point of the vision, the Lord. Each clause in Hebrew is shorter than the preceding; the first has seven words, the second six, and the third four:

> There was a stairway standing on the earth with its top reaching the heavens,
> And there were angels of God ascending and descending on it,
> And there was the Lord standing over it.

Attention is focused first on the setting, then narrowed to the participants, and then to the Lord.[12]

The first thing noticed is the stairway. סֻלָּם, translated "ladder" or "stairway," is a *hapax legomenon,* a word or form occurring only once in the biblical corpus. It has been traditionally connected to the root סָלַל, "to heap up, cast up." Related nouns are מְסִלָּה, "paved way" (but not of a street in a city), and סֹלְלָה, "a bank, siege-ramp" (2 Sam. 20:15). These suggested etymological connections, however, do not clarify the meaning.

The Greek text translated סֻלָּם with κλίμαξ, which can be translated "ladder" or "staircase." So too is the case with the Latin *scala.* The same uncertainty of meaning prevails with the versions.

Several specific interpretations have been offered for סֻלָּם,[13] but the one that has the most to commend it is the view that connects the סֻלָּם with Mesopotamian temple towers. The Akkadian word *simmiltu,* cognate to סֻלָּם, provides the link.[14] It is used to describe the "stairway of heaven" extending between heaven and the netherworld with messengers ascending and descending on it.[15] The comparison is certainly an attractive one. Another possible connection is with the celestial ladder found in the Pyramid Texts of Egypt.[16] But this may be too different. Pyramid Text 267 shows that the function of the stairway was to lead the deceased (king) to heaven.

The connection to Akkadian *simmiltu* with the Mesopotamian background is the most probable view. In the myth of *Nergel and Ereshkigal* communication between the netherworld and heaven takes place via the long stairway of heaven that leads to the gate of

Anu, Enlil, and Ea.[17] The idea of a ziggurat with its long staircase
to the temple top would be behind the idea. Nothing in Genesis
28, however, describes a ziggurat. The most that can be said is
that a word used in ziggurat settings is cognate to the word used
here, a word that fits the way of communication between heaven
and earth.[18] So Hebrew סֻלָּם is appropriate to the point of the
story—here was a place that heaven and earth touch, where there
is access to God.[19]

The second feature of the vision is the angelic hosts "ascending
and descending" on the stairway, suggesting their presence on
earth along with their access to heaven. Driver writes, "The vision
is a symbolic expression of the intercourse which, though invisible
to the natural eye, is nevertheless ever taking place between
heaven and earth."[20]

Nothing is said here about the function of the angels; likewise no
hint can be found in the corresponding episode at Mahanaim, which
simply reports that the angels "met him." Other references to angels
in Genesis are more helpful. Of course the cherubim in 3:24 guard
the way to the Tree of Life. Then in chapter 18 three visitors came
to Abraham and in chapter 19 two went on to meet with Lot in
Sodom. In 18:2 they are simply called "three men." That this may
be a manifestation of the Lord is suggested by the context and
reinforced by the use of נִצָּבִים עָלָיו in 18:2, which corresponds to
28:13. But in 19:1 the two who went to Sodom are called הַמַּלְאָכִים
שְׁנֵה. Their task was to rescue Lot before the judgment on the city.

The expression מַלְאַךְ יְהוָה, "the angel of the Lord," is used
interchangeably with "the Lord" in 22:11, 15–16. In 48:16 Jacob
apparently was referring to the Lord when he said, "The angel
(הַמַּלְאָךְ) who has redeemed me from all evil, bless the lads."

The activities in these passages are guarding, communicating,
rescuing, and protecting. In this vision, then, the angels of God
communicated God's protection for Jacob, the recipient of the
promises.

The third and central feature of the vision, however, was the
Lord who was standing over the stairway.[21] Later, in Genesis 48,
Jacob would identify the Lord as God Almighty (אֵל שַׁדָּי), explaining
that God had given him the blessing at Bethel.

The Promise

The word of the Lord in this vision took the form of a covenantal
communication and extended the patriarchal promises to Jacob.

The message begins with the identification of the Lord as the covenant God: "I am the LORD, the God of your father Abraham and the God of Isaac." This pattern of self-revelation was used in Genesis 15:7 for Abraham; it also appears in Exodus at the beginning of the covenant (Ex. 20:1) and throughout the Law when God stressed His covenant relationship to His people. The identification of Abraham as the "father" of Jacob shows the latter's continuity with the covenant.

The first part of the revelation guaranteed that Jacob would receive the blessings at first promised to Abraham. The wording of the promises is close to that in Genesis 13:14–16 and 22:17–18. Prominence is attached to the promise of the land, for it is mentioned before the seed promise and stressed by the word order: "The land on which you lie, I will give it to you and to your descendants."[22] The mention of descendants here would have been encouraging to Jacob, who was going to find a wife, and is further elaborated by the statement that the seed would "break out" ("spread out," NASB) and settle in every direction in this Promised Land (cf. 13:12–18).[23] Finally, the promise that all the families of the earth would be blessed in Jacob shows that the Abrahamic blessing had indeed been carried forward to Jacob (cf. 12:3).

These promises given to Jacob so dramatically would have provided him with confidence. Though he had been deceitful in gaining the blessing, God in His grace gave it to him, and even though he was fleeing from his land, God promised to give him the land.

The second part of the revelation guaranteed protection for Jacob in the sojourn. It begins with the promise of God's presence: "Indeed, I will be with you" (וְהִנֵּה אָנֹכִי עִמָּךְ). The promise of the divine presence carried God's chosen people through many times of danger and difficulty. It assured them that they did not have to accomplish His plan by themselves. Moses, for example, drew great comfort from this in his early career. When he was afraid to go to deliver the people, God said, "Surely I will be with you (עִמָּךְ כִּי אֶהְיֶה)." The writer of Psalm 46 also realized the benefits of God's presence: "The LORD of hosts is with us (עִמָּנוּ); the God of Jacob is our stronghold" (Ps. 46:7, 11). This passage also brings to mind Isaiah's oracle that promised "God is with us" (עִמָּנוּ אֵל, "Immanuel," NASB) (7:14).

That God's presence would guarantee safety is verified by the next verb, "and [I] will keep you" (Gen. 28:15). His presence,

then, meant that God would be Jacob's "keeper," so that no harm
would come to him wherever he should go.[24] Joshua also reminded
the people how God had protected them on their sojourn (Josh.
24:17). This is a theme that Psalm 121 develops for the pilgrim on
his way to Jerusalem, where he would hear the high priestly
blessing announce the same divine intent: "The LORD bless you
and keep you" (Num. 6:24). The promise of divine protection
does not exclude conflict and tension, but it does guarantee the
outcome for the good of the covenant and its recipient.

The promise concludes with the statement that God will restore
Jacob to the land to receive the promises. The statement "I will
not leave you *until* I shall have done" (Gen. 28:15, italics added)
need not imply that once God fulfills the blessing He will abandon
Jacob; rather it provides assurance that the promises just made
will be fulfilled. God's protective presence will work toward the
fulfillment of the promise.

The Realization

When Jacob awakened he was overwhelmed with the fact that
the Lord was "in this place" (v. 16). He had never imagined that
this rather ordinary place could be a holy place. Jacob here
realized what God had promised—His presence was with him.

Jacob's attitude of fear was appropriate for such a meeting with
the Lord. The term *fear* is used in the Bible to describe a mixture
of terror and adoration, a worshipful fear (cf. Ex. 19:16). People
may revere the Lord (the positive, worshipful, aspect of the word),
but when they comprehend more fully His sovereign majesty,
they shrink back in fear. All worshipful acts must begin with and
be characterized by reverential fear at the presence of the Lord
(Ex. 3:6; 19; Ps. 2:11). Of Jacob, Bush says, "His feelings upon
awakening were those of grateful wonder mingled with emotions
of reverential awe, bordering close upon dread."[25]

Jacob realized that this place was holy: "How frightening [KJV]
is this place! This is none other than the house of God, and this is
the gate of heaven." Here the motif of "house" is first introduced
(בֵּית אֱלֹהִים, "house of God"). By using this term Jacob designated
the place as a shrine. No literal house was there, nor an actual
gate. But it would now be known as a place where people could
find access to God, where God could be worshiped. He had "seen"
God in the heavens, and so God's "house" on earth was people's
gate to the heavens.

The Worship

Devotion. Early in the morning Jacob arose and stood the stone up as a pillar at which he could express his submission through worship. The preparation for worship by setting up a pillar raises questions about the custom. Graesser shows how standing stones in the ancient world would serve as markers, arresting the attention of the onlooker because they were not in their natural position.[26] Such a standing stone had to have been put that way; it would mark a grave (Rachel's pillar in Gen. 35:20), form a boundary (the treaty with Laban in Gen. 31:45), note some important event (Samuel's Ebenezer in 1 Sam. 7:12), or, as here, mark out a sacred area where God could be "found," where prayer could reach Him. This pillar would be a commemoration of the vision, recalling the stairway to heaven.

Jacob's offering took the form of oil poured on top of the stone, perhaps pointing to the Lord at the top of the stairway. Pouring the oil before the Lord was a gift to God, for it conveyed much the same attitude as making a sacrifice. It was a symbolic ritual act by which Jacob demonstrated his devotion to the Lord and consecrated the spot as holy to Him. Later, oil was used in worship to sanctify the holy places and holy things (Lev. 8:10–11). So this duly consecrated altar served to commemorate the appearance, to express the patriarch's devotion, and to guarantee the seriousness of the oath of the worshiper (cf. Gen. 12:8; 13:18; 26:25).

Commemoration. According to the story Jacob named the place "Bethel" because God had come near to him there. This naming actually transformed the place from being merely a Canaanite town called Luz into God's "house" for Jacob and his descendants to use for worship.[27]

Modern scholarship suggests that this spot was an original Canaanite shrine or sanctuary city, founded before the time of Abram and dedicated to the god El. Von Rad says that Bethel must have been known as a cult center before the time of Israel because a god named Bethel was worshiped there.[28] It is true that the name *Bethel* does not always seem to be a place name but at times is a divine name, perhaps developing metonymically through association with a shrine.[29] The evidence for this deity does not, however, include Phoenician or Ugaritic literature, and so the presentation of such a deity for the second millennium B.C. in Canaan cannot be convincingly defended. As far as the Hebrew account is concerned, the name of Bethel derives its significance from the fact that the Lord appeared to Jacob there. The motivation for the name came in the speech of verse 17, which is a stylized reaction to the theophany (cf. Gen. 16:13; Ex. 20:18; Deut. 5:24; Judge 6:22; 13:22).[30]

This part of the passage develops the theme of "house." The key is the patriarch's exclamation, "This is the house of God." He then preserved the vision by naming the place "House of God." But the word בַּיִת is repeated in verses 21a, b, and 22. It is as if this fugitive was saying that when he returned to settle in the land God would settle with him. God would go with him and bring him back to his father's "house" in peace. When he returned, there would be a "house" for God in the Promised Land.

Dedication. Jacob's promise to worship God at Bethel was solemnized by oath. Vows were not made to induce God to do something He was not willing to do. They were made to bind the worshiper to the performance of some acknowledged duty. Jacob made his vow on the basis of what God had guaranteed to do. So he was taking God at His word and binding himself to reciprocate with his own dedication.

The oath then must be divided between a *protasis* and an *apodasis*—"if . . . then." It is not easy to determine just where to make this division. The protasis should form the foundation for his promise and should include what God had promised to do. The apodasis should record what Jacob wanted to do for God. So the most appropriate place to start the apodasis may be in verse 22. The vow would then read:

> *If* the Lord God is with me,
> and keeps me in this way in which I am going,
> and gives me bread to eat and clothing to wear,
>   so that I return in peace to the house of my father,
> and the Lord becomes my God,
> *then* this stone which I set up as a pillar
>   will be the house of God,
> and all which you give me a tenth I will give to you
> (author's trans.).[31]

God had promised to be with him, keep him, bless him, return him in peace, in short, to be his God; Jacob promised that the spot would be a place of worship and that he would tithe.

The vow to tithe is the only part of Jacob's promise that is a real action. Moreover, the structure of the speech changes to the second person in a personal address to God directly. His gratitude and submission to God would be expressed through the paying of a tithe.

So Jacob did more than consecrate Bethel as a place of worship for the nation of Israel. He himself was moved to worship there, and his acts formed a pattern for later worshipers to follow in the offering of their devotion and their substance to God.

———

This brief account tells how God deals graciously with His covenant people. It tells how God suddenly and unexpectedly broke into the life of the deceiver who was fleeing for his life and assured him of the covenantal promises and His protective presence. But the point of the narrative is the effect on Jacob's life—he worshiped and prepared for the worship of his descendants at this "House of God."

The didactic level of the story for Israel would be clear. Jacob, who represents Israel in the story, who was anything but obedient at the outset, would spend a number of years outside the land (cf. Gen. 15:13–16). During that time God would protect and bless him (cf. Ex. 1:7, 12, 20) and ultimately return him to his inheritance. Such covenantal blessings should inspire worshipful devotion from God's people (cf. Ex. 5:1; 14:29–15:21; Josh. 4:19–24; 8:30–31).

The Christian experience is similar. The effectual revelation of God's gracious provision, those whom the Word of God has powerfully impressed, will respond with consecration and commitment. Where there is no reverential fear, no commitment, or no devotion, there is probably very little apprehension of what the spiritual life is all about. Like the revelation to Jacob, the written revelation of God makes the believer aware of the Lord's presence and prompts him to a higher level of living.

Chapter 7

Reexamining Biblical Worship

Kenneth O. Gangel

W orship in evangelical churches today is too often a congregational adaptation of good old American pragmatism—people do what they like and they like what they do. Worship experience has become a means to an end, as hymns, Scripture reading, and prayer serve as "preliminary activities" lead up to the focal point of worship, the preaching of God's Word. Without diminishing the importance of exposition, it is possible that one individual's comments about the Bible may be no more important than the worship pattern, no more truth-serving than singing God's Word or listening to it read in its purest, uninterrupted form.

Biblical worship is often corrupted by boredom, lack of purpose, and nonparticipational behavior that leads the congregation to go through the motions without genuine heart involvement. The opposite extreme offers little more than secular entertainment with a religious veneer, a packaged plastic program so perfect and professional that even the most sincere worshiper can scarcely break through its shrink-wrapped design to get his hands on true worship.

What Is Worship?

Webber defines worship as "a meeting between God and His people" and calls for renewal of worship based on the Scriptures and the history of the church.[1] He suggests that evangelicals actually suffer from an illness of which the failure to worship is a symptom. He warns that "the remedy consists of repentance, a *metanoia,* a turning away from all shallow and uninformed approaches to worship."[2]

Many people think the gospel of John focuses on evangelism, the message that whosoever will may come. But in his presentation of Jesus Christ the Son of God, John was concerned that people recognize His deity and bow before Him in worship. A blind beggar came to faith in the Savior after his sightless eyes saw light for the first time. Within hours he fell before the One who created sight "and he worshiped Him" (9:38).

In the Lord's encounter with the woman of Samaria (John 4) John mentioned "worship," "worshiped," or "worshipers" ten times (out of its thirteen occurrences in his gospel). The ten usages appear within five verses (4:20–24), dramatically demonstrating the difference between religion and Christianity. The Samaritan woman was deeply religious and knew precisely the appropriate place of worship, which in her view was Mount Gerizim. The Lord Jesus shoved aside the discussion of both place and time. Religion may emphasize the human struggle to find God, but the message of John's gospel identifies how God has revealed Himself to humans. It is not a matter of worshipers seeking for a hidden God but of a self-revealed God actively seeking the right kind of worshiper.

God is Spirit and His worshipers must worship Him "in spirit and truth" (John 4:23). The word "spirit" refers not to the Holy Spirit but to the spirit of the worshiper. One's posture in worship (kneeling, standing, bowing) is not the important thing. God is concerned with attitude before act, and wrong attitudes produce wrong acts.

To worship "in truth" means to be concerned for honesty before God and people. It also suggests that believers be biblical in their worship.

Small wonder that Paul affirmed, "God highly exalted Him, and bestowed on Him the name which is above every name, that at the name of Jesus every knee should bow, of those who are in heaven, and on earth, and under the earth, and that every tongue should confess that Jesus Christ is Lord, to the glory of God the Father" (Phil. 2:9–11). To the confused woman by the well the Lord offered the only voluntary declaration of messiahship in the entire New Testament—"I who speak to you am He" (John 4:26).

What then is worship? Worship is *affirmation*. In worship a believer acknowledges that God's revelation of Himself in Jesus Christ demands response. The self-revealed God awaits the reaction of His creation and that response is a duty for God's redeemed people, not some kind of emotion that sweeps over them in a certain hour on a certain day. In true worship believers affirm that they are His people and that He is their God. Worship looks above.

Worship is also *conservation*. The corporate worship of the people of God preserves and transmits the faith. They identify themselves with the people of God of all times and places. The Word and the words used to communicate the faith are a foundation to conserving and transmitting God's truth.

Worship is also *edification*. The worshiper gains increasing understanding of God's person and truth because proper worship teaches theology. In this sense biblical worship serves both the vertical and horizontal dimensions, though the latter should not be placed ahead of or even on a level with the former.

Worship is *celebration*. Believers celebrate their union with the Creator of the universe and with the Father of His people. They celebrate His marvelous works. They celebrate the birth, life, death, resurrection, and coming reign of the victorious Savior. And they invite others to join them in their homage.

> All people that on earth do dwell.
> Sing to the Lord with cheerful voice;
> Him serve with fear, His praise forth tell,
> Come ye before Him and rejoice.
>
> For why? The Lord our God is good,
> His mercy is forever sure;
> His truth at all times firmly stood,
> And shall from age to age endure.
>
> William Kethe
> "All People That on Earth Do Dwell"

Worship As Celebration

Celebration and joy are appropriate faith responses to God's work in His world. In ancient times Israel's leaders called the people to a festal mentality at times of worship. "Then Nehemiah the governor, Ezra the priest and scribe, and the Levites who were instructing the people said to them all, 'This day is sacred to the LORD your God. Do not mourn or weep.' For all the people had been weeping as they listened to the words of the Law.

"Nehemiah said, 'Go and enjoy choice food and sweet drinks, and send some to those who have nothing prepared. This day is sacred to our Lord. Do not grieve, for the joy of the LORD is your strength'" (Neh. 8:9–10 NIV).

How much more do church-age believers have reason to respond to God's grace as they are "speaking to one another in psalms and hymns and spiritual songs" (Eph. 5:19)! They rejoice in God's people as well as in God Himself, for their life together in the community of believers is cause for celebration. Not only this, but they also rejoice in their expectation of the Lord's return and the establishment of His kingdom on earth. True worship concentrates all one's physical, emotional, and spiritual faculties on a corporate self-giving to God in response to His love and in praise of His glory.

Often in the history of doctrine, worship has been viewed as the process of trying to give something to Someone who has everything. Thomas Aquinas, for example, concluded that worship is not for God's sake at all but for the sake of believers. Calvin responded that proper adoration of God is the prime purpose of Christianity.[3]

So dominant is the reality of grace, however, that believers find it extremely difficult to separate what God is from what God does. The question becomes, What can one give to Someone who gives everything? God's gifts provide an occasion to celebrate the Giver, and worship stimulates spiritual reaction. As Gilkey put it, "Worship is a response to the presence of God, our reaction to the appearance of the holy."[4]

When worship takes the form of response to a giving God, it honors grace by affirming that the heavenly Father has taken the initiative. The ultimate gift, of course, was the Cross. People's response to Calvary adorns the worship of the New Testament, causing it to stand in contrast to the cultic worship of first-century Mediterranean paganism. Christian worship was "decultified." Rather than secret rites practiced in darkened, scented cathedrals, worship is a normal, natural, and lifelike part of everyday behavior.

At certain times during the week Christians gather for collective praise. As Flynn put it in a book title, "Together we celebrate."[5] This corporate response of celebration does three things for the church:

1. It acknowledges God's supremacy by affirming who He is and what He has done. It agrees with God, honors Him, and says yes to His Word.
2. It rehearses God's goodness by affiliating with His great plan for the world in natural, personal, and special revelation (Ps. 100).
3. It proclaims God's truth by accenting that His message is more than just "Gospel"; it is the total scope of truth that always has its source in God (Ps. 93).

Clement of Alexandria (A.D. 150–220) described worship as celebration: "all our life is a festival: being persuaded that God is everywhere present on all sides, we praise Him as we till the ground, we sing hymns as we sow the seed, we feel His inspiration in all we do."

> I sing th'almighty pow'r of God
> That made the mountains rise,
> That spread the flowing seas abroad
> And built the lofty skies.
> I sing the wisdom that ordained
> The sun to rule the day;
> The moon shines full at His command
> And all the stars obey.
>
> I sing the goodness of the Lord
> That filled the earth with food;
> He formed the creatures with His word
> And then pronounced them good.
> Lord, how Thy wonders are displayed
> Where e'er I turn my eye,
> If I survey the ground I tread
> Or gaze upon the sky!
>
> There's not a plant or flow'r below
> But makes Thy glories known;
> And clouds arise and tempests blow
> By order from Thy throne;
> While all that borrows life from Thee
> Is ever in Thy care,
> And everywhere that man can be,
> Thou, God, art present there.
>
> Isaac Watts
> "I Sing the Mighty Power of God"

Practicing God's Presence

In ancient Israel the act of assembling focused on collectivity, the people of God in congregation. To be sure, there was a focus on place (tabernacle or temple). Sacred shrines and pious personnel are not essential ingredients of biblical worship, but the gathering of God's people, congregated in His presence, began at Mount Sinai where the assembling involved the actual formulation of a nation (Deut. 9:10, 14).

Many New Testament words express the act of gathering and reflect the sense of community so strategic in Paul's teachings. But none is more descriptive than the familiar word ἐκκλησία. Used more than one hundred times by New Testament writers, it speaks of people who are gathered out of the world.

Modern-day individualism has diminished and diluted the communal emphasis in Scripture. Piety has become compartmentalized, relegated to a private personal pocket of life. The result is a religious consumerism that describes worship as "attending the church of your choice." Western culture drowns in humanistic religion with its focus on "getting something out of the service."

Biblical worship, on the other hand, sees the Shepherd gathering the sheep, the Father gathering the children. The relational unity that God's people have with Him is, by its very strength, an antidote to individual loneliness (Ps. 106:47; Isa. 11:12; John 11:52; Eph. 1:7–10).

When Christians gather for worship, they practice God's presence by affirming His plan in their lives and in the entire world (Col. 1:15–20). People gather in groups for all kinds of reasons—fellowship, hospitality, fun, and even mutual service—but none other than worship exalts the glory of the triune God.

Many Christians have come to think of *orthodoxy* as correct doctrine when, as a matter of fact, a more specific use of the word would be "right worship." As the disciples gathered with Jesus in informal ways and places, they certainly were taught correct doctrine. But their communion with the Master stressed a relationship they were to cultivate, rather than merely a body of truth they were to learn. It is probably not incorrect to say that worship is *theantric,* or in other words, people and God coming together in a unique relationship designed and sustained by the Holy Spirit.

Practicing God's presence emphasizes the spirit of worship, not its forms. The church is an inn, not a fort. The gathered body is itself, even apart from its teaching and preaching, an act of evangelism, a symbol, a demonstration to an unbelieving world that the good news has been communicated and has been received (Acts 2:42–47).

> We gather together to ask the Lord's blessing;
> He chastens and hastens His will to make known;

The wicked oppressing now cease from distressing.
Sing praises to His name: He forgets not His own.

Netherlands folk hymn
"We Gather Together"

How Important Is the Day?

Ignatius of Antioch (A.D. 35–107) wrote, "Those who had walked in ancient practices attained unto newness of hope, no longer observing Sabbaths but fashioning their lives after the Lord's day on which our life also arose through Him."

Yet the Sabbath is grounded deeply in Old Testament history. Rooted in Creation, its observance hallowed time (Gen. 2:2–3). Rooted in the Mosaic covenant, its honor served as a reminder of God's creative work (Ex. 20:8–11), a reminder of the Exodus (Deut. 5:12–15), and as a sign between Israel and God (Ex. 31:13, 17). The Sabbath was to be hallowed by Israel (Lev. 23:3; Isa. 58:13–14).

But the Sabbath was made for man, not man for the Sabbath. Jesus often ministered on that great day, much to the horror of the Pharisees (Mark 2:27–28; John 5:17). That the early Christians were Jews makes their transition all the more remarkable. Keeping one day out of seven, they changed the emphasis from the seventh to the first day (John 20:1, 19, 26; Acts 20:7; 1 Cor. 16:2). By the end of the first century the first day had become known as "the Lord's day" (Rev 1:10). The Resurrection had brought assembly and rest under its first-day authority.

Justin Martyr (ca. A.D. 100–165) had opportunity to note how several generations of Christians understood the observance of Sunday. He concluded, "We all hold this common gathering on Sunday, since it is the first day, on which God transforming darkness and matter made the universe, and Jesus Christ our Savior rose from the dead on the same day."[6]

First-day worship has always been characterized by newness, freedom, joy, and the recognition of the day as one of God's great gifts. How tragic that through the years Christians have freighted it with the baggage of duty, guilt, and sadness.

Christians hold a sacred vow of the past with its glorious reminders of Creation, Incarnation, Crucifixion, and Resurrection. Believers treasure the precious hours of the present governed by the living Lord and indwelt by His vibrant Spirit. But essentially they are future-oriented since the first day looks at what is ahead as surely as the last day looked at what was behind.

The New Testament teaching regarding the church repeatedly affirms its function as a body and as a family. The images affirm the need for assembling together, for neither bodies nor families can work in a disjointed form. The church thrives, therefore, when it is together always in spirit, often in literal physical form. The day of gathering is a reminder of the believers' interdependence. In the late twentieth-century the Lord's followers need to heed again the words of apostle Peter:

> The end of all things is at hand; therefore, be of sound judgment and sober spirit for the purpose of prayer. Above all, keep fervent in your love for one another. . . . Be hospitable to one another without complaint. As each one has received a special gift, employ it in serving one another, as good stewards of the manifold grace of God. Whoever speaks, let him speak, as it were, the utterances of God; whoever serves, let him do so as by the strength which God supplies; so that in all things God may be glorified through Jesus Christ, to whom belongs the glory and dominion forever and ever. Amen. (1 Peter 4:7–11)

> O day of rest and gladness,
> O day of joy and light,
> O balm of care and sadness,
> Most beautiful, most bright;
> On these the high and lowly,
> Through ages joined in tune,
> Sing "Holy, holy, holy,"
> To the great God triune.
>
> Today on weary nations
> The heav'nly manna falls;
> To holy convocations
> The silver trumpet calls,
> Where gospel light is glowing
> With pure and radiant beams,
> And living water flowing
> With soul refreshing streams.
>
> New graces ever gaining
> From this our day of rest,
> We reach the rest remaining
> To spirits of the blest;
> To Holy Ghost be praises,
> To Father and to Son;

The Church her voice upraises
To Thee, blest, Three in One.

Christopher Wordsworth
"O Day of Rest and Gladness"

In Remembrance of Me

In the Passover feast, devout Jews remind themselves of who they are and whose they are. And though the Lord's Supper is no more a Christian Passover than Sunday is a Christian Sabbath, the worship life of the church is bound up with eating and drinking. Indeed, spiritual hunger and thirst rest at the foundation of the life in Christ (Ps. 23:5). Meals are shared both in family and in church. Animals grab a morsel and slink off to chew it alone, but believers fellowship together at food, both physical and spiritual. The English word *Lord* comes from the Old English words for "loaf" (*hlāf*) and "keeper" *(weard)*;[7] He is the "Keeper of the bread," the One to whom believers look to be fed. Promises of future gatherings for feasting abound in New Testament teaching (Matt. 8:11; Rev. 19:9).

New Testament believers ate together with regularity, sharing their homes with one another. But one meal stands out in the New Testament as "the Lord's Supper"—the *communion* of modern Christian worship (1 Cor. 11:23–25). How much like the early church do Christians today celebrate this ordinance? Why does the New Testament describe so little form, leading to such wide divergence of practice among God's people? When and how did the love feast and the Lord's Supper become divided? Did the early believers observe a fellowship feast as part of their worship?

Communion is the *Lord's* Supper. The focus is on Him and therefore celebration and affirmation become proclamation (1 Cor. 11:26). Any hint of duty or requirement rather than joy and freedom detracts from the reality of the worship experience.

The New Testament suggests that this meal sanctifies all others. Every communion meal offers an occasion for worship, an acknowledgment that believers are guests in God's world and that He is the Host. All worship gatherings of believers do not observe ordinances, nor are all the gatherings the sharing of a bounteous physical feast. But in reality all such gatherings recognize hunger and thirst, a desire to come to the Table of the Lord and be refreshed from His hand with song, prayer, Scripture, and other elements of the worship "meal."

As a fellowship feast the Lord's Supper emphasizes what the Lord's people have in common, "communion." The elements may be distributed in varying forms, but the emphasis on one loaf, one cup, and eating in unison focuses the celebration of the whole church without regard to denominational or even congregational boundaries. Deep historical significance underlies the celebration of the communion. It is a traditional thanksgiving to God, a form of prayer. The remembrance brings the reality of the Cross down to one's daily existence; believers' partaking of the elements of worship acknowledges a giving of themselves to God in response to what He gave and continues to give.

> Here, O my Lord, I see Thee face to face;
> Here would I touch and handle things unseen,
> Here grasp with firmer hand th'eternal grace,
> And all my weariness upon Thee lean,
>
> This is the hour of banquet and of song.
> This is the heavenly table spread for me.
> Here, let me feast and feasting still prolong
> The brief bright hour of fellowship with Thee.
>
> Feast after feast thus comes and passes by.
> Yet passing points to the glad feast above,
> Giving sweet foretaste of the festal joy
> The Lamb's great bridal feast of bliss and love.
>
> Horatius Bonar
> "Here, O My Lord, I See Thee Face to Face"

Worship As Service

The Germans say it well with their word *Gottesdienst,* commonly used for worship but literally meaning "service of God." Central to a New Testament understanding of service is the word διακονέω, from which comes the English word *deacon.* It denotes more an act of service than the state of servitude (Luke 22:27; Heb. 6:10; 1 Peter 1:12). Common acts of self-abasement are translated in New Testament theology to acts of service for each other. As Jesus put it to the disciples on the night of His crucifixion, the true guest takes the role of a waiter (Luke 22:24–27).

In a world of pagan religions full of temples and shrines, Paul told Christians that they are God's building (1 Cor. 3:9). Christian service purposes to build up the building and thereby build up the body and family. Is it fair to say that Paul does not emphasize worship as service to God, service to self, or service to a neighbor, but rather as service to the entire body of Christ? Perhaps the unity of ministry cannot be so divided.

Worship as service describes people allowing God to work through them in order to create a spiritual community. Worship as service involves the understanding and application of spiritual gifts and their role in the body of Christ (Rom. 12:6–8). The unity, diversity, and mutuality of the church abound when worshipers serve and servants worship. The worship affirmation in Romans 11:33–36 is followed by the appeal in 12:1 for "reasonable service" or "logical liturgy" ("spiritual worship," NASB). The apostle then describes the unity of Christ's body ("each member belongs to all the others," 12:5 NIV), details some of the spiritual gifts that carry out this worship-service, and discusses the whole lifestyle of the church active in worship and service.

The practical application of all this activates the involvement of the entire congregation in worship. Was Paul scolding the Corinthians when he said, "When you assemble, each one has a psalm, has a teaching, has a revelation, has a tongue, has an interpretation. Let all things be done for edification" (1 Cor. 14:26)? Or did he simply suggest that this kind of mutual sharing had taken on a dimension of disorder at Corinth and needed to be brought back into proper perspective and practice? The diversity of participation in New Testament worship can be easily defended. Worship was not one actor being watched by a multitude of spectators. Focus was not fixed; leadership was not single.

> Holy God, we praise Thy name;
> Lord of all, we bow before thee;
> All on earth Thy scepter claim,
> All in heav'n above adore Thee.
> Infinite Thy vast domain,
> Everlasting is Thy reign.
>
> Lo! the apostolic train
> Join Thy sacred name to hallow;
> Prophets swell the glad refrain,
> And the white-robed martyrs follow;
> And from morn to set of sun,
> Through the Church the song goes on.
>
> Holy Father, Holy Son,
> Holy Spirit, Three we name Thee;

While in essence only One.
Undivided God we claim Thee,
And adoring bend the knee,
While we sing our praise to Thee.

Attributed to Ignace Franz
"Holy God, We Praise Thy Name"

Marks of True Worship

True worship must be offered to God alone, in deep appreciation of His majesty and rulership in the world and in believers' lives. The worshiper engages God on a spiritual rather than physical level and the worship experience, private or public, must be *dominated by God's Spirit.*

An attitude of settled dependence on the Holy Spirit leads to cleansing, readiness, and a cultivation of the proper mind and heart attitude for worship. Worship becomes then a *total response* in which spiritual, emotional, and physical factors tune together to draw attention to the heavenly Father.

The biblical worshiper sees himself as Paul described him in Ephesians 1, the recipient of a vast undeserved bounty of spiritual riches provided entirely by the grace of God. He worships *in the truth* regarding triune Godhead and particularly Jesus Christ, the atoning Son. The preaching of the Word of God does not conflict with the solitude of quiet meditation, for both have their distinctive roles in the total worship experience. As God's people worship they focus their attention on the worthiness (worth-ship) of God. Then song and other forms of praise flow almost spontaneously from God's adoring, joyful people.

Certainly one of the marks of true worship is *confession of sin.* In the Old Testament the priests washed their hands before entering the tabernacle; an emphasis on cleansing dominates the Old and New Testaments alike. Too often the freedom of many churches generates a happy fellowship that makes the worship room sound like a busy airport before services are officially begun. Can they not learn to use the prelude time for personal preparation for true worship? Corporate worship particularly is an activity of the gathered body taught in the church during its formal meetings.

May the Lord give believers the wisdom and courage to purge themselves of clock-watching, spectatorism, cheap shoddiness, and self-centered emotionalism as they carry out their attempts at worship in harmony with the New Testament.

Immortal, invisible, God only wise,
In light inaccessible hid from our eyes,
Most blessed, most glorious, the Ancient of Days,
Almighty, victorious, Thy great name we praise.

Unresting, unhasting, and silent as light,
Nor wanting, nor wasting, thou rulest in might;
Thy justice like mountains high soaring above
Thy clouds, which are fountains of goodness and love.

To all, life Thou givest, to both great and small,
In all life Thou livest, the true life of all.
We blossom and flourish as leaves on the tree.
And wither and perish—but naught changeth Thee.

Great Father of glory, pure Father of light,
Thine angels adore Thee, all veiling their sight;
All praise we would render; O help us to see
'Tis only the splendor of light hideth Thee!

Walter C. Smith
"Immortal, Invisible"

Designing Creative Worship Experiences

Perhaps creative worship will take a nudge toward progress if Christians begin to realize that worship does not consist merely of Bible study or any other single activity. Certainly *prayer* will be involved, as will *praise;* but a third word beginning with the same letter clamors for more attention—*participation.*

The involvement of the people of God in the worship of God when they come to the house of God is a primary maxim on which all other plans for creative worship must rest. Too much time may be spent in the preparation of the sermon and too little time in preparation of the rest of worship. Some pastors want to rush through all the "preliminaries" to get to the "really important" aspect of the service, the preaching.

Innovations in worship must be carefully planned and the very element of variety itself can be a mark of creativity in worship. At the little church this writer serves, no two Sunday services are exactly alike. The order of service changes, people who are involved and what they do in the services often change, and the congregation has learned to expect a different approach to worship each time they meet.

Of course change simply for the sake of change is not desirable. The concern expressed here is for an upgrading of the quality of worship experience in the church. Here are a few specific examples of the kinds of things that can be done to bring about creative change in corporate worship. They might not work for all churches.

1. Read the Scriptures in unison or antiphonally or perhaps from various versions so that people who have brought the King James Version all stand and read a portion of the text of the week, people who have the NASB do likewise, the NIV the same, and so forth.
2. At different points in the service introduce helpful liturgical items such as leader-people response, original liturgies written by creative people in the church, and participational response of various kinds.
3. Introduce creedal recitation, on occasion using the Apostles' Creed or perhaps even the Nicene Creed.
4. The sermon could be delivered in sections divided by its major points and punctuated by hymns, other music, or congregational responses of various kinds.
5. A sermon reaction panel consisting of elders, young couples, or teenagers can interact with the pastor for five or ten minutes after the sermon.
6. If the church is not too large, a roving microphone can be handled by one of the ushers as people are allowed to ask questions about the sermon.
7. On occasion the familiar prelude and postlude can be replaced with meditative silence.
8. Vary the Scriptures and comments used in the communion service. First Corinthians 11 is fine but it is not necessarily the only passage in the Bible that speaks of communion in the Lord's Supper.
9. Use the bulletin creatively to include sermon outlines, interpretive verses, different names for the activities of worship, and for the printing of congregational response in whatever form it is used.
10. Take time to teach people how to worship. Explain the different things being done and why they are done. Worship must become meaningful.

All this, of course, must begin on an individual basis. People bring to corporate worship the attitudes and readiness (or lack of it) that set the standard not only for what they give and receive in a public service but how they influence family members and friends over a long period of time. May God's people never forget that the focus of worship is not themselves but their heavenly Father and His glorious Son, the Savior.

> Thine is the glory, risen, conqu'ring Son;
> Endless is the vict'ry Thou o'er death hast won.
> Angels in bright raiment rolled the stone away,
> Kept the folded graveclothes where Thy body lay.
>
> Lo! Jesus meets us, risen, from the tomb;
> Lovingly He greets us, scatters fear and gloom;
> Let His church with gladness hymns of triumph sing,
> For her Lord now liveth; death hath lost it sting.
>
> No more we doubt Thee, glorious Prince of Life!
> Life is naught without Thee; aid us in our strife;
> Make us more than conqu'rors, through Thy deathless love;
> Bring us safe through Jordan to Thy home above.
>
> Edmund L. Budry
> "Thine Is the Glory, Risen, Conquering Son"

CHAPTER 8

Believers' Spiritual Gifts

John F. Walvoord

One of the important ministries of the Holy Spirit to believers today is the bestowal of spiritual gifts on Christians at the time of their conversion. While Christians may have natural abilities even before they are saved, spiritual gifts seem to be related to the special purpose of God in calling them and saving them; in the language of Ephesians 2:10, they are "created in Christ Jesus for good works, which God prepared beforehand, that we should walk in them."

Spiritual gifts are divinely given capacities to perform useful functions of God, especially in the area of spiritual service. Just as the human body has members with different capacities, so individual Christians forming the church as the body of Christ have different capacities. These help them contribute to the welfare of the church as a whole, as well as bear an effective witness to the world. Spiritual gifts are bestowed by the sovereign choice of God and need to be exercised in the power and under the direction of the Holy Spirit.

Every Christian has at least some spiritual gifts, according to 1 Corinthians 12:7, "To each one is given the manifestation of the Spirit for the common good." After enumerating a partial list of such gifts, the apostle concludes in verse 11, "But one and the same Spirit works all these things, distributing to each one individually just as He wills." The analogy of the human body is then developed as illustrating the various functions of members of the body of Christ.

Spiritual gifts obviously differ in value, and the list of gifts in verse 28 is given in the order of importance. In chapter 13, the importance of the use of spiritual gifts in love is emphasized. Some gifts that were bestowed in the early church seem no longer to be operative today, and this introduces the important consideration of the extent of contemporary spiritual gifts.

Spiritual Gifts Used Today

Practically all serious expositors of the Word of God agree that some spiritual gifts continue throughout the present church age. These constitute the more important and essential capacities within the church that enable it to function and fulfill its divinely purposed role.

The gift of teaching or expounding the Scriptures is one of the more important gifts and is mentioned in Romans 12:7; 1 Corinthians 12:28; and Ephesians 4:11. Obviously the teaching of divine revelation to others is an important function for the members of the body of Christ. Although all believers have the capacity by the Spirit to receive divine revelation as is taught in the Word of God, all do not have the same gift in communicating this truth to others. The teaching gift does not necessarily require superior knowledge, but it does require the capacity for successful communication and application of the truth to an individual. No doubt the gift of teaching natural truth is similar to that of teaching spiritual truth, but the spiritual gift is especially adaptable to teaching the Word of God. Hence a person might be quite gifted in teaching natural truth who would not be effective in teaching the Word of God.

A common gift among Christians is that of ministering to each other, mentioned in Romans 12:7 and 1 Corinthians 12:28. This gift varies, depending on the person and the situation, and some are able to minister in one way and some in another. The total work of God depends on the capacity of the members of the body of Christ to minister in this way.

The gift of administration is related to wise direction of the work of God in the church and is mentioned in Romans 12:7 and 1 Corinthians 12:28. Comparatively few Christians are able administrators in the realm of spiritual things, and those lacking this gift should seek direction and guidance of those who are so gifted.

The gift of evangelism mentioned in Ephesians 4:11 refers to unusual capacity to preach the Gospel of salvation and to win the lost to Christ. While every Christian should be a channel of information to others and should do the work of an evangelist as Timothy was instructed to do (2 Tim. 4:5), nevertheless some will be more effective in preaching the Gospel than others.

The gift of being a pastor, or shepherd, of the flock also calls for special abilities. In Ephesians 4:11 pastors and teachers are linked, indicating that a true shepherd will also be able to teach or feed the flock and that a true teacher should have some pastoral abilities. While these qualities may be found in various degrees in different individuals, the link between teaching and shepherding the flock is inevitable for one who wants to be effective in preaching the Word of God.

The gift of exhortation mentioned in Romans 12:8 has the thought of presenting the truth in such a way as to stir to action. Sometimes those who have a gift of exhortation are not necessarily good Bible teachers, and vice versa, and people with these varied gifts are all essential to the work of the church.

Several other gifts are also mentioned in the Bible, such as the gift of giving, or having the special grace of sharing earthly possessions, as mentioned in Romans 12:8. The gift of showing mercy relates to the special ability to show empathy and sympathy for those in need and is mentioned in Romans 12:8. The gift of faith, or of special trust in the Lord, is included in 1 Corinthians 12:8–10. All these gifts abide throughout the entire church age and constitute the divinely appointed enablement for the church to fulfill its task.

Spiritual Gifts That Are Temporary

The question as to whether certain spiritual gifts are temporary is one of the debated areas of truth relating to the Holy Spirit in the contemporary church. While most believers agree that certain spiritual gifts were discontinued after the apostolic age, others are insisting that gifts given at the beginning of the church age continue in the same way throughout the entire period.

On the surface it is clear that the modern church does not function exactly like the apostolic church. There is an evident decline in miracles, though God is still able to perform the miraculous. No longer does the testimony of the church depend on its capacity to support its oral testimony by phenomenal miraculous works. It is also clear from the history of the Bible that miracles were evident in some periods for particular purposes, while almost absent in others. Three notable periods of miracles are mentioned specifically in the Bible: the period of Moses, the period of Elijah and Elisha, and the period of Christ and the apostles. In each of these there was a need to authenticate the message that God gave His prophets, but once this need was met the miracles receded.

The problems relating to the question of whether some gifts are temporary have been focused principally on the gift of tongues, the gift of interpreting tongues, and the gift of miracles or healing. Relatively little controversy has been aroused by considering certain other spiritual gifts temporary.

It seems evident from the Scriptures that the gift of apostleship was limited to the first-century church. Apostles were distinguished from prophets and teachers in 1 Corinthians 12:28. During the apostolic period they had unusual authority and were the channels of divine revelation. Often they had the gift of prophecy as well as that of working miracles. Generally speaking, those who were in the inner circle of the apostles were eyewitnesses of the resurrection of Christ or, like Paul, had seen the resurrected Christ subsequent to His resurrection. In Protestantism comparatively few claims have been advanced that any exist today with the same apostolic gift as was found in the early church.

The gift of prophecy, although claimed by a few, generally speaking, has also been recognized as having only passing validity. In the early church before the completion of the New Testament, authoritative revelation was needed from God not only concerning the future where the prophet was a forthteller, but also concerning the future where the prophet was a foreteller. The Scriptures themselves contain illustrations of such prophetic offices and their exercise. The gift is mentioned in Romans 12:6; 1 Corinthians 12:10; and 14:1–40. A number of illustrations are found, as in the case of Agabus, who predicted a famine (Acts 11:27–28) and who warned Paul of his sufferings (21:10–11). Among the prophets and teachers at Antioch were Barnabas, Simeon, Lucius, Manaen, and Paul (13:1). Women could also be prophets, as illustrated in the four daughters of Philip (21:9). Paul clearly had the prophetic gift as manifested in Acts 16:6ff.; 18:9–10; 22:17–21; 27:23–24. Among the others who were evidently prophets were Judas and Silas (15:32). These were authoritative channels through which God gave divine revelations, sometimes about the contemporary situation and sometimes about the future.

New Testament prophets were like prophets in the Old Testament who spoke for God, warned of judgment, and delivered the message from God, whether contemporary or predictive. The Old Testament prophet, however, was more of a national leader, reformer, and patriot, and the message usually was to Israel alone. In the New Testament the prophet principally ministered to the church and did not have national characteristics.

To be a prophet the individual had to have a message from God in the form of special revelation, had to have guidance regarding its declaration so that it would be given forth accurately, and the message itself had to have the authority of God. The prophetic office, therefore, was different from the teaching office in that the teaching office had no more authority than the Scripture on which it was based, whereas the prophetic office had its authority in the experience of divine reception and communication of truth.

In the early church the prophetic office was considered one of the principal gifts. It was discussed somewhat at length in 1 Corinthians 14 and was given more prominence than other gifts in the list in 1 Corinthians 12:28. Because no one today has the same authority or the experience of receiving normative truth, it is highly questionable whether anyone has the gift of prophecy today. No one has come forward to add even one verse of normative truth to the Bible. While individuals can have specific guidance and be given insight into the meaning of Scripture, no one is given truth that is not already contained in the Bible itself. So it may be concluded that the gift of prophecy has ceased.

The gift of miracles, while a prominent gift in the early church (1 Cor. 12:28) and frequently found in the New Testament, does not seem to exist today in the same way it did in Bible times. Throughout Jesus' earthly ministry He performed many miracles in attestation of His divine power and messianic office. After the ascension of Christ into heaven, miraculous works continued in the early church, on many occasions attending the preaching of the Word and constituting proof that it was indeed from God. With the completion of the New Testament, the need for such miraculous evidence in support of the preached Word seems to have ceased and the authority and the convicting power of the Spirit seem to have replaced these outer manifestations.

Holding that the gift of miracles is temporary does not mean there are no miracles today, as God is still able to do supernaturally anything He wills to do. Rather, in the purposes of God, miracles no longer constitute a mainline evidence for the truth, and individuals do not (as in the apostolic times) have the gift of miracles. While some who claim to have the gift of miracles today have succeeded in convincing many of their alleged supernatural powers, the actual investigation of their operation, which in some cases may be supported by individual miracles here and there, is often found to be quite deceptive, and often the alleged healings are psychologically instead of supernaturally effected. The thought is not that God cannot perform miracles today but rather that it is not His purpose to give to individuals the power to perform miracles by the hundreds as was true in the age of the apostles.

What is true of the gift of miracles in general seems also to be true of the gift of healing in the early church mentioned in 1 Corinthians 12:9, 28, 30. In Bible times there were special acts of divine healing, and undoubtedly there were hundreds of instances where the apostles were able to demonstrate the divine power that was within them by restoring health to those who had various physical disabilities.

A survey of the present church, while not without its segment of those who claim divine healing, does not support the contention that it is the same gift as was given in the early church. That God has the power to heal supernaturally today is obvious, and that there may be cases of supernatural healing is not to be denied. Healing as a divine method for communication or authenticating the truth, however, is not the present divine purpose, and those who claim to have the gift of healing have again and again been proved to be spurious in their claims. While Christians should feel free to pray and to seek divine healing, it is also true that frequently it is God's will even for the most godly of people that, like Paul, they should continue in their afflictions as the means to the end of demonstrating the sufficiency of God. Cases of healing are relatively rare in the modern church and are not intended to be a means of evangelism.

Probably the most controversial of the gifts of the Spirit is the gift of tongues. On the day of Pentecost, Jews who had come to Jerusalem for the feast were amazed to hear the apostles speak in their language, and they asked the question, "And how is it that we each hear them in our own language to which we were born? Parthians and Medes and Elamites, and residents of Mesopotamia, Judea and Cappadocia, Pontus and Asia, Phrygia and Pamphylia, Egypt and in districts of Libya around Cyrene, and visitors from Rome, both Jews and proselytes, Cretans and Arabs—we hear them in our own tongues speaking of the mighty deeds of God" (Acts 2:8–11). This was clearly a supernatural work of God and a testimony to the authority and truth of the apostles' message concerning Jesus Christ.

Two other instances occurred in Acts—one in Acts 10:46 on the occasion of Peter speaking to the house of Cornelius. In Acts

11, Peter, analyzing their speaking in tongues, said, "And as I began to speak, the Holy Spirit fell upon them, just as He did upon us at the beginning" (Acts 11:15). In the other instance, mentioned in Acts 19, when Paul encountered certain disciples of John the Baptist at Ephesus, as Paul "laid his hands upon them, the Holy Spirit came on them, and they began speaking with tongues, and prophesying" (19:6). It would seem reasonable to conclude that in all of these three instances in Acts there was a supernatural manifestation of the Spirit in the form of empowering people to speak in languages that were not known to them. It should also be observed, however, that these are the only three instances mentioned in the book of Acts and that apart from the discussion in 1 Corinthians 12–14 there is no other reference to speaking in tongues in the New Testament. What is the explanation of this gift, and can it be exercised today?

Though some writers have distinguished between the instances in Acts that were clearly in known languages and the experience of the Corinthians in 1 Corinthians 12–14, there does not seem to be adequate basis for this distinction as the same expressions are used in both places. The term "unknown tongue" in the King James Version in 1 Corinthians 14:2 is, of course, inaccurate as the word "unknown" is not in the original. There is no evidence that the gift of tongues used languages that were unknown to people, although there is reference to the theoretical possibility of speaking in the tongues of angels in 1 Corinthians 13:1. The instance in Acts 2 was clearly in known languages as the recognition of a language as a known language is essential to any scientific confirmation that genuine speaking in tongues has taken place. If those speaking in tongues had only babbled incoherent sounds, this would lend itself to fraudulent interpretation that could not in any way be checked. Thus, it should be assumed that speaking in tongues in the Bible was a genuine gift, that it involved speaking in existing languages unknown to the speaker, and that actual communication took place in such experiences. Hence, genuine speaking in tongues, as experienced in the book of Acts, cannot be explained simply by hypnosis or psychological emotionalism but was a genuine gift of the Holy Spirit.

The purpose of speaking in tongues is clearly defined in the Scriptures. It was intended to be a sign in attestation to the Gospel and a proof of the genuineness of the work of the Holy Spirit (1 Cor. 14:22). Though words were expressed and the glory of

God was revealed, there is no instance in Scripture where a doctrine was revealed through speaking in tongues, and it does not seem to have been a major vehicle for revelation of new truth.

In all three instances in Acts, speaking in tongues served to prove that what was taking place was a genuine work of God. In Acts 2, of course, it was the gift of the Spirit and the beginning of the New Testament church. In Acts 10 it was necessary as an evidence to Peter of the genuineness of the work of salvation in the household of Cornelius and was designed to teach Peter that the Gospel was universal in its invitation. The experience in Acts 19 served to identify the twelve men mentioned as being actually converted to Christianity instead of being simply followers of John the Baptist. In all instances, tongues were a sign that the work of the Holy Spirit was genuine.

The only passage in the New Testament that deals theologically with the gift of tongues is 1 Corinthians 12–14. The Corinthian church was plagued with many doctrinal and spiritual problems. It is rather significant that three chapters of Paul's epistle to Corinth are devoted to expounding the purpose and meaning of tongues, giving more attention to this problem than to any other in the Corinthian church. On the whole, the chapters are designed to correct and regulate speaking in tongues rather than to exhort them to the exercise of this gift. In the light of the fact that none of the other epistles or New Testament books apart from the book of Acts deal at all with this subject, it would seem apparent that speaking in tongues, although it existed in the early church, was not a major factor in its evangelism, in its spiritual life, or in its demonstration of the power of God. It seems to have been prominent only in a church that was notoriously unspiritual.

The gift of tongues is introduced in 1 Corinthians 12 as one of many gifts and as the least of the gifts enumerated in 1 Corinthians 12:28. It is number eight in the list, and immediately afterward the apostle made plain in the questions that are asked that all spiritual gifts are not possessed by all the church and only a few would necessarily speak in tongues. The entire next chapter of 1 Corinthians is devoted to motivation in speaking in tongues, and Paul pointed out that the only proper motivation is love. Therefore they were not to exalt the gift nor to use it as a basis for spiritual pride. Speaking in tongues without love was an empty and ineffectual exercise.

In chapter 14 the discussion on the significance of the gift of tongues deals with the subject in some detail. At least five major points are made. First, tongues is defined as a gift that is not nearly so important as the other gifts, such as the gift of teaching or the gift of prophecy. The problem was that speaking in tongues could not be understood without the gift of interpretation and was limited in its capacity to communicate divine revelation. So Paul said it is better to speak five words with understanding than ten thousand words in a tongue unknown to the hearer (14:19). It is clear from this that Paul exalted the gifts that communicate truth rather than the phenomenal gift of tongues, which was more of a sign gift.

Second, Paul pointed out that speaking in tongues should not be exercised in the assembly unless an interpreter is present. The principal exercise of speaking in tongues was to be in private, but even here Paul indicated that praying with understanding is better than praying in an unknown tongue (14:15).

Third, the importance of speaking in tongues is found in the fact that it is a sign to unbelievers, that is, a demonstration of the supernatural power of God, and that tongues is not primarily intended for the edification of believers (14:21–22). The Corinthian church, however, was told that unless speaking in tongues was conducted with proper order, it would not achieve its purpose of convincing unbelievers but would rather introduce an element of confusion (14:23). In the public assembly the exercise of the gift of prophecy, that is, the communication of a revelation from God in a known language, was more important and more effectual in leading to faith and worship than the exercise of the gift of tongues (14:24–25).

Fourth, the spiritual gift of speaking in tongues as well as the exercise of the gift of prophecy should be regulated and should not be allowed to dominate the assembly. The principle should be followed that they should be exercised when it was for the edification of the church. Ordinarily only two or three in any given meeting should be allowed to speak in tongues and none at all if an interpreter was not present (14:27–28). A blanket prohibition was laid down against women speaking either as prophets or in tongues in the church assembly (14:34–35). The general rule is applied that all things should be done decently and in order.

Fifth, Paul permitted tongues to be exercised, but he stated that its limitations should be recognized and its exercise should be in keeping with its value. From this thorough discussion of the gift of tongues in 1 Corinthians 14, as well as in chapters 12 and 13, it is evident that speaking in tongues was not intended as a primary source of revelation or a primary experience of power in the church. It was, rather, collateral and auxiliary as a proof of the truth of God.

If speaking in tongues was truly exercised, however, in the early church and, under proper regulation, was beneficial, the question, of course, still remains as to whether a similar experience can be had by the church today. Because it is almost impossible to prove a universal negative in an experiential matter such as this, especially in the light of many who claim to have exercised the gift, a practical line of approach is, first, to examine the question as to whether the Scriptures themselves indicate that speaking in tongues was a temporary gift and, second, on the basis of the total evidence, to ask the question as to what one should do in the light of the claims of many that they have the gift of speaking in tongues today.

At least four arguments lead to the conclusion that the gift of tongues was temporary. First, it is clear that there was no exercise of speaking in tongues before Pentecost. Christ and the apostles and John the Baptist did not exercise the gift of speaking in tongues before the day of Pentecost. There is no evidence that such a spiritual gift was given in the Old Testament period. It follows that if such a gift was given at Pentecost, it also could be withdrawn according to the sovereign will of God.

Second, according the Scriptures, tongues were especially a sign to Israel. Isaiah 28:11 prophesied, "He will speak to this people through stammering lips and a foreign tongue." This is quoted in 1 Corinthians 14:21–22 as being fulfilled in the exercise of the speaking in tongues. Such a sign gift would be fitting and effective at the beginning of a new age, but it would not necessarily be required throughout a long period of time.

Third, though it is debated, it seems evident that some other spiritual gifts were temporary such as the gift of apostleship, the gift of prophecy, the gift of miracles, and the gift of healing. If these gifts, so effective in establishing the church, were used in the apostolic period but seem to have faded thereafter, it would follow that the gift of tongues might have a similar withdrawal from the church.

Fourth, the statement is made in 1 Corinthians 13:8 that tongues would cease. It, of course, can be debated as to whether this means that tongues will cease now or whether they will cease at some future time. The point is, however, in either case that tongues are temporary and not a continued manifestation indefinitely in the purpose of God. These evidences seem to point to the conclusion that speaking in tongues is not a gift that can be expected to be exercised throughout the entire church period.

The natural question, however, is how can one account for the exercise of speaking in tongues today as it is claimed by many individuals? The answer is threefold.

First, most of the phenomena of speaking in tongues today seems to be babbling without known words or language. This can be completely explained by psychological means and without supernatural inducement.

Second, claims are made in some cases that speaking in tongues is in definite languages recognizable by those who are familiar with these languages. Though such claims are few and far between and difficult to confirm, if such a claim can be substantiated the question is how can it be explained? This introduces a second possibility for explaining a portion, at least, of the tongues phenomena today.

It seems clear that Satan is able to counterfeit the gift of tongues and occasional reports are received of those claiming to speak in tongues who actually express the most horrible blasphemies against God.

A third possibility in explaining the contemporary claim for speaking in tongues is, of course, to recognize that in some rather remote instances it is a genuine spiritual gift. Many evangelical Christians do not feel that there has ever been evidence in this century of the exercise of the genuine gift, but if such could be substantiated in a particular case it still would not justify the great majority of instances of speaking in tongues that apparently are not at all what the Scriptures refer to as speaking in tongues.

Much of the difficulty in the modern Pentecostal movement is found in the fact that rarely will it submit the exercise of the speaking in tongues to scientific demonstration. If a given instance of speaking in tongues was put on electronic tape and played separately to several individuals who claimed to have the gift of interpretation and their evaluation or translation would prove to be identical, it would be a scientific demonstration of the genuineness of speaking in tongues like that on the day of Pentecost. Unfortunately the Pentecostal movement has not been willing to submit speaking in tongues to such a scientific test and in fact objects to such a process. Until this is done, questions continue to be raised about the genuineness of the so-called gift of tongues in the contemporary situation. Even if proof were advanced of one genuine instance of speaking in tongues today, it would not prove the genuineness of any other instances.

It is also obvious that while speaking in tongues was a genuine gift in the early church, it was peculiarly adapted to abuse. In the Corinthian church it was a source of pride on the part of unspiritual people who exercised the gift but who had little spiritual power or holiness attending its exercise. Unfortunately the same tendencies sometimes are observed today in those claiming to speak in tongues who make it a source of pride instead of effective testimony for the Lord. It is not true, as often claimed, that speaking in tongues is a proof of either the filling of the Spirit or of spiritual power. There is no basis for pride in the exercise of such a gift.

The danger of the abuse of tongues may be itemized as existing in four areas. First, speaking in tongues is not, as sometimes claimed today, a prominent spiritual gift but is the least of all spiritual gifts and is the least effective in propagating Christianity.

Second, tongues is not a required sign of salvation and by its very nature as a gift would be given only to a few, not to all Christians. The lack of reference outside the books of Acts and 1 Corinthians is proof that it was not an important feature of Christianity in the first century.

Third, clearly, speaking in tongues is not in itself a proof of spirituality. The church that seems to have exercised it the most was the least spiritual. The history of the tongues movement seems to have given rise to emotionalism and excesses of various sorts that have not been beneficial to the propagation of the Gospel.

Fourth, it is not true that speaking in tongues is an inseparable evidence of the baptism of the Spirit. While one who spoke in tongues in the early church obviously, if it were a genuine gift, was also baptized into the body of Christ, it is clear from 1 Corinthians 12:13 that every Christian is baptized by the Spirit into the body of Christ, but only a few speak in tongues. So it is wrong to attempt to make tongues a necessary sign of either spirituality or salvation.

A practical approach to the problem of speaking in tongues is probably not one of attempting to prove to Pentecostals that they do not have the gift, though this may be our own conclusion. It is rather that evangelical Christianity should insist that Pentecostalism should confine the exercise of its supposed gift of tongues to the regulations and limitations proposed by the Scriptures themselves. If the Pentecostal movement followed closely the regulations laid down in 1 Corinthians 12–14, there would be little harm, if any, in exercising the supposed gift, for it would be regulated and kept within bounds and properly evaluated. The improper use and promotion of the gift of tongues, however, is detrimental to the exposition of Bible doctrine as a whole and confuses the issue of both salvation and spirituality. Evangelical Christians are duty-bound to speak out on this subject and in Christian love to reaffirm what the Scriptures teach on this theme.

If the gift of tongues as exercised today is suspect, it follows that the gift of interpreting tongues would not be given today either. Because of the nature of the gift of interpreting tongues, it is difficult to verify it. If a bona fide case could be found of one who, without knowledge of a foreign language, is able to interpret such a foreign language exercised in the gift of tongues and this can be verified by someone who knows the language naturally, there would be scientific evidence for a supernatural gift. (There still might be the question of whether this was of God or of Satan.) However, the Pentecostal movement has seldom come forward with any such proof, and until it does it is reasonable to question whether the gift of interpreting tongues can be exercised today.

The gift of discerning spirits, while not related to speaking in tongues, is another gift that seems to be temporary in the church. This was the gift of discerning whether a person supposedly speaking by the Spirit was speaking by God or by Satan. It is probably true that Christians today who are spiritually minded can discern whether someone is Spirit-directed or demon-possessed, but it does not seem to be bestowed on the church today as a particular gift.

In approaching these controversial matters, Christians should avail themselves of the revelation of Scripture and attempt to find a workable basis for solving these problems. The important truth is that there are spiritual gifts bestowed on the church today. The proper use of these gifts in the power of the Spirit is essential to fulfilling God's work in and through His church. While the temporary gifts are no longer necessary, the exercise of the permanent gifts is vitally important and is the best demonstration of the power of the Holy Spirit.

CHAPTER 9

Victory Over Indwelling Sin in Romans 6

Kenneth S. Wuest

In Romans 6 Paul answered two questions with which he was
often confronted as he preached on grace. The first has to do
with habitual sin in the Christian life (present subjunctive,
v. 1); the second pertains to infrequent, occasional acts of sin
(aorist subjunctive, v. 15). This chapter addresses the first of
these, habitual sin.

The Power of Sin Is Broken

The words "What shall we say then?" (v. 1) take the reader
back to 5:20–21: "Where sin increased, grace abounded all the
more, that, as sin reigned in death, even so grace might reign
through righteousness [resulting in] eternal life through Jesus
Christ our Lord." Paul's hearers, not understanding grace, may
have reacted with the question, "Are we to continue in sin that
grace might increase?" (6:1). "Sin" is preceded by the article in
the Greek text, which points out an object previously referred to in
the context. The reference is to the "sin" of 5:21 which is said to
reign. Here sin is personified as a king; it is sin not in the abstract,
as an act of sin, but in the concrete, as indwelling sin or the sinful
nature. This is the key to the understanding of Romans 6. Where
the word *sin* is found as a noun, as in verses 1–2, 6, 10–11, 13–14,
16–18, 20, 22–23, reference is made to the totally depraved
nature. (Paul continued this discussion in chapter 7 by referring to
"sin which dwells in me," v. 17.)

"Continue" renders μένω, "to remain, stay, dwell, remain in
fellowship with someone." When used of persons in the Gospels
the word speaks of fellowship, communion, friendship, the
relationship of a guest and a host. "Mary stayed with her" (Luke
1:56); the Samaritans begged Jesus "to stay with them" (John
4:40); Jesus said to Zacchaeus, "Today I must stay at your house"

(Luke 19:5). Paul used it here in the present subjunctive mood, which always speaks of continuing action. The question then is, "Shall we habitually continue to sustain an attitude of dependence on, yieldedness to, and cordiality with the sinful nature in order that grace may abound?"

Paul's answer is first an emotional one. Using the optative of wishing, he wrote, "May it never be!" Second, it is a rational one, "How shall we who died to sin still live in it?" The word for "how" is πῶς, "how is it possible?" Paul was declaring the impossibility of saints sustaining habitually the same attitude toward the sinful nature they did before they were saved. "Died" is aorist indicative, referring to a past fact. Death is separation. The ἀπό prefixed to the verb means "off, away from." The case that follows this preposition is the ablative, which is the case of separation. The apostle said that when a person was saved he "died off" (ἀπεθάνομεν) to the sinful nature. That means he was separated from it. At the moment of salvation, God performs a major surgical operation in the inner spiritual being of the sinner, cutting him loose from the sinful nature yet allowing that nature to remain in him until his death. Actually a disengagement is effected. How is it possible for a believer, who has been separated once for all from the sinful nature, to live any longer in the sphere of its grip? Here is one of the secrets of the victorious life, the realization that the believer is set free from the clutches of the sinful nature with the ability to say no to it, the realization that one has the same power over this fallen nature one has over, for example, a radio. The believer can turn it off at will and in an instant. It has no more control over him than he allows it to have.

Then the apostle told his readers how this surgical operation was performed. Each believer was baptized into Christ and, thus, into His death (6:3). The separation of the believing sinner from the sinful nature is an act of God, not a human act. This separation is the result of this baptism. Therefore this baptism, which resulted in the person being united to Christ in His death (a death that occurred almost two millennia ago, bringing to pass the separation), must have been a supernatural baptism. The word "baptize" translates βαπτίζω, "to dip into, to place into." Paul therefore wrote, "Do you not know that all of us who have been baptized into [placed in] Christ Jesus have been baptized into His death?" This refers to the act of God the Holy Spirit placing in Christ at the cross all sinners who in the sovereign grace of God were selected for salvation, so that by sharing His death, a separation might be effected at salvation between the believing sinner and indwelling sin.

The Divine Nature Is Imparted

Not only are believers delivered from the power of the sinful nature, they are also made recipients of the divine nature. Paul wrote, "Therefore we have been buried with Him through this being placed in His death, in order that in the same manner as Christ was raised up out from among those who are dead, through the glory of the Father, thus also we by means of an imparted new life may order our behavior" (author's paraphrase). Death with Christ results in believers being delivered from the power of the sinful nature. Resurrection with Him results in the believer being given a new nature. However, the believer has two natures within, the sinful and the divine. The sinful nature, the result of Adam's fall, is not his nature after he is saved. The divine nature is the believer's nature as a saint, the result of the regenerating work of the Holy Spirit. The sinful nature energized him before salvation to acts of sin. The divine nature is there to provide spiritual energy both for the willing and the doing of God's will. The sinful nature, because of the checks and balances of God's salvation, is not able to exercise habitual control over the saint and has control only when yielded to. The divine nature, when the believer is living victoriously, exercises control moment by moment.

In the first four verses Paul presented two major facts: the believer's separation from indwelling sin and the imputation of the divine nature. These facts are accomplished through union with Christ in His death and resurrection and make impossible a life of habitual sin. The apostle has shown such a life to be a spiritual impossibility. In verses 5–10 Paul answered the question again, but differently. The contents of these verses are the expert teacher's "in other words," his effort to make absolutely clear what he was teaching.

In verse 5 Paul declared, "For in view of the fact that we are those who have become permanently united with Him with respect to the likeness of His death, certainly also we shall be those who, as a logical result, have become permanently united with Him with respect to the likeness of His resurrection" (author's paraphrase). Here Paul picked up the thread of his discourses presented in verses 3 and 4 in order to elaborate on the truth of verses 2 and 4. He then wrote in verse 6, "Our old self was crucified with Him." The word for "self" is ἄνθρωπος, the generic term for humankind, referring here to the individual self whether male or female. "Old" is not ἄρχαιος, "old in point of time," but πάλαιος, "old because of use; outmoded, antique, worthless, decrepit, worn out." "Our old, decrepit, worthless, worn out self [that person we were before salvation: body, soul, and spirit dominated by the sinful nature] was crucified with Him" (author's paraphrase). This was brought to pass that "our body of sin might be done away with." "Body" is σῶμα, referring to the physical body of the unsaved person. "Sin" is in the genitive case, here the genitive of possession, the body possessed or dominated by the sinful nature. "Done away with" translates καταργέω, "to make ineffective, to render inoperative."

Paul's thought in verse 6 might be expressed like this: "Knowing this, that our old, decrepit, worthless, worn out self was crucified with Him in order that the 'physical' body [which before salvation was] dominated by the sinful nature might be rendered inoperative [in that respect]." The purpose of this was "that we should no longer be slaves to sin." But Paul was presenting the mechanics of the victorious life. He delayed speaking of ethics until chapters 12–16. Paul's thought here is expressed thus: "with the result that no longer are we rendering a slave's habitual obedience to the sinful nature." He explained the actuality of this wonderful truth in the words of verse 7: "For the one who died once for all stands in the position of a permanent relationship of freedom from the sinful nature" (author's paraphrase). That is, God has separated the believer once for all, by one stroke of His surgical knife, from the sinful nature. "Now, maintain that position of freedom moment by moment, and do not allow yourself to become entangled in the tentacles of the sinful nature any more" (author's paraphrase).

After presenting the fact of the believer's identification with Christ in His death with the result that there has been a permanent cleavage between the believer and the sinful nature (vv. 5–7), Paul spoke of the other aspect of inward salvation, the impartation of the divine nature. The Greek of verses 8–10 may be rendered, "Now, in view of the fact that we died once for all with Christ, we believe that we shall also live by means of Him, knowing that Christ, having been raised up from among those who are dead, no longer dies. Death over Him no longer exercises lordship. For the death He died, He died with respect to our sinful nature once for all. But the life He lives, He lives with respect to God."

The words "we shall also live with Him," speak of relationship or fellowship. Paul was writing of the means of the victorious life, explaining the "how" of living that life. The fellowship he mentioned here is not one of companionship but of joint participation. Believers participate in Jesus' life, deriving their spiritual existence from Him.

In verse 10 Paul said Jesus "died to sin" (i.e., with respect to the sinful nature). There are two aspects of the Lord's death. He died in relation to acts of sin, paying their penalty. This is dealt with in Romans 3:21–5:11, where the subject of justification by faith is presented. But in Romans 6 Paul dealt with sanctification. Here the Lord is seen as dying with respect to the believer's sinful nature in that His death effected the separation from that sinful nature. Thus, in the words of the hymn writer, the blood of Jesus is "the double cure"; it provides for both justification and sanctification.

Reckon It to Be True

In verses 11–13 Paul moved to another unit of thought. In verses 1–10 he dealt with the inner spiritual "machinery" of the victorious life, namely, the power of indwelling sin broken and the divine nature imparted. In verses 11–13 he gave instruction on the care and operation of this machinery. Just as an automobile motor works best only when it is regularly serviced, so this spiritual machinery in the inner being of believers operates most efficiently only when they obey the directions in these verses.

In living the Christian life God's children are to reckon on the fact that they have been separated from the indwelling sinful nature, "dead to sin," and that the divine nature has been implanted: "alive to God," verse 11. "Reckon" (KJV) or "consider" (NASB) translates λογίζομαι, "to calculate, take into account." The fact that a believer takes into account the change God wrought in his inner being when He saved him does not make it so, but his act of reckoning puts into operation the machinery that gives him victory over sin and enables him to lead a life pleasing to God. When a saint counts on the fact that the power of indwelling sin is broken, he is encouraged to refuse to obey it and to fulfill Paul's admonition—paraphrasing verses 11–13a—"Thus also, as for you, be constantly counting on the fact that on the one hand you are those who have been separated from the sinful nature, and on the other hand that you are living ones with respect to God. Stop, therefore, allowing the sinful nature to reign as king in your mortal body with a view to obeying it [the body] in its passionate cravings. Moreover, stop putting your members at the disposal of the sinful nature as weapons of unrighteousness." And when a believer takes into account the fact of the indwelling divine nature, he will obey the apostle's exhortation in verse 13b: "By a once-for-all act and at once, put yourselves at the disposal of God as those who are actively alive out from among the dead, and put your members as weapons of righteousness at the disposal of God" (author's paraphrase). Then when he has done all that, he has God's promise: "For sin [the sinful nature] shall not be master [exercise lordship] over you, for you are not under law, but under grace" (v. 14).

Paul has answered the first question, "Shall we habitually continue to sustain an attitude of dependence on, yieldedness to, and cordiality with the sinful nature so that grace may abound?" (author's paraphrase) by showing the impossibility of a Christian's habitually sinning as he did before he was saved. Then Paul voiced another question: "Shall we sin, because we are not under law, but under grace?" (v. 15). Here Paul used the aorist subjunctive, whereas in the first question he used the present subjunctive. The latter construction speaks of continuous action, the former, merely of the fact of the action. In effect, Paul's hearers said, "Since grace makes it impossible for a Christian to sin habitually, may we provide for a life of occasional, spasmodic, infrequent acts of sin since we are not under law, which is unyielding and firm, and are under grace, which is tolerant and mild?"

Paul answered in verses 16–20, "Do you not know that to whom you put yourselves at the disposal of as slaves resulting in obedience, slaves you are to whom you render habitual obedience, whether slaves of the sinful nature resulting in death, or obedient slaves [of Christ] resulting in righteousness? But God be thanked that [whereas] you were slaves of the sinful nature, you obeyed out from the heart as a source a type of teaching into which you were handed over. And having been set free once for all from the sinful nature, you were constituted slaves of righteousness. For just as you placed your members as slaves at the disposal of uncleanness and lawlessness resulting in lawlessness, thus now place your members as slaves at the disposal of righteousness resulting in holiness. For when you were slaves of the sinful nature, you were those who were free with respect to righteousness" (author's paraphrase).

Paul's argument is based on the Greek word δοῦλος, "slave," which speaks of one whose will is swallowed up in the will of another. Paul said, in effect, "Do you think that a believer, one whose will is swallowed up in the sweet will of God, would live a life of planned, occasional sin?" Δοῦλος speaks of one who serves another without regard for his own interests. A Christian who serves the Lord Jesus with the thought of bringing glory to his Lord and not out of concern for his own interests surely will not live a life of planned, occasional sin. Since a Christian by nature serves the Lord Jesus, he will surely follow the dictates of his divine nature and not live a life of planned occasional acts of sin. The saint has changed masters because he has changed natures. In his unsaved condition he served the Devil because his totally depraved nature impelled him to do so. In his saved state he serves the Lord Jesus because his new nature, received in regeneration, impels him to do so.

The apostle concluded his presentation of God's prescribed method of obtaining victory over indwelling sin with these words: "Therefore what benefit were you then deriving from the things of which you are now ashamed? For the outcome of those things is death. But now, having been freed from sin [the sinful nature] and enslaved to [made bondslaves of] God, you derive your benefit, resulting in eternal life. For the wages of sin is death, but the free gift of God is life eternal in Christ Jesus our Lord" (vv. 21–23, author's paraphrase).

CHAPTER 10

Christlikeness in Ephesians 4:13

Richard L. Strauss

W hen starting on a trip, it is normally wise to have the final destination clearly in mind. This is also true in the spiritual realm. The Christian life is likened to a pilgrimage (1 Peter 2:11), and everyone involved in Christian ministry should have the terminus of the pilgrimage in clear focus. Ministry is most effective when the goal is kept in plain view.

The apostle Paul had a lucid understanding of what God wants to accomplish in the body of Christ and in the lives of its members. He always kept that goal before him and shared it with others on a number of occasions. One verse in his epistle to the Ephesians sums it up concisely and cogently, a verse appearing in a powerful statement on Christian unity (Eph. 4:1–16). The passage begins with an impassioned plea to guard the unity that the Spirit of God has produced in the body of Christ (v. 3). Then it describes that existing unity in graphic detail (vv. 4–6).

But unity does not necessarily mean sameness. The parts in the body of Christ are not all identical. The genius of this body is the wide variety that exists among its members and the great diversity of spiritual gifts they possess. This is unity in diversity. The Lord Jesus in His sovereign grace gives to every member the ability to make a unique and profitable contribution to the whole (v 7). Furthermore He provides gifted leaders to help the other members develop their gifts, thus better equipping them for meaningful service (vv. 11–12). As they all use the abilities God has given them, the body of Christ is built up.

But what does it mean for the body to be built up? How is it possible to know when true edification is taking place? That is the point of the next verse. While explaining the meaning of edification, Paul was also defining the end of this entire process. Here is the goal of ministry: "until we all attain to the unity of the faith, and of the knowledge of the Son of God, to a mature man, to the measure of the stature which belongs to the fulness of Christ" (v. 13).

113

The word *attain* (καταντάω) means "to reach, to arrive at, to come down to the goal." At least eight times in the book of Acts this verb is used of travelers arriving at their destination. The subjunctive mood used here in a temporal clause with μέχρι (until) indicates purpose.[1] So Christians are pictured figuratively as travelers whose purpose is to reach a destination that is described in a threefold way—with three phrases each introduced by the preposition εἰς (to), each phrase closely related to the other two. Lenski suggests that the second is appositional to the first, and the third is appositional to the second.[2] Barth says they seem to interpret one another mutually.[3] They do seem to build in intensity. Maturity explains how unity can be attained, and Christlikeness describes what true maturity entails. The three together, culminating with Christlikeness, define God's goal for believers.

Commentators differ sharply on the meaning of the verse. Barth sees it strictly as eschatological. He renders καταντάω as "to come to meet," and he says it refers to Christ's second coming. According to Barth "the mature man" is none other than Christ Himself, and only when the church meets Him will it measure up to the stature of His fullness.[4] But that interpretation ignores the emphasis on progressive growth that permeates the context (vv. 12, 15–16).

Others see in the verse the quantitative growth of the body of Christ.[5] "The mature man" is understood as being the church, the one new man mentioned in 2:15. And in 4:13 attaining "the measure of the stature which belongs to the fulness of Christ" means the church in its completion, the full number of believers who will eventually take their positions as members of the body of Christ (cf. 1:23 and 1 Cor. 12:12). But the word "man" in Ephesians 2:15 is ἄνθρωπος, whereas ἀνήρ is used in 4:13. It is doubtful that these two words refer to the same thing. And "we all" attaining to the church would be a strange concept indeed.[6]

A third view is that Paul was referring to the spiritual growth of the church corporately. "The mature man" is the whole church in a perfect state, corresponding perfectly to its Head.[7] This would be difficult to deny in view of verse 12, which refers to "the building up of the body of Christ."

But the maturing of Christ's body will come through the maturing of its individual members. "We all" is a personal notation portraying the whole body made up of its individual parts. The contrast to spiritual babies in verse 14 would corroborate a reference here primarily to individuals. The spiritual growth of individual believers is one of Paul's major concerns in Ephesians (cf. 3:16–19). Understanding the verse in that sense would be consistent with the purpose of Paul's life and ministry as stated in Colossians 1:28: "that we may present every man complete [τέλειος, the same word used in Eph. 4:13] in Christ," a clear reference to individuals.

The thrust of the verse then is God's aim for each individual member of the body of Christ. This is the destination that all believers shall someday reach, but it is also the path along which every believer should be making daily progress. This is life's purpose for the child of God. Heeding it carefully will help keep ministers of Christ on track, investing their time, energies, and abilities in the things that are dearest to the heart of God. It should prove helpful, then, to examine this threefold goal more fully.

Unity of the Faith and of the Knowledge of the Son of God

Earlier (in 4:5) Paul affirmed that there is but "one faith." Faith can mean either a body of truth (as in Jude 3) or an attitude of trust. There is only one system of truth that reveals how sinful human beings can become acceptable to a holy God, and there is only one attitude by which they can avail themselves of His salvation. In other words there is only one true faith. But in the reality of daily living, Christians are not always one in the faith. They do not always agree on what they believe, nor are they always agreed on what it means to trust Christ. The existence of so many denominations and religious organizations dramatizes that disagreement.

But the goal of true believers is ever and always unity of the faith. Their goal should be to agree. As Paul wrote to the Corinthians, "Now I exhort you, brethren, by the name of our Lord Jesus Christ, that you all agree, and there be no divisions among you, but you be made complete in the same mind and in the same judgment" (1 Cor. 1:10). The aim of believers should be to highlight their areas of agreement without compromising any clearly revealed truth. A growing ability to agree will be one indication that spiritual progress is being made.

Christians usually find it easier to emphasize areas of difference rather than areas of agreement. The former holds people at arms length from each other and makes it difficult for them to dispense with their preconceived notions and cherished prejudices. But as

Bruce put it, "The higher reaches of the Christian life cannot be attained in isolation from one's fellow-believers."[8] The goal is togetherness, agreement, unity of the faith.

Unity of the faith is then coupled with unity of the knowledge (ἐπίγνωσις) of the Son of God. This is more than intellectual knowledge; this is intimate, experiential heart knowledge, a growing personal relationship with the Savior. The more all believers get to know Christ, the more they will agree with each other. When they focus their primary attention on horizontal relationships, they often meet with frustration because new areas of difference keep appearing to distract and divide them. But when they focus their attention on getting to know Christ better, their differences begin to fade and their mutual knowledge of Him and love for Him begin to draw them to each other. The better they know Him, the closer they are drawn to each other.

Mature Man

The second facet of the believer's destination is maturity. The word τέλειος refers to reaching a set goal. When applied to people and contrasted as it is here in verse 14 with little children, it means reaching the goal of growth, that is, "full grown, fully developed." Then to that word the apostle added another reference to maturity—the word ἀνήρ (man). To use ἄνθρωπος here would have been inadequate, for babies are human beings too.[9] Paul chose a word that conveyed the full, mature, robust strength of adulthood.

The believer's destination is spiritual adulthood, mature manhood. And that goes naturally with unity. In fact maturity is a condition for attaining unity. People who are growing in unity of the faith and knowledge of God's Son must first be growing toward mature adulthood. Contentious and quarrelsome Christians have not yet grown up. Critical and complaining believers are revealing that they are still spiritual children. They contribute to disunity and disharmony in the body.

God's goal for believers is that they grow up, that they become responsible, self-disciplined, well-adjusted, spiritually minded, loving, and considerate human beings. He wants them to fulfill their humanity, to be the men and women He envisaged when He created the human race. That is their destination.

People tend to think they are reasonably mature. They think this because they compare themselves with others who are weaker than they. The proper measuring rod for maturity is revealed in the third element of the believer's destination. It explains what true maturity involves.

The Measure of the Stature That Belongs to the Fullness of Christ

Here is the proper standard for measuring maturity, for measuring human life as God intended it to be. Here is the goal toward which the believer is to grow. It is the fullness of Jesus Christ Himself. "The fullness of Christ" means the fullness that belongs to Christ, all He is in His humanity with all the graces and qualities He possesses. He in His fullness is the essence of perfect adulthood. And the stature He attained in His incarnation, the spiritual maturity level He possessed, is the measure toward which every believer should be progressing.

Becoming perfectly like Him is the believer's *ultimate* destiny. Nothing can deter him from reaching that goal, for God has predestined him "to become conformed to the image of His Son" (Rom. 8:29). That perfect transformation into Christ's image will occur when he enters His presence (1 John 3:2). Meanwhile, there is no higher calling in life than to keep moving toward that goal.

God is not trying to produce successful Christian business people who can impress the world with their money and affluence. He is not to seeking to fashion successful church leaders who can influence people with their organizational and administrative skills. Nor is He attempting to fashion great orators who can move people with persuasive words. He wants to reproduce in His followers the character of His Son—His love, His kindness, His compassion, His holiness, His humility, His unselfishness, His servant attitude, His willingness to suffer wrongfully, His ability to forgive, and so much more that characterized His life on earth.

The world desperately needs to know Christ. But how can they meet Him when they cannot see Him? Earlier in this epistle, Paul explained that Christ is the Head of His spiritual body, which includes every believer (Eph. 1:22–23). And while the Head is physically present in heaven, much of the body is on the earth. As each member of that body begins to reflect His attributes, His graces, His characteristics, His qualities, the world will see Him and be attracted to Him.

The same thought is repeated in 4:15, where Paul wrote that "we are to grow up in all aspects into Him, who is the head, even

Christ." The goal is for the members of the body to match the
Head. Paul had the same burden for the Galatians, agonizing over
them until Christ be formed in them (Gal. 4:19), that is, until
Christ's character be built into them and Christ's life be expressed
through them. If every servant of Christ would establish this as the
goal for his own life and make it a priority in his ministry, the
body of Christ would be built up and the world would experience
the impact of the Gospel more powerfully.

CHAPTER 11

The Christian Life According to Colossians

H. Wayne House

A muscle will not function properly if the bone to which it is attached is broken or is in a state of degeneration. The same is true of the Christian life. Orthodoxy serves as the skeletal framework for the saint of God. If that framework is faulty and does not affirm truth, the result will be a defective lifestyle.

In the epistle to the Colossians Paul demonstrated this point. The Colossian congregation was under attack by syncretistic Jewish mysticism, which promoted "legal ordinances, circumcision, food regulations, the Sabbath, new moon, and other prescriptions of the Jewish calendar."[1] In response to this heterodoxy, Paul sought to make clear how the infection of false doctrine would affect their Christian living. This chapter examines the union between doctrine and practice by noting four themes in the book of Colossians: walking in divine wisdom, living in Christ, putting off sinful works, and putting on Christ.

Walk in Divine Wisdom (2:6–10)

In Colossians 2:6 Paul affirmed the association between correct theology and correct living. The Colossians, or at least some of them, were abandoning the doctrines espoused by Paul and were pursuing theological opinion in addition to deprecating the superiority and efficacy of Christ. Paul reminded them to live according to the truth that had been taught them.

HOLD TO TRUTH, NOT OPINIONS (2:6–7)

Paul was concerned that the Colossians might succumb to a philosophy completely estranged from his apostolic message. In 2:1 he said he wanted his readers to know of his willingness to suffer for the saints. He did this so the Colossians would come to experience "all the wealth that comes from the full assurance of understanding, resulting in a true knowledge of God's mystery, that is, Christ Himself" (v. 2). He wanted to prevent their being led astray by malignant "persuasive" speech (πιθανολογία, v. 4, persuasive speech that is plausible yet false[2]). However pleasing and logical this new philosophy seemed, it was heresy, not truth. The Greco-Roman world of the first century did not lack an abundance of views, philosophies, and religious trends. The populace was probably accustomed to hearing rhetoric and oratory promoting one cause or another.

Paul urged the Colossians to live in accord with the fact that they had received Jesus Christ: "As you therefore have received [παρελάβετε[3]] Christ Jesus the Lord, so walk in Him" (v. 6). Paul's concern was not that they simply possess the right Christology and theology in general but that they also live in accord with it (v. 7). The Colossians were to be rooted and established in the truth. Ellicott remarks that the two words "rooted" (ἐρριζωμένοι) and "established" (ἐποικοδομούμενοι) refer to "the image[s] of a root-fast tree (hence the perf. part.), [and] a continually uprising building (hence the pres. part.) marking the stable growth and organic solidity of those who truly walk in Christ."[4] The authority and priority of orthodoxy serves as a filter through which any grain of wisdom, whether true wisdom or false, must be strained.

AVOID PHILOSOPHIES THAT REJECT CHRIST (2:8)

The Colossians were also warned not to allow anyone to take them captive through philosophy and empty deception. The verb "take captive" translates συλαγωγέω, "to carry off as booty or as a captive, rob."[5] In employing the term figuratively, Paul symbolized Colossians being carried "away from the truth into the slavery of error."[6] The pundits who harbored this wayward philosophy were an imminent threat to the Colossian congregation. In the Greco-Roman world the word *philosophy* included a broad spectrum of religious and intellectual perspectives. "In Hellenistic language usage the word 'philosophy' (φιλοσοφία) was used to describe all sorts of groups, tendencies and points of view and thus had become a rather broad term."[7] This deviant and mystical philosophical skew not only posed a threat to the intellectual understanding of the Christian faith, but also served as a potential barricade against true Christian virtue.

The heresy in Colossians 2 echoes a form of Jewish mysticism known as Merkabah mysticism,[8] which was characterized by supposed ascents of the initiates to heaven to converse with beings in the heavenly realm. The name *Merkabah* comes from "the literary tradition that associates these celestial revelations with the biblical accounts of angelic figures surrounding the Throne of Glory (Ezek. 1:22–28) and the chariot (1 Chron. 28:18) on which it descended."[9] This early phase of Jewish mysticism grew out of Palestine and eventually became grafted into Christian Gnosticism and Greek mystery religions.

Merkabah mystics yearned for religious experiences apart from the Scriptures. "To experience God, i.e., to behold him, the mystic must undergo a total transformation induced by ascetic practice and the recitation of hymns declaring the holiness and majesty of God."[10] Along this journey angelic beings would attempt to expel the mystics from the realm of the heavenlies. To avoid confrontation and expulsion it was necessary for the mystics to know the names of all the angels. In Merkabah, "there was no love for God nor a desire to attach oneself to him, but only the ecstatic, albeit passive, vision of God and his realm."[11]

Scholars do not agree on the exact nature of the Colossian heresy.[12] However, the view that it involved a Jewish form of mysticism is held by Bornkamm, Lightfoot, Lyonnet, and Francis.[13] Lexical evidence in Colossians 2 may indeed point to a Merkabah-like experience, particularly the use of the word ἐμβατεύων,[14] which occurs in the New Testament only in Colossians 2:18. (The *New American Standard Bible* renders it "taking his stand on," and the *New International Version* translates it, "goes into great detail about.") The Jewish-Gnostic philosophy of the Colossian heretics suggests that ἐμβατεύων means "to approach something with a view to examining it."[15] "What they try to achieve by way of ecstasy and asceticism is for Paul opposed to adherence to the exclusiveness of Christ the Head in whom all wisdom and knowledge are given."[16] "Ἐμβατεύων is to be taken as a quoted word, containing a sarcastic reference to the man of the mysteries with his false worship and fleshly mind."[17]

The earthly and fleshly orientation of this heretical viewpoint was not at all amenable to the Christian life as it had been proclaimed by Paul. It is clear that Paul's tenor in 2:8 is polemical. He referred to this philosophical stream as "empty deception" (κενῆς ἀπάτης), originating from men and from the "elementary principles [or, elements] of the world" (κατὰ τὰ στοιχεῖα τοῦ κόσμου).

Concerning the phrase κενῆς ἀπάτης, O'Brien states that Paul "exposes it as a hollow sham, having no true content, seductive and misleading," using a phrase that "can describe the seduction which comes from wealth, Mark 4:19; the deceitfulness of sin, Heb. 3:13; wicked deception generally, 2 Thess. 2:10; or deceptive desires, Eph. 4:22."[18] Though the heretical leaders may have possessed the ability to charm people, their tantalizing ideas parted company with doctrinal soundness. There was no inherent value in accepting concepts that were void of substance and lacking worth.

Also the apostle considered this heresy mundane as opposed to celestial, for it was confined to the depraved ingenuity of the human mind, a mind inclined to earthly and carnal things of no spiritual and eternal import. This heresy was in keeping with "the tradition of men" (κατὰ τὴν παράδοσιν τῶν ἀνθρώπων, Col. 2:8). Through this phrase "Paul rejects any suggestion of divine origin. This was a human fabrication standing over against the apostolic tradition which centered on 'Christ Jesus as Lord.'"[19] The clause κατὰ τὰ στοιχεῖα τοῦ κόσμου, "according to the elementary principles of the world," parallels and emphasizes the idea of human origination and tradition.[20] "Elements [στοιχεῖα] is a common word in the language of the philosophers when they treat of the matter or the elements out of which every thing is formed."[21] *Elements* can also imply "the fundamental principles which provide the basis for every thing that is to be built upon it."[22] It seems plausible that Paul employed *elements* in this fashion. In Colossians 2 Paul emphasized establishing a credible basis for theology and life and refuting any principles that were groundless.

The apostle asserted that the false philosophy did not find its roots in Christ Jesus (οὐ κατὰ Χριστόν). If everything were built on a faulty foundation of speculation and deceit, the lifestyle of the Colossian believers would no doubt reflect the fallacy of this thinking. Verse 16 serves as an indicator of what the logical end of this fallacious reasoning would be. The result would be the needless practice of customs and sacerdotal mannerism meant to appease angels. Paul implored the Colossians not to allow anyone to entice or browbeat them into ascetic practices or make them feel obligated to participate in feasts, new moon festivals, or rites pertaining to the Sabbath.

Paul wanted the Colossians to be established in Christ Jesus and to grow in Him. Christ was to be the basis of every aspect of life. The only way to ensure this was to beseech the Colossians to reject any doctrine or teaching that did not have Christ as its bedrock. In addition, the teaching concerning Christ had to do with what they had received originally (2:6). Thus the door would be closed to any wayward religious idealism that attempted to infiltrate Colossae by merely using the name of Christ. Any interpretation of Christ proffered by advocates of Jewish mysticism or any other Gnostic-like mystery religions was not to be tolerated.[23]

Syncretism posed a great threat to the integrity of the Christian faith. The shared nomenclature of the mystery religions and Christianity made doctrinal interference and confusion easy. For example πλήρωμα (fullness, completeness) was a word common to the mystery religions; however, Paul utilized the same term to reflect the completeness of the deity of Christ.[24] Since such lexical congruities existed, heretics sought to redefine the person and work of Christ in terms that mitigated His role in both salvation and sanctification. Therefore Paul emphasized the superiority of Christ over and above that of angels (2:10; Eph. 2:20–21).

ENJOY THE FULLNESS OF CHRIST (2:9–10)

The Colossian saints were to live the Christian life by adhering to the soundness of the apostle's Christ-centered message. The resonance of this doctrine was rich and full. There was no need for any philosophical or esoteric embellishments. Furthermore, when one's life is based on Christ, the result is virtue and not false humility associated with the worship of angels (2:18).

Christ is to be regarded above all. The causal "for," ὅτι (because), with which verse 9 begins, introduces the reason He should be the ground for "Christian philosophy": "In Him all the fullness of Deity dwells in bodily form." "The high Christological statement serves as the basis for the application to the particular needs of the congregation."[25] Colossian believers needed to know that Christ is superior to all, even above the angels who were the objects of worship for the heretics. Since Christ possesses in Himself "all the fullness of Deity," He is to be revered, honored, and obeyed. Moreover, this fullness was not shared, certainly not with lesser beings such as angels. As O'Brien states, "the expression 'the entire (πᾶν τὸ) fullness' is tautologous and this suggests Paul is writing polemically to underscore the point that the *'plēroma'* is to be found exclusively in Christ."[26]

The Colossian heretics worshiped angels as intermediaries

between God and humans. Paul's counterattack focused on the fact that *Christ* is the sole intermediary and that access to the πλήρωμα (fullness) was through Christ and Him alone. The words τῆς θεότητος (deity) refers to the "quality of being divine."[27] Σωματικῶς (in bodily form) underscores the reality of Christ's incarnation. Paul then associated the fullness of Christ with the fullness the Colossians had in Christ because of the symbiotic relationship they shared with Him. This can be seen through the use of the root πληρ- in Christ's fullness (πλήρμα) and in the participle πεπληρωμένοι, "have been made complete," (v. 10), which refers to the believer's position in Christ as complete.[28] The passive voice of the participle πεπληρωμένοι indicates that the action of making the believer "full or complete" was accomplished by an outside agent, namely, God.[29] Thus the status and well-being of the Christian life is predicated solely on Christ Jesus, who indwells the saints (cf. 1:28). Compared to Christ, all other entities ("all rule and authority," v. 10, or, powers and principalities) are inferior, irrelevant, and impotent.

Live in Christ (2:11–23)

Because believers are in Christ, who has forgiven them, they are to conduct themselves in a holy manner, while laying aside all rules of conduct based on terrestrial principles concocted by false teachers.

POSITIONAL TRUTH (2:11–12)

Two of the many benefits of being in Christ are treated in Colossians 2:11–12. The first benefit was that of having a circumcision "not done with hands" (ἀχειροποιήτῳ). Circumcision in the Old Testament was a sign of consecration. Abraham was circumcised to demonstrate his relationship with God and the efficacy of the promises of God accompanying that relationship. In Israel's history circumcision grew from a sign of a relationship with God to a stumbling block for Jews. As Unger states, "circumcision became the pride of Israel, they looking with contempt upon all those people not observing it (Judg. 14:3; 15:18; 1 Sam. 14:6; Isa. 52:1, etc.)."[30] However, the circumcision mentioned here in Colossians was different. In Ephesians 2:11 Paul belittled the legitimacy of the circumcision done in the flesh by hands. "Handmade" righteousness was of little use to God. Lincoln remarks, "This term [χειροποίητος] and its opposite are frequently used in the NT for the contrast between external material aspects of the old order of Judaism and the spiritual efficacy of the new order (cf. Col. 2:11; also, for example, Mark 14:58; Acts 7:48; Heb 9:11, 24)."[31] The circumcision of the Jews was only a shadow of things to come, but the circumcision Paul discussed here was the real thing, namely, *spiritual* consecration.

> The circumcision of Christ which every member of the community has experienced is nothing other than being baptized into the death and resurrection of Christ. The formulation of the sentence depends on expressions used in the primitive Christian teaching on baptism. Such expressions also underlie Rom. 6:4f. Christianity believes and acknowledges that Christ died for our sins, that he was buried and that God raised him from the dead (1 Cor. 15:3–5).[32]

A second benefit of being in Christ is that the believer participates in the death of Christ, "buried with Him," and the resulting ramifications of His resurrection, "raised up with Him" (Col. 2:12). The burial of Christ served as proof of His death. The result of His death was that a penalty had been paid on the cross for the remission of sin. Christ's death removed the requirement of sentencing for all who receive Him as their Savior. Therefore since an individual, at the moment of belief, participates in Christ's burial, the penalty for his sin is considered paid. No further charges can be brought against the one who believes in Christ (Rom. 8:11, 31–34).

Christ's resurrection, then, indicated that all matters of divine justice were settled and a new day could commence. The believer therefore is to live according to his resurrected life, because his old life met its demise in Christ. In Romans 6:2 Paul pondered the question, "How shall we who died to sin still live in it?" The connection between a believer, born from above in Christ, and sin is an unnatural relationship. Death has no fellowship with life.

NEW LIFE AND FORGIVENESS (2:13–15)

God's forgiveness of the believer is the impetus for a new position and outlook on life. The believer acquired this newness not through any merit of his own. Paul's perspective was that although "you were dead in your transgressions and the uncircumcision of your flesh, He made you alive together with Him, having forgiven us all our transgressions" (v. 13). A dead person has no means of raising himself from his grave. This is especially true of sinners who are dead in their sin. Thus forgiveness, which enables the believer to enjoy spiritual life, should be exemplified in his daily conduct.

The forgiveness provided for by Christ is final (v. 14). "God has not only removed the debt; he has also destroyed the document [χειρόγραφον, 'certificate of debt,' NASB] on which it was recorded."[33] A χειρόγραφον was a note of indebtedness in one's own handwriting as proof of his obligation.[34] The mention that this certificate of indebtedness was nailed to the cross was notification that the debt was paid in full by Christ's death.

As Lohse explains, this means that on the cross Christ divested the "powers and principalities of their authority" (v. 15).[35] Thus Paul was implying that the heretics' practice of worshiping angels or elevating their status beyond that of Christ was wrong.

THE RESPONSE OF FAITH TO WORKS (2:16–23)

In 2:16–23 Paul wrote against succumbing to standards of living inappropriate for Christians. In no way were the tenets of the Colossian heresy requisites for a genuine Christian experience. Asceticism and the observance of festivals were only shadows of reality. The mysterious tactics used by the heretics produced false humility and arrogance. Paul remarked that such practices caused them to be "inflated" (φυσιούμενος, lit., "puffed up") in their earthly minds (ὑπὸ τοῦ νοὸς τῆς σαρκὸς αὐτου, lit., "by the mind of his flesh"). Christian virtue fosters true humility and meekness in light of the forgiveness of God, not arrogance. Living in light of forgiveness helps sustain believers in both doctrinal orthodoxy and orthopraxis. A Christian who neglects the truth of his marvelous position in Christ and of the forgiveness wrought through Him is opened to influence by "every wind of doctrine" (Eph. 4:14) and empty, deceitful philosophy.

Put Off Sinful Works (3:1–11)

THE BELIEVER'S POSITION IN CHRIST (3:1–4)

Because of the believer's participation in the death and resurrection of Christ and his victory over "the elements of the world," he is to "keep seeking the things above" (τὰ ἄνω ζητεῖτε, 3:1). This continual, ongoing process of seeking, suggested by the present imperative, is to be the consequence of having "been raised up with Christ." For Paul there was no reason for anyone to be "seeking the things above" if he had not been raised with

Christ. The road to the heavenly realm was through Christ not through asceticism or mysticism.

The believer's position in Christ is his only hope of glory. There should be no boasting of a meeting with God apart from Christ. The believer is to "set" his "mind on the things above" (v. 2), that is, to seek spiritual wisdom and guidance from the One who sits "at the right hand of God" (v. 1). This wisdom from above is superior to human traditions and "the elementary principles of the world" (2:8). The contrast is striking. From Christ, the Source above, there is wisdom. On the other hand the world and all that is a part of it, "the things that are on earth" (3:2), are under a curse and doomed for destruction. Believers are to have a mind-set that avoids all that is at enmity toward God (cf. Rom. 8:6).

The believer's death in Christ terminated his relationship with the old self and the things of the earth. To ensure its safety, the new life is protected and vouchsafed in Christ. As Paul wrote, "your life is hidden with Christ in God" (Col. 3:3). "The verb κέκρυπται ('hidden') is a perfect tense, in contrast to the preceding aorist, ἀπεθάνετε ('you died,' drawing attention to the specific occasion of their death with Christ), and stresses the ongoing and permanent effects: your life has been hidden with Christ in God and it remains that way."[36]

When Christ will return, "when Christ, who is our life, is revealed" (v. 4), the believers' glory will be disclosed as well. Meanwhile they can live life to the fullest because of Jesus' power sustaining them.

THE BELIEVER'S RESPONSE TO HIS POSITION IN CHRIST (3:5–11)

In light of their security, believers pursue righteousness while putting to death (νεκρώσατε) "the members of [the] earthly body" (lit., "the members that are on the earth"). This command means to "put to death whatever in your nature belongs to the earth"[37] (cf. Rom. 6:11; 8:10). "Man cannot distance himself from his actions; he is so intimately bound up with them that his actions are a part of himself. Only through the death in which the old self dies, can the way to new life be opened."[38]

With the aorist imperative νεκρώσατε, Paul moved from the theological to the practical, into the realm where the believer is responsible for his actions. Five things Christians should exclude are fornication (πορνείαν), impurity (ἀκαθαρσίαν), lust (πάθος), evil desire (ἐπιθυμίαν κακήν), and greed or covetousness (πλεονεξίαν). The order of these terms in Colossians 3:5 moves "from the outward manifestations of sin to the inward cravings of the heart, the acts of immorality and uncleanness to their inner springs."[39] These sins emerge from a heart that feeds on earthly philosophies of living. Because of such filth God's wrath will come on those who willfully disobey Him (v. 6). This includes not only flagrant unbelievers, but also those in the Colossian congregation who said they believed in Christ but who actually were unbelievers, as their evil actions revealed. As already noted, Paul wrote this epistle to dissuade some who might delude themselves with alleged visions of glory through mystic encounters. Though false teaching may be enticing, it is bankrupt with respect to life-sustaining principles and as a result, the heresy leads to moral turpitude.

The apostle reminded the Colossian believers that moral misconduct was part of their former demeanor: "in them you also once walked" (v. 7). The words "but now" (νυνὶ δὲ), which begin verse 8, introduce a temporal contrast, pointing to the fact that the Christian life must contrast with the person's former life (cf. 1:21–22).[40]

Paul commanded the Colossians to "put . . . aside" (ἀπόθεσθε, "rid themselves"[41]) of other vices, including wrath (ὀργήν), anger (θυμόν), malice (κακίαν), slander (βλασφημίαν), and foul talk (αἰσχρολογίαν). The aorist imperative ἀπόθεσθε emphasizes that "the process and repeated efforts which lead to a transformed daily walk are all incorporated into the imagery of 'putting off the old life with its deeds' and 'putting on the new life' of righteousness and Christ-likeness."[42]

> Believers are to discard their old repulsive habits like a set of worn-out clothes. Ἀποτίθημι, meaning to "put away," was used literally with reference to clothes at Acts 7:58 (cf. 2 Macc 8:35; Jos[ephus] *Ant[iquities] of the Jews]* 8, 266) and in a metaphorical and ethical sense at Romans 13:12; Ephesians 4:22, 25; Hebrews 12:1; James 1:21; and 1 Peter 2:1.[43]

Believers also are not to lie to each other. The present tense in the prohibitive imperative μὴ ψεύδεσθε, "do not lie" (Col. 3:9), connotes an action that is to be habitual. In Ephesians 4:15 the present participle ἀληθεύοντες (being truthful) demonstrates this same idea. Dishonesty characterized the former life, the old self, which was crucified and buried with Christ, but now honest speech and conduct are to characterize believers.

Since the old self (παλαιὸν ἄνθρωπον, lit., "old man") and his proclivities are to be purged, a new and invigorating self, or lifestyle, must fill the void left by the absence of the old (Col. 3:10). The new life is to be lived in conformity to the image of the One who created it (κατ᾿ εἰκόνα τοῦ κτίσαντος αὐτόν). Thus Christ alone starts as the Christian's paradigm.

This newness also implies that former distinctions of race or social caste bear no significance on the status of saints as image-bearers of God. In verse 11 Paul emphatically denounced the notion that one group had any greater advantage in Christ than any other. Greeks and Jews were adversaries. Greeks viewed Jews as unsophisticated and lacking wisdom, and Jews viewed the Greeks as uncircumcised aliens estranged from "the covenants of promise" (Eph. 2:12). Barbarians and Scythicans were viewed as crass and repulsive peoples, the scorn of Greco-Roman society. Slaves and masters in general bore mistrust and animosity toward one another. Yet the enmity between these groups departs when these individuals come to Christ. An unregenerate life gives birth to racism and classism, attitudes stemming from the heart. By contrast, it is improper for believers to harbor disdain for races and classes of people different from their own (cf. Rom. 3:22; 10:12). Being renewed at salvation to a new perspective and knowledge (ἐπίγνωσιν, Col. 3:10), the believer's conduct is to be "in conformity with the Creator's will."[44] Skin color and socioeconomic status, being merely aspects of external appearance and circumstance, are inadequate barometers of character.

Put on Christ (3:12–4:6)

The believer's new life, based on his status in Christ, means that every relationship and activity is to be patterned after the model set forth by Christ.

GENERAL ADMONITION (3:12–17)

Believers are to "put on" (ἐνδύσασθε, lit., "clothe themselves") righteousness and its accompanying amenities. Ephesians 6:11 uses the same word in reference to believers clothing themselves with the armor of God in order to be victorious in spiritual warfare. The redeemed are to don spiritual garb fitting for God's elect (ἐκλεκτοί).

> The phrase "as God's chosen ones" (ὡς ἐκλεκτοὶ τοῦ θεοῦ) is not meant as a comparison, as if Christians try to become equals of the heavenly elect. Rather the community is addressed as the chosen, holy and beloved

people of God. Just as Israel had been singled out by God as his possession (Dt 4:37; 7:7; Ps 33:12, etc.) and the Qumran community understood itself to be the assembly of the chosen ones.[45]

The Christian's attire is to include "compassion, kindness,
humility, gentleness and patience" (Col. 3:12). Furthermore
Christians are to be lovingly tolerant of each other and forgiving
in the same manner as Christ forgave them (v. 13).

Love, however, is the supreme virtue (v. 14). This is the same
love God manifested on the cross (John 3:16). Peace, which
comes from Christlikeness,[46] serves as an umpire (βραβευέτω) on
all the fields of endeavor for Christians (Col. 3:15). This peace
can be understood as subjective inner peace and also as objective
peace in reference to interpersonal relations. That is, the lives of
Christians who apply the blessings brought to them by virtue of
their position in Christ are marked not by a chaotic, argumentative
demeanor but by harmony and rapport. In addition their lives are
to be characterized by gratitude (mentioned in each of the three
verses of 3:15–17), appropriation of God's Word (v. 16), worship
that expresses itself in music (v. 16), and conduct that is focused
on "the name of the Lord Jesus" (v. 17).

PRACTICAL OUTWORKING OF THE
CHRISTIAN LIFE (3:18–4:6)

The house rules (3:18–4:1). There is no greater testing ground
for the authenticity of one's faith than the family. For this reason
Paul set forth rules of conduct for Christian households. "Luther
called this scheme of household duties a *Haustafel,* which means
'a list of rules for the household,' but it is usually translated into
English as 'house-table.'"[47] This "house-table" established the
rules of order and conduct in the Christian household. In Greco-
Roman society emphasis focused on three major relationships:
husband and wife, parent and child, and master and slave. All
these relationships were in the home. Paul contrasted the
relationships in Christian households with secular families.[48] For
example, fathers held extensive control over their sons.[49] This
extensive control, coupled with a depraved nature, could make for
some harrowing experiences between fathers and their offspring.
The Christian household, however, was to have no such discord
(vv. 20–21). The impetus for maintaining better parent-child
relationships rests on the fact that Christian fathers and sons are to
exhibit Christlike qualities, as addressed in verses 12–17.

Though Paul had much more to say about the union of husband and wife in Ephesians 5:22–33, the gist is the same in Colossians 3:18–19. Wives should respect their husbands because "it is fitting in the Lord" (ὡς ἀνῆκεν ἐν κυρίω). The goal is to do what the Lord expects and not what society accepts. Husbands are commanded to love their wives and not to treat them with bitterness or harshness (μὴ πικραίνεσθε). In Ephesians 5 Christian husbands are challenged to follow Christ as their model. They are to hold their wives in the highest esteem, viewing them in the same way Christ views the church.

The master-slave relationship was also to differ from the secular order (Col. 3:22–4:1). Slaves had no rights. Their well-being was totally in the hands of their masters on earth (lit., "lords according to the flesh"; cf. Eph. 6:5). One of the most vivid examples of how this relationship was to differ from the secular world is seen in the epistle to Philemon. In the Roman world Philemon, a master, had every right to punish his runaway slave, Onesimus, even to the point of death. Yet Paul, appealing to Philemon's faith and appreciation for the sovereignty of God, encouraged him to rejoice in his spiritual obligation to forgive. "Perhaps the reason he was separated from you for a little while was that you might have him back for good—no longer as a slave, but better than a slave, as a dear brother" (Philem. 15–16, NIV). The believer's position in Christ transforms the nature of relationships, for the power of Christ overshadows even the most despicable institutions in society.

Christian attitudes and graces (4:2–6). The attitudes and graces of the Christian community serve as an excellent public-relations tool for the Gospel. The Christian life is to be expressed in an attitude of thanksgiving (ἐν εὐχαριστία, 4:2; cf. 3:15–17). In this attitude of thanksgiving believers are to devote themselves to alertness and prayer so that the mystery of the indwelling Christ may be proclaimed (4:2–4). Paul implored the believers at Colossae to live wisely before "outsiders" (τοὺς ἔξω, lit., "the ones outside"), a reference to unbelievers (4:5). They were to make the most of every opportunity for spiritual gain "by redeeming the time."[50]

Conclusion

The book of Colossians clearly mandates that all facets of one's Christian experience must be in harmony. The basis of this harmony is correct theology regarding Christ Jesus. One cannot redefine or mitigate the role of Christ in salvation and expect to enjoy right practice. Correct living is driven by hope and conviction stemming from the work of Christ. A proper understanding of Christ serves as the platform for the Christian life. With the Cross in view, believers are enabled to strip away behavioral characteristics of sinners and to clothe themselves in the righteousness befitting those who have been redeemed.

CHAPTER 12

Christian Apparel in Colossians 3:5–17

S. Lewis Johnson Jr.

Christianity is not just theology nor simply a system of ethics, but incorporation into Christ. To use one of James Denney's favorite expressions, union with Christ is the "diamond pivot" of Christian truth, when considered from the human side. From the divine side, of course, it is the Cross.

Since this is true, then it is seen more clearly than ever that Christian doctrine and Christian duty go together. Years ago, P. T. Forsyth, Scottish theologian of unusual brilliance, wrote, "The same act which sets us 'in Christ,' sets us also in the society of Christ."[1] Acceptance of doctrine about Christ must lead to a decisive modification in duty. Creed should be followed by conduct, it is said, and quite correctly. As Paul put it, "For you have died. . . . Put to death therefore your members which are upon the earth" (Col. 3:3, 5).

Colossians 3:5 begins the more definitely ethical, or practical, section of this epistle. Terrible damage is often done to the Christian church by an unethical mysticism. Paul with all his genuine Christian mysticism was eminently practical in his teaching. There was no divorce between doctrine and ethic in him, such as existed even in Stoicism.

The figure around which Paul built his opening paragraph (3:5–17) is that of the divesting and reinvesting with apparel. In verse 8 he wrote, "put off" (KJV), and in verse 12 he commanded, "put on." The use of this figure may be related to the rite of baptism, as Moule suggests. "This particular language—that of divesting and reinvesting—was no doubt dramatically symbolized by the baptizand's unclothing before immersion and reclothing after it."[2] Pilots, soldiers, and athletes must dress their part, and so too must believers. If the old man has been put off and the new man put on, the moral apparel of the old man must be laid aside and new apparel donned. Clothes do not make the man, but a person is often reflected in his clothes, and Paul would have the new man reflected in new moral attire after the image of Him who created him.

The Negative Precepts (3:5–11)

WHAT THE CHRISTIAN MUST PUT OFF (3:5–9a)

Paul connected this passage with the preceding doctrinal section by the use of οὖν, "therefore." The sense of the inferential particle is plain. In the light of the exalted standing of the Colossian believers before God in the risen Christ, there must follow a life in conformity with it. They are to become what, in fact, they are. The indicative contains an implied imperative. Position and practice are to agree. The imperative is necessary because within the church in all ages are Demases who may yearn to go back to the worldly life, Peters who may deny, Thomases who may doubt, and Ananiases who may lie.

The key word in the section is the imperative νεκρώσατε (consider as dead). The verb means "to put to death," but obviously not in the physical sense, though some have taken it this way. The members to be put to death are defined as vices. The verb νεκρώσατε is similar to καταργέω and θανατόω in Romans 6:6 and 8:13 and to expressions like that found in Romans 6:11, λογίζεστε . . . νεκρούς, "consider yourselves to be dead." The last-named expression differs in that the verb is a present and looks at the reckoning as a process, while in the Colossian passage νεκρώσατε is an aorist imperative and pictures the act as urgent and decisive. Perhaps Bruce is correct in saying, "There must be a decisive initial act (aorist), introducing a settled attitude (present)."[3] At any rate the apostle intended that the Colossians render impotent[4] their members as instruments of the various vices he mentioned (cf. Rom. 6:6). Undisciplined self-expression has no place in the Christian life. While mortification has acquired Roman Catholic connotations in its historical usage, such as self-denial for the purpose of control of the body (a genuine sense, as 1 Cor. 9:24–27 shows) or of gaining merit (a wrong sense), nevertheless it is a genuine biblical word that believers must heed. They ought to note that the very expression indicates that the exercise of mortification is not painless. To put to death is never pleasant.

This practice of reckoning dead finds an excellent illustration in the gardener's practice of grafting. Once the graft has been made on the old stock the gardener is careful to snip off any shoot from the old stock that may appear. So in the believer's life, since he has now been grafted into the Last Adam and His new life, he must by the Spirit put to death any products of the old life that may appear (cf. Rom. 8:13).

There is also a word of encouragement that ought to be offered struggling saints. In the exhortation there is implied, of course, an assurance of power to perform the command.

The phrase τὰ ἐπὶ τῆς γῆς, "which are upon the earth" (KJV), is an allusion to verse 2, where the identical expression is found. Earth is the sphere of the existence and operation of the vices, so the believer is to set his affection on things above, not on things on the earth.[5]

The identification of covetousness with idolatry is not surprising, because the covetous person is guilty of erecting a rival object of worship in the place where God should be supreme.[6] He worships gain instead of God (Matt. 6:24).[7]

In Colossians 3:6 the apostle stated that the vices are the reason for the judgment of God. The expression "the wrath of God" is usually eschatological in the New Testament and refers to the coming tribulation period (cf. 1 Thess. 1:10; 5:9; Rom. 5:9). If this is the sense here, then the ἔρχεται, "will come," is a futuristic present. The expression does not mean the vindictive anger of God, as Moule points out.[8] He suggests the rendering, "the disaster from God," and this vividly brings home the fact that the tribulation period is a period of God's mighty judicial acts in vindication of His righteousness.

The transforming power of the Gospel of Christ shines through Paul's words in verse 7. The Colossians had walked in pagan vices and had even lived in them, but now they were new people in Him. Such is the power of the truth of God in every age. The contrast in the tenses of περιεπατήσατε, "walked," and ἐζῆτε, "living," is quite vivid. The first verb, an aorist, views all the ungodly acts as a whole, and the second, an imperfect, views the ungodly life in its progress.

When Stephen was stoned to death, the witnesses, according to Luke, "laid aside their robes at the feet of a young man named Saul" (Acts 7:58). The words, "laid aside," translate the Greek word ἀοτίθημι, rendered "put aside" or "put off" in Colossians 3:8. The metaphor is that of the divestiture of clothes. Thus the Colossians were exhorted by the apostle to lay aside as an old and

useless garment the old life's vices. The last words of Colossians
3:8, "from your mouth," are redundant if taken only with "abusive
speech." Most likely they go with "put aside," as do also the other
sins that are mentioned. Hence the verse has in mind the sins of
the tongue primarily. For example, "anger" and "wrath" are the
forms of these vices that manifest themselves in speech: θυμόν,
"wrath," is the outburst of temper, and βλασθημίαν is slander. No
wonder the psalmist prayed, "Set a guard, O LORD, over my
mouth; keep watch over the door of my lips" (Ps. 141:3).

Colossians 3:9 opens with an exhortation against lying, the
present imperative referring to the forbidding of the habit.[9]

WHY CHRISTIANS CAN AND MUST
PUT THEM OFF (3:9b–11)

The causal participle ἀπεκδοσύμενοι, literally, "having laid
off," sets forth the basic transformation through the work of
Christ out of which the new life is to grow. A change of nature
precedes a change of dress. Forsyth was referring to something
similar when he wrote, "A conversion which is but a wave of
spiritual experience is not the passage from death to life."[10]

Several important things may be noted in connection with this
transformation. First, the word ἀπεκδύω is a familiar Colossian
word, having occurred in Colossians 2:11 and in its noun form in
Colossians 2:15. In both places it is used in connection with the
effects of the work of Christ on the cross. There He stripped off the
body of the flesh and also the powers of evil. Bruce suggests that
the word has much the same meaning as συνσταυράω, "crucified
with," in Romans 6:6.[11] The word is an intensive double compound,
a stronger word than ἀποθέσθε, "put off," which occurs in verse 8
and is translated in identical fashion. The sense of the two is
adequately represented by the distinction between the two English
expressions, "to put off" and "to strip off."[12] Second, the participle
is an aorist and cannot be contemporaneous in time with the subject
of φεύδεσθε, "do not lie." It refers to the events of the Cross (cf.
Eph. 4:21–24). There the great change took place. This past fact is
the ground of all apostolic exhortation and true spiritual life. As
Nicholson says, "This is the great secret of the believer's power, not
a realization of it. We are never exhorted to crucify ourselves."[13]
Third, the fact that the participle is causal marks this stripping off of
the old man as the reason for the admonition to resist the habit of
lying. A new position obligates the believer to new life and action.

The identity of the old man has occasioned considerable discussion, but it may be defined fairly accurately as the whole unregenerate man, conceived of as a member of the first federal man, Adam. The expression, then, has corporate associations.[14]

The positive side is presented in Colossians 3:10. With the stripping off of the old nature there has come a new nature, the new man. The participle ἐνδυσάμενοι, "have put on," also causal and aorist in tense, is the complement of the preceding ἀπεκδυσά. The believer, having been severed from his connection with Adam the first, has now been clothed with and joined to Adam the last in all His fragrance and beauty.[15]

The constant renewal of the new man (the participle is present) is according to the image of Christ and wrought by the God who created the new man. Christ is the image of God (cf. Col. 1:15), and the new man is undergoing a constant renewal in the likeness of Christ. He is the great pattern for all spiritual life, and God engages Himself to recreate believers in His likeness, both individually (cf. Rom. 8:29) and corporately (cf. Eph. 4:7–16).

The new man lives in a new environment where all racial, national, religious, cultural, and social distinctions are no more. Rather, Christ is now all that matters for He is in all who believe.[16] The statement is one of the most inclusive in the New Testament and is amply supported by the preeminence of Christ in New Testament theology. It is a particularly appropriate statement for the Colossians and affords an excellent summary statement of the teaching of the letter. There are three realms, relevant to the Colossians, in which He is all. He is everything in salvation; hence there is no place for angelic mediation in God's redemptive work (cf. Col. 1:18–22; 2:18). He is everything in sanctification; hence legality and asceticism are out of place in the Christian life (cf. 2:16–23). He is the believer's life (3:3–4). And He is everything necessary for human satisfaction; hence there is no need for philosophy or the deeds of the old man (1:26– 28; 2:3, 9–10). He fills the whole life, and all else is hindering and harmful.

The Positive Precepts (3:12–17)

WHAT CHRISTIANS MUST PUT ON (3:12–14)

The οὖν, "therefore" (KJV), of verse 12 makes the connection with the preceding. A new character demands new characteristics! But the appeal is based not only on the preceding; it is also based

on the following words that describe the love of God that led to
His sovereign election and free forgiveness of the Colossians.
Paul never got far away from these soul-stirring truths. There is a
genuine logic in the necessity of Christian commitment. Since
believers owe all to Him, He should have all of them. But there is
something more moving than logic; it is love. There is something
suggestive in the fact that the Greek word χάρις does duty not
only for "grace" but also for "thanks" (as does *gratia* in Latin).
There is a close connection between the source of God's action
toward the children of God and the source of their response to
Him. Furthermore is it not also significant that the central act of
corporate worship, the Lord's Supper, is called the Eucharist (lit.,
the "Thanksgiving," from εὐχαριστέω, 1 Cor. 11:24)? Grace and
gratitude are the closest of kin. Baillie summed it up in this way:
"A true Christian is a man who never for a moment forgets what
God has done for him in Christ, and whose whole comportment
and whole activity have their root in the sentiment of gratitude."[17]
Paul was in thorough agreement. The following virtues he
inculcated have their root in the grace of election and forgiveness,
rooted and grounded in a love that has no end. Paul's use of the
perfect participle ἠγαπημένοι, "beloved," stresses the permanence
of God's love.

The climax of the virtues is, as one might expect, love (v. 14).
The ἐπὶ in verse 14 may mean "in addition to" (instead of "above,"
KJV). In that case the apostle conceived of this virtue as one that
holds the other virtues together and completes them. Moule
suggests that just as Christ is the principle of coherence in the
physical universe (Col. 1:17), so love (which He embodies) gives
coherence in the practical life.[18] If ἐπὶ is elative and means "above
all," then love is the most important moral quality in the believer's
life, a sentiment certainly compatible with New Testament teaching.
Love gives unity to all the graces and is the mark of maturity.
Christians recognize that God is in this age bringing believers into
the likeness of His Son, and therefore it is only natural that love
should be the sphere and consummation of maturity, because God
is love (cf. 1 John 4:8,16).

PRECEPTS CHRISTIANS MUST OBSERVE (3:15–17)

Four imperatives in this section single out the precepts believers
must follow.

The first imperative, βραβευέτω. "rule," is related to the word βραβεύς, an "umpire." The verb then means "to act as umpire" and represents an athletic metaphor. As Lightfoot says, "Wherever there is a conflict of motives or impulses or reasons, the peace of Christ must step in and decide which is to prevail."[19] Paul has in mind primarily the relationships between members in the body, the church, as the remainder of verse 15 indicates, but the principle has individual application too. In fact it forms, with the Word of God and the witness of the indwelling Spirit, one of the most important principles of guidance in the Christian life. F. B. Meyer wrote about a man aboard a ship crossing the English Channel toward a continental port on a dark starless night. One of the passengers was chatting with the captain over the difficulty of making port under such circumstances. The captain pointed to the distant shore and said: "Do you see the three lights shining faintly ahead on land? Well, I steer our ship until the three lights merge into one, and then I head straight into port with the light ahead of me. I know that course is the right course." In similar fashion the believer may trust the united witness of the Word of God, the witness of the Spirit, and the peace of Christ. When the three agree on or approve of a particular decision, the believer may have strong assurance of the will of God.

The second imperative, "be thankful," concludes verse 15. As already stated, grace must issue in gratitude. Paul elsewhere extended this exhortation to cover everything in the believer's life (1 Thess. 5:18). One is reminded of an entry in the diary of Matthew Henry, the famous Bible commentator, after he had been robbed: "Let me be thankful: 1st, because I was never robbed before; 2nd, because, although he took my purse, he did not take my life; 3rd, because, although he took all I possessed, it was not much; 4th, because it was I who was robbed, and not I who robbed."

The third imperative is found in verse 16. The apostle encouraged believers to assimilate the word of Christ in their meetings, as they admonish and teach one another amid the psalms and hymns of praise.[20] The expression "the word of Christ" occurs only here. In view of this, as well as the fact that the phrase occurs in this practical section of the letter, it may be that the words refer not to the Scriptures as such but to the word that Christ constantly speaks in the heart of the believer. Lightfoot agrees, saying that the expression "denotes the presence of Christ in the heart, as an inward monitor."[21]

With the peace of Christ, this word of Christ forms a second inward monitor. The word χάριτι, "grace" (KJV), probably means "thankfulness" (NASB), as the following words suggest. It should be noted that the singing is to be "in your hearts," as well as "to God." What a difference this would make in congregational singing!

It has often been noted that the Colossian passage is parallel with Ephesians 5:18–20. In the latter passage the hymns and songs are the outgrowth of the filling of the Spirit, while in Colossians they are the result of the deep assimilation of the word of Christ. Undisciplined emphasis on the Holy Spirit is accompanied too frequently by shallow grounding in the Word of God.

The final imperative is an implied one in verse 17. Everything is to be done in the name of the Lord Jesus. The present imperative ποιῆτε should be supplied with the second clause of the verse. One notices here that doing may be in "word" as well as in "deed." The expression, "in the name of the Lord Jesus," means under His authority and approval. George Goodman used to tell a story that illustrated action under the approval of the Lord Jesus. He wrote:

> I remember hearing a story of a man who was walking behind a gipsy woman, and when they came to a place where the road divided, the gipsy woman threw her stick up into the air, and let it fall on the ground. Then she did it a second time; and a third time. By this time the gentleman had caught up with her, and, being curious, he enquired: "Why do you throw your stick up into the air like that?" She replied: "That is how I determine which way to go; I go whichever way the stick points." "But you threw it up three times?" he said, wondering why she had done so. "Yes, I did!" she answered, "for the silly thing would point that way, and I wanted it to go this!"[22]

Colossians 3:5–17 points out the need for a marriage between the believer's position and the believer's practice, between creed and conduct. In these verses the apostle has outlined the Christian apparel, and it is indeed a heavenly wardrobe. These garments are the products of the enabling power of the Spirit of God. May He motivate believers by reminding them of their cost in His blood, and may He enable believers to don them in His name and for His glory.

CHAPTER 13

Sarah As a Model for Christian Wives (1 Peter 3:5–6)

James R. Slaughter

In 1 Peter 3:1–4 the apostle offered Christian wives instruction on how to relate to their husbands in a Christlike way. He explained that even in difficult situations wives should behave with deference toward their husbands, voluntarily submitting to them. Such submission should be characterized by a sincere, respectful, nonargumentative spirit. These qualities would be attractive to an unbelieving husband, who thus might be led to Christ through the gentleness and beauty of his wife's character. Behavior that reflects a spirit of deference, rather than a self-assertive, rebellious spirit, displays Christlikeness, and thus serves as an effective witness to unbelieving husbands.

Models of Deference in Godly Wives of the Past

In verses 5–6 Peter offered an example of the behavior he advocated in the preceding verses. His οὕτως γάρ, "for in this way" (v. 5), introduces the reference to godly women of the past who serve as models to Christian women. The lifestyle they are to follow has been exhibited by those who came before them—the holy women of former times (αἱ ἅγιαι γυναῖκες). Although Peter mentioned Sarah specifically in verse 6, the plural "women" refers generally to godly women in the Old Testament.[1] While Best may be correct in saying the church had not been in existence long enough to furnish examples,[2] it seems natural that Old Testament personalities might be familiar models.

Peter already had used the word "holy" (ἅγνος) to challenge his readers to do good: "But like the Holy One who called you, be holy yourselves also in all your behavior" (1:15), and to describe the nature of their priesthood as believers: "You also, as living stones, are being built up as a spiritual house for a holy priesthood, to offer up spiritual sacrifices acceptable to God through Jesus Christ" (2:5). The women in Peter's audience were holy (ἅγιαι) in that they were set apart by God and belonged to Him. They were chosen by God (2:4) and possessed an eternal inheritance and salvation through Christ (1:4–5, 9). The word "holy," when used in 3:5 of women of ages past, seems connected to this thought previously expressed. There were women in the past who also had been set apart by God. Whether the apostle was referring to some specific holy women or holy women in general is not stated. Michaels suggests Peter had in mind a specific group of women, namely, the four matriarchs of Jewish history: Sarah, Rebekah, Rachel, and Leah (the wives of Abraham, Isaac, and Jacob).[3]

Whoever they were, these models of holiness were characterized by their hope in God (αἱ ἐλπίζουσαι εἰς θεόν). Selwyn relates this hope to the dream of every Old Testament woman to be the mother of Messiah,[4] but this interpretation seems forced and does not fit the context of the passage well. Peter's point seems to be that these women characteristically rested in God.[5] Even in the face of hardship they lived their daily lives expecting that God would do for them what He had promised. Earlier in his letter Peter affirmed that believers, whose hope is in God, look forward to a future inheritance and salvation in spite of suffering in all kinds of trials (1:3–6, 13, 21). This is the same hope entertained by holy women of old who trusted in God, looking forward to His future redemption,[6] a redemption Peter knew had been realized in Christ but would be fulfilled when He returns.

Because the Christian women Peter addressed placed their hope in God, they and the Old Testament women had a similar perspective.[7] Such a perspective was crucial in light of the persecution experienced by Peter's initial readers and here by Christian wives. Some of these wives were being treated unfairly by their husbands but were nonetheless instructed to be models of deference through their submission to those husbands (3:1–2). Wives were to submit not out of a desire to avoid hardship or in an attempt to manipulate but on the basis of their expectation that God would act on their behalf. Later the apostle would confirm to all his readers, including these wives, "The eyes of the Lord are upon the righteous and His ears attend to their prayer" (3:12).

The way in which Christian wives were to adorn themselves (i.e., with a "gentle and quiet spirit," v. 4) was the same way in which these Old Testament models "dressed." The verb "adorn" (v. 5) is related to the noun "adornment" in verse 3, and its imperfect tense indicates continuing or repeated action over time in the past.[8] As before, fashion is a metaphor for conduct.[9] The Old Testament women fulfilled the ideal set forth in 1 Peter 3:3–4 through their godly conduct, or behavior, demonstrated through their submission to their husbands (ὑποτασσόμεναι τοῖς ἰδίοις ἀνδράσιν). Grudem observes that quiet confidence in God produces in a woman the imperishable beauty of a gentle and quiet spirit, but it also enables her to submit to her husband's authority without fear that it will ultimately be harmful to her.[10]

Sarah As a Representative of Godly Wives

Rabbinical literature exalted Sarah as being surpassingly beautiful[11] and exceedingly modest.[12] Though the characteristic of modesty is consistent with Peter's message to wives, he singled her out as exemplary because of the spirit in which she honored her husband.[13] Verse 6 affirms that Sarah "obeyed Abraham, calling him lord." Here the author substituted the word "obey" (ὑπακούω) for the term "submit" (ὑποτάσσω). The verb ὑπακούω (obey, follow, be subject to)[14] reflects the idea of ὑποτάσσω and the substitution may simply represent a stylistic variation.[15]

On what occasion did Sarah call Abraham her "lord"? The only Old Testament passage in which Sarah used the title "lord" of Abraham is Genesis 18:12. Responding to the news she overheard about her forthcoming son, she "laughed to herself, saying, 'After I have become old, shall I have pleasure, my lord being old also?'" But this was not an event in which Sarah obeyed or followed Abraham nor was it an occasion when she encountered unfairness, which is the special focus of Peter's exhortation. This problem causes Beare to assert that Sarah's calling Abraham lord is introduced arbitrarily by the apostle.[16] On the other hand, in ancient literature *lord* is not commonly used of husbands; therefore Michaels concludes that Sarah's use of it is highly significant.[17] Sly accuses Peter of chauvinistically stereotyping Sarah as the perfect Hellenistic wife, but this position necessitates an exceptionally low view of Scripture.[18]

It is likely that Jews in Peter's day saw Sarah's reference to her husband as "lord" as evidence of a proper and respectful attitude toward a husband, a spirit of deference Peter commended. The aorist ὑπήκουσεν, "obeyed," summarizes Sarah's habitual response to Abraham. Similarly, the present, active participle, καλοῦσα, "calling," represents her customary, respectful attitude and behavior toward him. Johnstone remarks that though no act of obedience may be found in Genesis 18:12, Sarah's use of "lord" in speaking to herself becomes "a kind of discourse which brings out with special exactness the real habits of thought and feeling."[19] Peter's use of the aorist and of the present participle indicates Sarah's attitude and customary pattern of conduct, whether or not Genesis 18:12 is the specific event the apostle had in mind.

Wives As Sarah's Daughters

In the final portion of verse 6 Peter affirmed that wives become Sarah's daughters (τέκνα) if they do what is right without being afraid of any fearful thing. Some see in Peter's use of the aorist ἐγενήθητε (you became, have become) a reference to conversion or baptism as the point at which these women became Sarah's "children."[20] In this case doing what is right without being afraid refers to godly behavior resulting from their salvation.[21] But because Peter's words to wives in verses 1–6 are a strong exhortation, it makes better sense to interpret the aorist in verse 6 as "you have become, you are." The following participles then would be conditional, "if you do what is right without being afraid of any fearful thing." The King James Version, *New American Standard Bible,* and *New International Version* translate the passage in this sense. Peter suggested that in submitting to their husbands, wives are thereby following Sarah's example of submissiveness. This view is consistent with the similar New Testament usage of *sons of* (υἱοὶ τοῦ) to mean "be like," as in Matthew 5:44–45: "But I say to you, love your enemies, and pray for those who persecute you in order that you may be sons of your Father who is in heaven; for He causes His sun to rise on the evil and the good, and sends rain on the righteous and the unrighteous." Bigg catches the meaning accurately when he writes, "Those [wives] who exhibit the same character as Sarah may be called in a figure her children."[22] Or as Davids puts it, "It is in moral likeness that they show their heritage."[23]

Earlier in the letter Peter instructed his readers to do what is right. Often they will be commended for doing so (2:14) but not always. Sometimes they will suffer for it (2:18–20). In 3:6 the apostle used this instruction specifically of a wife's submission to her husband even when he may cause her suffering. While

Michaels correctly observes that doing what is right may include disobeying the husband if he requires his wife to disobey God,[24] Peter's point is that godly wives characteristically show deference to their husbands by submitting to them. For Peter doing "what is right" means refraining from evil deeds and doing good deeds (2:11–12). Foh contends that doing what is right refers to following God's commands.[25] But Kassian observes that, though every woman must make her own choices, in most instances obedience to God means submission to one's husband.[26]

"Without being frightened by any fear" (μὴ φοβούμεναι μηδεμίαν πτόησιν) seems somewhat vague and has been variously interpreted. Kassian believes what the wife should not fear is the loss of her rights.[27] Beare relates the term to fear of the husband or of intimidation by him.[28] Wand and Reicke suggest that it refers to fear of being charged with a violation of religious laws and having to leave the church.[29] While it is possible to view fearful things in a broader context, such as fears relating to the raising of children or the management of household servants,[30] Peter's focus seems sharper. He is not addressing doubts about competency as a parent or about setting up a household. Fear relates to intimidation. Immediately following his instructions to husbands and wives Peter wrote, "And who is there to harm you if you prove zealous for what is good? But even if you should suffer for the sake of righteousness, you are blessed. And do not fear their intimidation, and do not be troubled" (3:13–14).

If, as some contend, Peter's words in 3:6 are an allusion to Proverbs 3:25, the issue of intimidation may be relevant: "Do not be afraid of sudden fear, nor of the onslaught of the wicked when it comes." In the case of the wives Peter addressed, the "onslaught of the wicked" would be intimidation from their unsaved husbands' hostility to the Christian message.[31]

Sarah serves as a good example to wives in Peter's exhortation because of her response to her husband. Several times submitting to her husband (though he was not an unbeliever) meant trusting God in uncertain, unpleasant, and even dangerous situations.[32] Moving with Abraham from Ur to Canaan (Gen. 12:1–8) may have been frightening for Sarah. Perhaps even more frightening may have been following her husband to the courts of Pharaoh (12:10–20) and Abimelech (Gen. 20). Kiley sees in these two events the basis for Sarah's credentials as a wife who models submission to her husband.

The author of 1 Peter is concerned with exhorting to submissive obedience even if in the midst of an unjust situation. This is revealed in his comments both to slaves (2:18–20) and to the community at large (3:9, 17). The same concern informs his comments to Christian wives, for whose paraenesis he draws in 3:6 on the story of Sara as recounted in Genesis 12 and 20. Her comportment in those chapters establishes her not just as a model of obedience but as a model of those wives who obey their spouses *in an unjust and frightening situation in a foreign land/hostile environment.*[33]

When a Christian wife trusts God as she submits to her husband, even when his requests seem unreasonable and the situation frightening, the Lord is pleased with her and commends her.

Summary and Conclusion

Godly women of the Old Testament, especially Sarah, serve as models for Christian wives. These holy women, like the women to whom the apostle wrote, anticipated future glory through the ultimate fulfillment of God's covenant promises. Trusting God daily enabled the godly women of former times to submit voluntarily to their husbands even when their husbands led them into dangerous, frightening situations.

Sarah serves as a representative of exemplary Old Testament women in her obedience to Abraham, whom she called "lord." Though it remains difficult to relate Sarah's reference to her husband as "lord" to any one historical incident, Peter may have had in mind Genesis 18:12, for it is the only Old Testament reference in which Sarah used that term of Abraham. The episode may not suggest that Sarah was submitting to her husband in an obvious way or that she was being subjected to unfair treatment. But Sarah's reference to her husband as "lord" revealed a respectful attitude toward him. In other accounts Sarah submitted to her husband by following him in the face of what must have seemed unreasonable requests: leaving Ur, entering the courts of Pharaoh and Abimelech, and perhaps seeing Abraham take Isaac to be sacrificed.

Peter affirmed that Christian wives married to unbelievers become Sarah's children if they do what is right and are not fearful. Here the apostle used "children" as a figure for those women who exhibit Sarah's character by their submission to their husbands even in difficult circumstances. Doing what is right refers to refraining from doing evil and doing good deeds including submitting voluntarily to their husbands. "Without being afraid of any fear," in light of Peter's argument, means a Christian wife need not be afraid of the intimidation of an unbelieving husband or of the alarming circumstances into which he might lead her. Submitting to a husband under such conditions means trusting God for one's well-being even in uncertain, unpleasant, and perhaps even in dangerous circumstances. A wife's trust in God in the face of fearful circumstances demonstrates the genuineness of her faith (1 Peter 1:7). This trust is strengthened by her anticipation of future glory and by the conviction that she is following the example of her Lord.

A tendency of some people is to argue or even belittle an unbeliever into making a profession of faith. A Christian wife may be tempted toward heated debate with her unsaved husband. But in 1 Peter 3:1–6 the wife is encouraged not to manipulate her husband with argumentation or false affection. Instead, she is reminded of the impact of Christlike behavior. The Holy Spirit touches the heart and mind of an unbeliever through deference when a Christian encounters unfair circumstances. Peter's words constitute both incentive and comfort for wives who are aware that their obedience to God and to their husbands will not be in vain.

First Peter 3:1–6 also shows that an unequal marriage, here the marriage of a Christian wife to an unbelieving husband, serves as an opportunity for the wife to achieve spiritual goals. Marriage to an unbelieving husband often causes great distress and emotional pain. But Peter's words to those wives point out the potential for spiritual gain in such a situation. By her sincere, respectful behavior she may win her unbelieving husband to Christ. What may seem a curse from the human perspective may result in blessing for the husband and wife individually and in their relationship as a couple.

In addition to the potential for winning a husband to Christ is the potential for personal spiritual growth of the believing wife. Though Peter did not state this, other New Testament writers point out that spiritual growth is produced by trials. Paul wrote, "And we exult in hope of the glory of God. And not only this, but we also exult in our tribulations, knowing that tribulation brings about perseverance; and perseverance, proven character; and proven character, hope; and hope does not disappoint, because the love of God has been poured out within our hearts through the Holy Spirit who was given to us" (Rom. 5:2–5).

And James stated, "Consider it all joy, my brethren, when you encounter various trials, knowing that the testing of your faith produces endurance. And let endurance have its perfect result, that you may be perfect and complete, lacking in nothing" (James 1:2–4).

Trials often produce in the believer greater dependence on God for help through a closer devotional relationship with Him. Reading the Scriptures, meditation, prayer, and, for some, fasting, often become much more consistent practices in trials than at any other time. It is only reasonable to expect a Christian wife of an unbelieving husband to strengthen her relationship to Christ as she seeks God's help in her unequal marriage yoke. Through such hardship God promises to pour out His power, His righteousness, His faithfulness, and His mercy.

CHAPTER 14

Living in the Light of Christ's Return (1 Peter 4:7–11)

D. Edmond Hiebert

The hope of Christ's return is an essential part of the believer's equipment for fruitful Christian living. In 1 Peter 4:7–11 the apostle discussed aggressive Christian service in the light of the impending end. The anticipation of the Lord's return must have an impact on present Christian conduct.

In the face of persecution from without, believers, inspired by their hope of the future, must band together in loving service to each other to the glory of God. Peter here asserted the end is near (v. 7a), he delineated Christian living in view of the end (vv. 7b–11a), and he pointed to the true goal of all Christian service (v. 11b).

The Assertion Concerning the End

The clause, "The end of all things is at hand" (v. 7), summarizes the Christian anticipation concerning the future. "Of all things" (πάντων), standing emphatically forward, underlines the comprehensive nature of the end in view. The genitive "all" could be taken as masculine, "all men, all people"; in 4:17 reference is made to "the outcome for those who do not obey the gospel." But here this comprehensive term is best taken as neuter, "all things," depicting the eschatological end. "The end" (τὸ τέλος), the consummation of the present course of history, implies not merely cessation but also the goal toward which this present age is moving. It is the prophetic message of Christ's return.

It is unwarranted to limit this comprehensive designation to "the end of the temple, of the Levitical priesthood, and of the whole Jewish economy" in A.D. 70.[1] Neither is it to be understood as a reference to the impending death in martyrdom awaiting the readers.[2] These views offer no proper basis for the exhortations that follow.

The verb "is at hand" (ἤγγικεν) is used in the New Testament of the approach of the kingdom of God in relation to the First Advent (cf. Matt. 3:2; 10:7; Mark 1:15; Luke 10:9, 11) as well as to the Second Advent (Rom. 13:12; Heb. 10:25; James 5:8). The verb means "to approach, to draw near"; in the perfect tense, as here, it portrays the event in view as having drawn near and now being in a position as near at hand, ready to break in. It thus depicts the return of Christ as impending. Newell characterized His return as "the next thing on the program."[3] Peter's statement expresses the conviction of the early Christian church (Rom. 13:12; 1 Cor. 7:29; Phil. 4:5; Heb. 10:25; James 5:8–9; Rev. 1:3; 22:20). Christ's anticipated return was "always near to the feelings and consciousness of the first believers. It was the great consummation on which the strongest desires of their souls were fixed, to which their thoughts and hopes were habitually turned."[4]

The delay in the expected return of Christ did create a problem for some in the early church (2 Peter 3:4–7). Yet the passing of the centuries has not invalidated this hope. No dates for the return of Christ were revealed to the apostles (Matt. 24:36); they did not know when their Lord would return; they were instructed to be expectant and ready for His return. They were not conscious of anything that expressly precluded such an expectation; much that they saw encouraged it.

The lengthy time interval between Christ's first and second coming must be understood in the light of God's chronology (2 Peter 3:8–9), not humankind's. Peter's assertion that the end is "at hand" and ready to break in expresses the Christian concept of the nature of the present age. With the Messiah's first advent the reality of the eschatological kingdom broke on human history, but with the King's rejection, His eschatological kingdom was not established. It awaits the day of His return. But that eschatological encounter introduced a new element into the nature of history. Human history now moves under the shadow of the divinely announced eschatological kingdom.

> Up to Christ's coming in the flesh, the course of things ran straight towards that end, nearing it by every step; but now, under the Gospel, that course has (if I may so speak) altered its direction, as regards His second coming, and runs, not towards the end, but along it, and on the brink of it; and is at all times near that great event, which, did it run towards it, it would at once run into. Christ, then, is ever at our door.[5]

As human history moves along the edge of the eschatological

future, "it is always five minutes to midnight," and "that edge at times becomes a knife-edge."[6] Only God's long-suffering holds back the impending manifestation of that day (2 Peter 3:8–9). This consciousness must have an impact on present Christian living.

The Duties in View of the End

"Therefore" (οὖν) grounds the duties now depicted in the consciousness of the impending end. In the New Testament this eschatological hope is frequently used to motivate Christian conduct (Matt. 24:45–25:13; Rom. 13:11–14; 1 Cor. 15:58; 1 Thess. 4:18; Heb. 10:25; James 5:8–9; 1 John 2:28; 3:2). "The return of our Lord," Erdman observes, "has always furnished the supreme motive for consistent Christian living."[7] The proper apprehension of this hope does not lead to uncontrolled excitement and fanatical disorder (cf. 2 Thess. 2:1–3; 3:6–16) but rather to self-discipline and mutual service. In 1 Peter 4:7 Peter set forth the believer's duty concerning the personal life, and in 4:8–11 he described proper community relations.

THE DUTY CONCERNING PERSONAL LIFE

"Therefore, be of sound judgment and sober spirit for the purpose of prayer." Two aorist imperatives set forth the urgent and decisive nature of these personal duties.

The first verb, "be of sound judgment" (σωφρονήσατε), was used of a person who was in his right mind in contrast to one who was under the power of a demon (Mark 5:15; Luke 8:35). It was also used more generally of one who was reasonable, sensible, and prudent, one who retained a clear mind. The readers are thus urged to be self-controlled and balanced in their reactions, able to see things in their proper place. Cranfield remarks, "The sound mind is equally far removed from the worldliness and unbelief of those who think to explain away the promise of Christ's coming again, and from the fanaticism and sensationalism of those who would fain predict the hour of it and the manner."[8]

The second verb, "sober" (νήψατε), conveys the thought of sobriety as the opposite of intoxication. The King James Version renders this "watch," but it is a watchfulness related not to sleepiness but to drunkenness. It is a call to remain fully alert and in possession of one's faculties and feelings. The eschatological context of this passage indicates that believers must "be free from every form of mental and spiritual 'drunkenness'"[9] resulting from befuddled views and feelings about the future.

The two verbs, similar in meaning, are connected by "and" (καὶ), marking a connection between the two duties. It is a question whether both imperatives or only the latter is to be connected to the words "for the purpose of prayer." The former seems to be the intended view of the *New American Standard Bible,* as quoted above. The *New International Version* also supports this position by joining both verbs with prayer: "Be clear minded and self-controlled so that you can pray." The *American Standard Version,* by putting a comma after the first verb, keeps the two commands as distinct duties: (1) Believers must maintain a personal disposition of balance and self-control as they face life, and (2) they must be alert in mind and attitude so that they can pray. This rendering seems preferable.

The phrase, "for the purpose of prayer" (εἰς προσευχάς, "unto, with a view to prayer"), implies that prayer is a normal and expected activity of the Christian life, but it is easy to become distracted and unfitted for its performance. "Prayer" is a general term and includes prayer in all its aspects. But the original is plural, "prayers" of all kinds, both private and public. What follows suggests that Jesus' followers must maintain the practice of prayer in relation to their own lives as well as in their community relations.

THE ACTIVITIES IN THEIR COMMUNITY RELATIONS

The close connection between personal and familial relations is underlined by the fact that verses 8–11, consisting of a series of participles, depend grammatically on the imperatives of verse 7. Though the participles are subordinate, the words "above all" (πρὸ πάντων) make clear that the duties now enjoined are of primary importance. Peter urged the practice of fervent mutual love (vv. 8–9) and depicted two broad areas of mutual service (vv. 10–11).

The duty of mutual love (vv. 8–9). "Keep fervent in your love for one another." Peter already mentioned love several times (1:8, 22; 2:17; 3:8), fully realizing its importance. "At a never-to-be-forgotten interview, the Master thrice reminded him that the supreme qualification for ministry was love."[10]

"Your love for one another" underlines the mutual nature of the love being urged. The noun *love* denotes a love of intelligence and purpose that desires the welfare of the one loved. The use of the definite article, "the love," points to the love they have already experienced. Its mutual character is underlined by the attributive position of "for one another" (τὴν εἰς ἑαυτοὺς) before the word ἀγάπην, literally, "the into-yourselves love." Peter's reflexive pronoun brings out the thought that they are all members of one body (cf. 1 Cor. 12:12) and that love for other members promotes one's own spiritual well-being.

Assuming that this love is already operative among them, Peter urged that his readers' love be "fervent" (ἐκτενῆ, "stretched out" and up to full capacity). The term was used to describe a horse at full gallop or to picture "the taut muscle of strenuous and sustained effort, as of an athlete."[11] "Keep" represents a present tense participle (ἔχοντες, "having" or "holding") and indicates that they must maintain their mutual love at its highest level. Such love can be actively cultivated.

The words "because love covers a multitude of sins" justify the demand for fervent love. It has a beneficial impact on social relations because it "covers" sins. The meaning is not that love condones or hushes up sins, either before God or others. The reference is not to sin in its Godward relations but rather to sins and failures in human relations. Love refuses deliberately to drag out the sins it encounters to expose them to the gaze of all; it prefers to refrain from and discourage all needless talk about them. It prefers to throw a veil over these sins, like the conduct of Shem and Japheth in throwing a covering over their father's shame, in contrast to Ham's viewing of it (Gen. 9:20–23). This gracious action of true love promotes the peace and harmony of the community and is the very opposite of hatred, which deliberately exposes sin in order to humiliate and injure. "Only when Christians become mean and ugly do they favor the devil by dragging each other's failings out into the public and smiting each other in the face."[12]

Love's action is necessary because believers are still weak and failing. In their close associations with each other, believers do, regrettably, encounter a multitude of sins. "Sins" (ἁμαρτιῶν), "the most comprehensive term for moral obliquity"[13] in the New Testament, basically denotes all that misses the mark in falling short of the standard of right; it may thus include sins of weakness and moral shortcomings as well as overt acts of sin. Love will deal with these sins according to the principles Jesus set forth in

Matthew 18:15–17. Peter here was thinking of believers in their mutual relations and not of their individual personal relationships to God. It is unwarranted to assume, as some do (e.g., Moffatt[14]), that such covering of sins wins forgiveness of one's sins before God. That would be a form of salvation by works.

The command, "Be hospitable to one another without complaint" (v. 9), widens the application of this principle of love. As indicated in Young's literal rendering,[15] Peter continued his directive without any verbal form: "hospitable to one another, without murmuring." He thus named a positive expression of the presence of love.

"Hospitable" (φιλόξενοι) is a plural adjective describing those who have an affectionate concern for strangers, which expresses itself in offering them food and shelter. The practice of hospitality was highly valued in the early church, and it is frequently mentioned in the New Testament (Rom. 12:13; 16:1–2; 1 Tim. 3:2; Titus 1:8; Heb. 13:2; 3 John 5–8; cf. Matt. 25:35). This fruit of familial love strengthened mutual ties among the churches, often widely scattered. Without its practice the early missionary work of the church would have been greatly hindered. When travelers or delegates from other churches arrived, their hospitable reception was regarded as a matter of course (cf. Acts 10:5–6, 23; 16:15; 21:15–17). Believers who were on journeys found it highly desirable to find lodging in Christian homes, fostering mutual fellowship and strengthening the ties between churches. Even more important was it for believers to find refuge in Christian homes whenever they were fleeing from their persecutors.

But Peter's use of the reciprocal pronoun (εἰς ἀλλήλους) implies that hospitality within the local group is involved. Since there were no separate church buildings for the first two centuries, each local congregation met in the home of one of its members (cf. Rom. 16:5; 1 Cor. 16:19; Philem. 2). This practice put their hospitality to a practical test.

"Without complaint" (ἄνευ γογγυσμοῦ) is a frank recognition that the practice of hospitality could become costly, burdensome, and irritating. The Greek term denotes a muttering or low speaking as a sign of displeasure. It depicts the opposite of cheerfulness. Such a spirit negates the value of the hospitality rendered and destroys the recipient's enjoyment of it. It is a ministry to be shouldered cheerfully if it is to be worthwhile. The addition simply emphasizes the true character of Christian hospitality and does not imply that Peter's readers were chronic grumblers.

The duty of mutual service (vv. 10–11). The thought now passes from mutual love to mutual service. The participial construction again ties this picture of Christian service to what has gone before. Verse 10 describes the ministry of believers individually as stewards serving the needs of the household of God with the means their Master has entrusted to them.

"Each one" (ἕκαστος), standing emphatically first, stresses that the duties and functions of a steward have been assigned to each believer. Each member of the body of Christ has been entrusted with at least one spiritual gift (1 Cor. 12:7; Eph. 4:7). Each member has his own distinct function, "as each one has received a special gift." The word "as" (καθὼς, "just as") indicates that the service of each one is to be governed by the nature of the gift received. Since each member has received a gift, it is clear that these gifts are not offices in the church. The term "gift" (χάρισμα), derived from the same root as "grace" (χάρις), denotes something bestowed freely and graciously. The term includes any capacity or endowment that can be used for the benefit of the church. It is not to be restricted to miraculous gifts; included is any "natural endowment or possession which is sanctified in the Christian by the Spirit."[16] Each should be employed as an expression of Christian love.

Believers must employ their gifts "in serving one another." The reflexive pronoun ἑαυτοὺς again points to the mutual benefit when these gifts are used for the sake of the whole body of Christ. God has made the members interdependent; what benefits others has a reflexive benefit for the one exercising the gift. The participle "serving" (διακονοῦντες) denotes any beneficent service freely rendered to another.

All must minister in the personal consciousness of being "good stewards of the manifold grace of God." Christians are "stewards," not owners of the means and abilities they possess. A steward was one to whom property or wealth was entrusted to be administered according to the owner's will and direction. A steward was entrusted with its use not for personal enjoyment or personal advantage but for the benefit of those served. This entrustment involved responsibility and demanded trustworthiness (1 Cor. 4:2). "As good stewards" means that they not merely resemble but actually are such; they must render their service in a noble and attractive manner.

Each believer has his share in ministering "the manifold grace of God." The collective singular, "the grace of God," comprehends all the gifts graciously bestowed, while the adjective "manifold" (ποικίλης) displays the many-colored gifts in their infinite variety. The Lord of the church has distributed His bounty with masterly variety to enable His people successfully to encounter the "manifold trials" (1 Peter 1:6) to which they are subjected.

In verse 11 Peter divided these gifts into two functional categories: the speaking gifts and the service gifts. The two categories are given in two conditional sentences, but no verbal form is expressed in the conclusion, which the Greek did not feel essential. In English one feels compelled to insert some verbal form, either an imperative, "let him," or a participial form.

"Whoever speaks" (εἴ τις λαλεῖ, "if anyone speaks") assumes the speaking function in operation. The verb may be general, simply denoting use of the faculty of speech; it is frequently used in the New Testament of teaching and preaching, and so here the speaking may be in the form of teaching, prophesying, or exhorting. While speaking in the assembly seems primarily in view, the verb is broad enough to include speaking outside a church setting, such as ministering to the sick or personal communication.

Speaking "as it were, the utterances of God" (ὡς λόγια θεοῦ) marks the necessary subjective feeling of the speaker as he exercises his gift. He must be conscious that what he says is God's message for the occasion. In classical Greek the λόγια were the utterances or responses of some deity. In the Septuagint the term is often used of "the Word of the Lord," and elsewhere in the New Testament it has reference to the Old Testament Scriptures (Acts 7:38; Rom. 3:2; Heb. 5:12). Here the sense seems to be that the speaker utters his message with the consciousness that he is giving not merely his own opinion but God's message under the leadership of the Spirit.

"Whoever serves" (εἴ τις διακόει) seems best understood as including all forms of Christian ministry other than speech. The one rendering the service (τις, "anyone") is again left entirely indefinite. It is unwarranted to limit the reference to the office of the deacon, as Demarest does.[17] The context simply limits the service to the realm of deeds.

The phrase "by the strength which God supplies" is a timely reminder that Christian service must be rendered in a spirit of humility and divine enablement. The one serving must avoid the conceit that the strength and ability to perform the service are his own. If his service promotes well-being of others, he must realize that this ability is "by" (ἐκ, "out of") divine enablement (cf. John 15:4). God abundantly "supplies" (χορηγεῖ) the needed strength to carry out His work. In classical Greek the verb was used of paying the expenses of a chorus in the performance of a drama. Since the performance reflected on the prior provision of all that was needed, the term came to denote supplying in abundance. Christian service must be humbly yet aggressively performed in full reliance on God's enablement.

The Goal in Christian Living

The added purpose clause, "so that in all things God may be glorified" (v. 11), declares the true goal in all Christian living. The comprehensive "in all things" (ἐν πᾶσιν) is best understood as looking back to the entire paragraph. All that they have and do must magnify "God" (ὁ θεὸς), the God whom they now know and serve. He is the Fountain of all their gifts and blessings. In all they are and do, they must desire to thank Him and to extol and ascribe honor to His name.

"Through Jesus Christ" is a reminder that only through the reconciliation achieved in Him can God be truly glorified (cf. 1:21; 2:5; 3:18). "There is only one way to God, and our incense must be scattered on coals taken from the true altar, or it can never rise up acceptable and pleasing to Him."[18]

Peter's own grateful heart moved him to glorify God: "to whom belongs the glory and dominion forever and ever. Amen." The use of the indicative verb "belongs" (ἐστιν, "is") marks his words as an assured declaration, not merely a devout wish. "To whom" may refer to either Jesus Christ or God the Father. In favor of Jesus Christ is the fact that He is the nearer antecedent here and that in Hebrews 13:20–21; 2 Peter 3:18; and Revelation 1:5–6 the glory is ascribed to Christ. In favor of God the Father is the fact that He is the subject of the sentence. Best cites three considerations in favor of God the Father as the intended antecedent:

> (i) The reference to the glorification of God in the preceding clause links with "glory" here; (ii) The majority of NT doxologies are offered to God, and in particular the very similar doxology of 5:11 is offered to him; (iii) To speak of glorifying God "through Jesus Christ" and then to speak of glory belonging to Christ seems odd.[19]

It is preferable to take God the Father as the subject of this doxology.

God is magnified as possessing "the glory and dominion" (ἡ δόξα καὶ τὸ κράτος). The definite article in the Greek with both nouns marks them as separate and distinct possessions, rightfully belonging to Him. He possesses the glory, the radiant majesty and sublimity characteristic of deity, and He exercises the dominion (κράτος, "might and power in action"), marking Him as the sovereign Ruler over all.

To Him belong the glory and the dominion "forever and ever" (εἰς τοὺς αἰῶνας τῶν αἰώνων), literally, "unto the ages of the ages." This strengthened form of "forever" emphasizes the thought of eternity in the strongest way. The expression depicts eternity as "a series of ages flowing on endlessly, in each of which a number of other shorter ages are gathered up."[20]

"Amen" is a transliteration (alike in Greek and English) of the Hebrew word meaning "so let it be." So used, it is not a wish but rather a strong affirmation, placing a seal of approval on what has just been said. Its use was common in the early Christian worship services as an expression of devout assent (cf. 1 Cor. 14:16). The practice was adopted from the Jewish synagogue.

This brief paragraph offers insight into Peter's understanding of Christian life and service. For him the hope of the impending return of Jesus Christ was a living reality. But he firmly held that this eschatological hope must promote loving Christian relations and faithful Christian service. The hope of the future is to have a sane, sanctifying impact on the present. In waiting as well as in serving, the true goal of the Christian life must ever be to glorify God.

CHAPTER 15

Growth in the Christian Life (2 Peter 1:5–11)

D. Edmond Hiebert

The contents of 2 Peter clearly fall into three parts, appropriately marked by the chapter divisions. The sequence of these parts well serves to accomplish the apostle Peter's purpose of fortifying his readers against the false teachers who would harass the church. The first chapter vividly portrays the nature of the Christian life with its challenge to spiritual growth and maturity, built on a sure foundation. The second part of the epistle is a ringing polemic against the false teachers who allure and seek to mislead God's people, while the third chapter deals with the heretical denial of the return of Christ and concludes with some fitting exhortations to the readers.

In seeking to prepare his readers against the danger from the false teachers, Peter stated in chapter 1 that their safety lies in their clear apprehension of the nature of the new life in Christ and their spiritual growth and maturity in the faith as the best antidote against error. In verses 3 and 4 he set forth the amazing bestowal of a new life whereby they were made "partakers of the divine nature." In verses 5–11 Peter stressed the necessity that believers grow in this new life. Its proper development requires diligent cultivation, calling for the strenuous involvement of believers. He enumerated the needed qualities that must be developed (vv. 5–7), pointed out two incentives for such growth (vv. 8–9), called for personal assurance through effective growth (v. 10a), and underlined the results of such growth (v. 10b–11).

> Now for this very reason also, applying all diligence, in your faith supply moral excellence, and in your moral excellence, knowledge; and in your knowledge, self-control, and in your self-control, perseverance, and in your perseverance, godliness; and in your godliness, brotherly kindness, and in your brotherly kindness, [Christian] love. For if these qualities are yours and are increasing, they render you neither useless nor unfruitful in the true knowledge of our Lord Jesus Christ. For he who lacks these

qualities is blind or short-sighted, having forgotten his purification from his former sins. Therefore, brethren, be all the more diligent to make certain about His calling and choosing you; for as long as you practice these things, you will never stumble; for in this way the entrance into the eternal kingdom of our Lord and Savior Jesus Christ will be abundantly supplied to you (2 Peter 1:5–11).

The Qualities Involved in Spiritual Growth (vv. 5–7)

"Now for this very reason also" (καὶ αὐτὸ τοῦτο δὲ) summarizes verses 3–4 as the basis for a logical demand. Καὶ indicates that something new is being added, while δὲ indicates that what is added differs from what has preceded. The adverbial accusative "for this very reason" (αὐτὸ τοῦτο) introduces the duty to grow spiritually. It stresses the logical duty involved in the divine bestowal of new life. "The divine nature we receive must be daily exercised in the endeavors of moral living."[1] Peter was anxious that they not frustrate the grace of God by resting content with "faith without works" (James 2:20).

THE NEEDED DILIGENCE FOR GROWTH (v. 5a)

"Applying all diligence" points out the basic requirement for effective growth. "Diligence" (σπουδὴν), placed emphatically forward, denotes quick movement or haste in the interest of a person or cause. But it also commonly denotes earnestness or zeal in performance; at times it is used in contrast to sloth.[2] Peter was calling for an attitude of eagerness and zeal, the opposite of sluggishness and self-indulgence. "All" underlines the comprehensiveness of the duty; their diligence must be neither halfhearted nor selective.

"Applying" (παρεισενέγκαντες) is literally "bringing in alongside of" and pictures this diligence on their part as something brought in alongside of what God has already done (vv. 3–4). Human effort must follow the work of God, but the participial construction indicates that such human effort is subordinate to the divine bestowal and flows out of it (cf. Phil. 2:12–13). The aorist tense of the participle calls for effective action on the part of the readers. The concern is not with the process of procuring this needed diligence but with its actual operation. This compound form, which occurs only here in the New Testament, was at times used in the papyri to refer to importing something quietly along byways.[3] (Compare the action of the false teachers in Jude 4.) Perhaps the implication is that diligence should characterize the believer and the readers should bring it into operation "quietly and without ostentatious display."[4]

"Supply" (ἐπιχορηγήσατε) specifies the task they must effectively perform. In the task of Christian character development, believers must contribute what is rightly demanded of them. This aorist imperative carries a note of urgency; it states a peremptory command. It calls for a generous and lavish provision or equipment for an intended task. The original imagery was that of a rich patron lavishly supplying every need for the training and staging of a grand chorus for some public celebration. This idea has faded, but the concept of a generous cooperative activity remains. "The Christian must engage in this sort of cooperation with God in the production of a Christian life which is a credit to Him."[5]

THE SPIRITUAL QUALITIES TO BE NURTURED (vv. 5b–7)

The words "in your faith supply" do not ask believers to supply faith; it is accepted that they already have it (v. 1). Their spiritual lives began with this life-bringing faith. "Your faith" (τῇ πίστει ὑμῶν) marks the faith as personal, but it has an objective content, involving their firm adherence to the divine realities portrayed in verses 3–4. But their faith must attain its full potential in spiritual fruitfulness through daily exercise in moral living

Peter listed seven qualities or traits of character in this moral development. Each new trait is introduced as being "in" (ἐν) or "in connection with" the preceding. Each is inherent in the preceding, which in turn is supplemented and perfected by the new, giving it more abundant fruitage. All are empowered by a living faith that constantly draws on the divinely implanted life.

The definite article is used with each new trait mentioned; the possessive "your" occurs only with faith, which believers already possess. The article makes each trait specific, not just any trait they may wish to substitute.

Moral excellence. "In your faith supply moral excellence" names the first feature in Christian character development. The precise force of ἀρετήν, here rendered "moral excellence," is not certain.[6] English Bible versions show a wide variety of renderings.[7] The term basically characterizes anything that properly fulfills its purpose or function. Then generally it may be taken to denote one who fulfills the purposes and implications of the Christian calling. Accepting such a general meaning here, it denotes "moral excellence" or "virtue" (KJV, et. al.). But since the term is used here in a series of character traits, it may well have a more specific meaning. As a specific quality it may denote "moral courage" or "energy in the exercise of their faith, translating it into vigorous action."[8]

Knowledge. Connected with moral excellence, or with Christian courage and moral energy, believers must have "the knowledge" (τὴν γνῶσιν). This is not the compound form ἐπίγνωσις, used in verses 2 and 3, but the simple form, which denotes a practical knowledge in which one can grow. Grounded in the verities of the Christian revelation, this practical knowledge enables a discernment between right and wrong in facing the duties of life. A resolute and aggressive faith must be governed by practical intelligence and moral insight. Barnett observes, "where moral and religious values are concerned, the good man thinks more clearly and discriminatingly than the licentious man."[9] This knowledge stands over against the spurious "knowledge" of the false teachers. The cure for false knowledge is not less knowledge but a knowledge characterized by moral insight.

Self-control. "The self-control" (τὴν ἐγκράτειαν) points to the inner power to control one's own desires and cravings as the fruit of true knowledge. While the term was often used in connection with sexual desires, it extends to all areas of life. It involves the discernment between good and evil that true knowledge brings. "Where virtue, guided by knowledge, disciplines desire and makes it the servant instead of the master of life, self-control may be said to supplement faith."[10] Any religious system claiming that religious knowledge emancipates from the obligations of morality is false.

Perseverance. "The perseverance" (τὴν ὑπομονήν) designates that inner power of endurance developed by persistent self-control. The cognate verb, composed of the preposition ὑπο, "under," and the verb μένω, "to stay, abide, remain," portrays a picture of steadfastly and unflinchingly bearing up under a heavy load. The noun conveys the concept of steadfastness and endurance. It has in it a forward look, the ability to look beyond the current pressures (cf. Jesus' perseverance; Heb. 12:2). It fosters the ability to "withstand the two Satanic agencies of opposition from the world without and enticements from the flesh within."[11]

Godliness. Christian endurance is motivated by "godliness" (τὴν εὐσέβειαν), the attitude of reverence that seeks to please God in all things. It desires to be rightly related to both God and people and brings the sanctifying presence of God into all the relationships of life. The characteristic distinguishes true believers from ungodly false teachers (2 Peter 2:5–22; 3:7).

Brotherly kindness. "Brotherly kindness" (τὴν φιλαδελφίαν) denotes the warm, familial affection between those who are spiritually related in the family of God. It is more than a passing disposition of fondness for other believers; it manifests itself in overt acts of kindness toward them (Gal. 6:10). True godliness does not permit the Christian life to be "a sullen solitary habit of life."[12] This affectionate relationship in the early church between Christian converts, in spite of their diverse status and varied backgrounds, amazed the pagans around them.

Christian love. "The love" (τὴν ἀγάπην), the greatest of Christian virtues (1 Cor. 13:13), forms the natural climax in this portrayal of character development. It is not restricted to other believers but reaches out to all. The preceding term implies personal warmth and affection; this word denotes a love that springs from intelligence and good will and purposefully desires the welfare of the one loved. It has its origin not in the desirability of the object but in the agent who deliberately desires the highest good for the one loved. It does not condone or gloss over sin in the one loved but willingly engages in self-sacrificing action to procure that person's highest good.

All the elements named are inherent qualities of a maturing Christian character. All may not be equally developed in any one believer, but they cannot be compartmentalized and one quality selected to the disregard of the others. They are all the fruit of the Spirit's work in the life of the believer.

The Incentives to Spiritual Growth (vv. 8–9)

The word "for" (γὰρ) at the beginning of verses 8 and 9 introduces a positive and a negative incentive to grow.

THE EFFECT OF ABUNDANT GROWTH (v. 8)

The clause "for if these qualities are yours and are increasing" depicts the marks of abundant growth. "These qualities" (ταῦτα) summarizes the seven elements in the growth elaborated in verses 5–7. The abundance of the growth is depicted by two participles: "these things unto you belonging and abounding."[13] Most English Bible versions render these participles as a conditional construction since they relate to the exhortation in verse 5. But the Greek implies no doubt as to the readers' possession of these qualities in some measure. "Are yours" (ὑμῖν ὑπάρχοντα), a strong expression in the Greek, denotes what actually exists as one's possession. The implication is that these qualities have become a rightful part of the character, not a mere fleeting manifestation.

The added participle, "are increasing" (πλεονάζοντα), indicates Peter's real concern for his readers. The verb may mean "to be present in abundance," or "to increase, to bring forth in abundance." The present tense depicts a continuing process: their growth must be a process involving continuing increase leading to abundance. Lack of such growth is a sign of inner deterioration and impending death.

"They render you neither useless nor unfruitful in the true knowledge of our Lord Jesus Christ" states the assured result of such growth. Their abundant possession of these qualities "renders" (καθίστησιν, "constitutes" or "places") them in the category of being "neither useless nor unfruitful." The direct object "you" is understood and the two negative adjectives are predicative, "as neither useless nor unfruitful." The negative (οὐκ, "not") with both negative adjectives gives the force of a strong positive assertion.

"Useless" (ἀργούς) is literally "unworking"; it denotes not one unavoidably unemployed but one who avoids labor for which he should assume responsibility. In James 2:20 the term is used of a faith that fails to show itself in works. The double negative pictures believers as diligently cultivating these qualities. "Unfruitful" (ἀκάρπους) pictures a fruit tree that remains without fruit under the most favorable conditions. "Nor" (οὐδὲ) again reverses the picture. The believers are viewed as "active and productive."

The phrase "in the true knowledge of our Lord Jesus Christ" has been understood in two ways. Some, like Mounce,[14] take the preposition "in" (εἰς) to mean "in respect to" and understand the meaning to be that they will be neither useless nor barren in regard to their knowledge of Christ as believers. Others prefer to retain the usual meaning of the preposition εἰς ("unto") as denoting the goal toward which their growth looks. Knowledge of Jesus Christ is "the aim toward an ever greater measure of which they are continually to advance."[15]

"Knowledge" (ἐπίγνωσιν) is not the simple form used in verse 6 but the compound form used in verses 2 and 3. It implies an intimate and growing knowledge of One whom they already know. It is knowledge of, not merely about, the Person whom Peter and his readers acknowledged as "our Lord Jesus Christ." It is a part of the divine nature that has been bestowed on them, but by its very nature it can never be fully apprehended in this life. This knowledge is both the root and the goal of the Christian life. "The best evidence that can be given of 'knowing' the Lord is to 'follow on to know' Him."[16]

THE BLIGHT FROM THE FAILURE TO GROW (v. 9)

"For" points to the blighting effort of the failure to grow as a further incentive for growth. "For he who lacks these qualities" ("he to whom these things are not present," Rotherham) states the tragic condition of the one who claims to have faith without resultant works. The switch to the third person, "he who," makes the picture abstract, while the negative μὴ places it in the realm of thought. Peter does not think of his readers as being in this condition. "Lacks" (μὴ πάρεστιν, "are not present") forms a sharp contrast to "are yours and are increasing" in verse 8. Such a believer shows no evidence of a productive faith.

Peter described the true status of such an individual by using an adjective and two participles. "Blind" (τυφλός) metaphorically describes his moral and spiritual condition. The absence of the spiritual qualities just set forth shows that personally he has no eyes for them. Two participles further define his condition. "Short-sighted" (μυωπάζων) clarifies his true condition. The term, occurring only here in the New Testament, portrays him as so shortsighted as to be indeed blind to the spiritual qualities under consideration. They are beyond the scope of his earthbound vision.

Peter has been understood to picture a person who shuts his eyes and will not see. This implication of willful blindness is drawn from the fact that a nearsighted person usually blinks his eyes when trying to see something at a distance. But such a person does not close his eyes because he does not want to see; his defective eye condition constrains him to blink in trying to see something distant. Therefore the thought of a deliberate refusal to see is probably not in Peter's picture. Rather, Peter was saying that the shortsighted person's spiritual condition leaves him *unable* to see the need for these spiritual realities.

"Having forgotten his purification from his former sins" points out that an inner change has taken place. The unique expression, "having forgotten" (λήθην λαβών, "forgetfulness having received"), pictures the person as subject to spiritual amnesia. The failure of his "faith" to produce any of these spiritual qualities has effectively dimmed and blotted out the memory of "his purification from his former sins." The reference is to his public initiation into the Christian life through baptism, which symbolized cleansing from his sins and the beginning of a new life. But his failure to cultivate the qualities of the new life has caused him to forget the implications of that event.

Is this the picture of a saved person who has lost his salvation, or is it the picture of a "converted" but unregenerated person who fails to live up to his baptismal commitment? The problem of the true status of such an individual has agitated the thinking of the Christian church from earliest times. Peter was apparently thinking of the false teachers who had professed to receive new life but continued to live in open sin.*

The Exhortation to Spiritual Growth (v. 10a)

"Therefore" (διὸ, "for this reason") marks the exhortation in verse 10 as logically arising out of the incentives just cited. "Brethren" (ἀδελφοί), the only occurrence of this term of address in the Petrine Epistles, adds intimacy and affection to the appeal. It recalls the family to which they mutually belong as believers.

The imperative "be all the more diligent" (μᾶλλον . . . σπουδάσατε) carries a sense of urgency. If taken with the verb, the adverb "more" urges greater diligence than they have been showing. But the adverb may be taken with the force of "rather," to mark a contrast to the careless life just described in verse 9.[17] The word order seems to give a slight preference to this view. "Be diligent" urges the readers to be eager or zealous, thus safeguarding themselves against the spiritual blight just pictured.

In urging his readers "to make certain about His calling and choosing you," Peter was not merely urging them to engage in more strenuous activities. He was concerned about their personal assurance that they are the called and chosen of God. The middle infinitive "to make" (ποιεῖσθαι), standing emphatically at the end, underlines their own interest in the matter, while the present tense suggests that it is a lifelong responsibility. "To make certain" indicates that their personal assurance of being called and chosen

---

*Editor's note: A third view, not mentioned by Hiebert, is that Peter was referring to believers who are not growing spiritually.

must be based on the appropriate evidence in their own lives. Believers' robust spiritual growth confirms that God has called and chosen them. The blighted condition pictured in verse 9 destroys such assurance.

The two nouns "calling and choosing" (τὴν κλῆσιν καὶ ἐκλογὴν) are united under one article as intimately connected. Since it is implied that the calling and election can be rendered insecure, some suggest that "both words should be taken of the entering into communion with God in this world."[18] Thus viewed, the calling came through the preaching of the Gospel and the election came through the admission of the converts into the church. This would explain Peter's order here. But elsewhere the two terms relate to the divine side of salvation. The calling is certainly the act of God; the union of the two under the one article demands that the election must also be the divine act. Chronologically divine election precedes the call (Rom. 8:30), but Peter's order here is in accord with his concern for the believer's certainty of the divine initiative in salvation. One's consciousness of God's calling is mediated through the preaching of the Gospel; only after a person responds to His call can he begin to understand God's pretemporal election (Eph. 1:4). Election becomes a certainty to believers after they have experienced His transforming call (cf. 2 Thess. 2:13–14). Green remarks,

> *Make your calling and election sure* is an appeal that goes to the heart of the paradox of election and free will. The New Testament characteristically makes room for both without attempting to resolve the apparent antinomy. So here; election comes from God alone—but man's behaviour is the proof or disproof of it.[19]

The Results of Spiritual Growth (vv. 10b–11)

Peter named two results that will follow, the first relating to the present life (v. 10), the second to the eschatological future (v. 11). The repeated "for" (γὰρ) again marks the logical connection.

ASSURED STABILITY IN THE PRESENT LIFE (v. 10b)

"For as long as you practice these things" again recalls the tie between divine grace and human responsibility. The forward position of "these things" (ταῦτα) is best understood as referring back to the qualities mentioned in verses 5–7. A flourishing spiritual life is the safeguard against failure. "As long as you practice" renders a present tense participle (ποιοῦντες) that again (cf. ποιεῖσθαι) points to the continuing process of nurturing and developing these Christian qualities. "Obedience is not optional in any consideration of Christian safety."[20]

"You will never stumble" (οὐ μὴ πταίσητέ ποτε) declares their assured stability. The double negative with the aorist subjunctive has the force of a categorical and emphatic denial.[21] "Stumble" is metaphorical, denoting a fall or failure. The aorist tense here points to a stumbling that is final, a fall from which there is no arising (cf. Rom. 11:11). This does not mean that they will never sin but that, kept from an irretrievable fall, they will complete their journey to their destination. They are assured spiritual surefootedness on their way to the eternal kingdom.

TRIUMPHANT ENTRY INTO THE ETERNAL KINGDOM (v. 11)

"For in this way the entrance into the eternal kingdom . . . will be abundantly supplied to you." The adverb rendered "in this way" (οὕτως) is parallel to "as long as you practice these things" (v. 10) and once more recalls the necessary human response. The human activity does not earn the entry; it is the way that leads into the eternal kingdom.

"Will be abundantly supplied" (ἐπιχορηγηθήσεται) picks up the verb used in verse 5; God will reciprocate to their activity of diligently supplying the necessary development of Christian character by supplying them an abundant entry into the eternal kingdom. "Abundantly" (πλουσίως, "richly") suggests a warm welcome, as of a son returning in triumph. The underlying picture may be that of the return of a victor in the Olympic games; he would be welcomed home with honor and escorted into the city through a specially prepared entrance through the city wall.[22] The passive voice of the verb indicates that this entry will be God's generous provision, but provided in response to their faithfulness in the use of God's gifts.

"The eternal kingdom" (τὴν αἰώνιον βασιλείαν) names the goal of their pilgrimage. Both terms are common in the New Testament, but this combination occurs nowhere else in the New Testament or the apostolic fathers, except in the *Apology* of Aristides of Athens (ca. A.D. 129) where this verse is cited.[23] But Luke 16:9 and 2 Corinthians 5:1 offer close parallels. This kingdom has the quality of being "eternal," which means more than endless duration. "Eternity will not be endless sequence as much as it will be the presence of the One in whom time ceases to have significance."[24]

As "partakers of the divine nature" (2 Peter 1:4), Peter's readers had already entered into the kingdom about which Jesus spoke to Nicodemus (John 3:3, 5). This present phase of the kingdom involves suffering for those who enter it (2 Thess. 1:3–5). For believers, the future aspect of the kingdom is associated with reward (Matt. 25:31–33; Acts 14:22). Peter viewed this kingdom, conceived under messianic forms, as belonging to Christ (cf. Luke 1:33), its Ruler.

The risen Christ is now enthroned at the Father's right hand (Col. 3:1; Heb. 1:3; 8:1; 10:12; 12:2); when He returns to earth, His kingdom will be visibly manifested (Matt. 13:40–43; 25:31). His return will inaugurate the earthly messianic phase of the kingdom (Rev. 20:1–6).

> In this mediatorial capacity, Christ must reign till He has put all enemies under His feet (1 Cor. 15:25), and when that glorious end shall have come, He will relinquish His mediatorial character, delivering up the kingdom to God, even the Father; but the kingdom itself will continue forever.[25]

It will be the eternal kingdom "of God and of the Lamb" (Rev. 22:1).

Believers now acclaim this sovereign Ruler as "our Lord and Savior Jesus Christ." This familiar double designation occurs only in this epistle (2 Peter 1:11; 2:20; 3:2, 18). "Our" is confessional. Believers acclaim Him as "Lord" of their lives since He first came into their lives as "Savior."

CHAPTER 16

Fellowship and Confession in 1 John 1:5–10

Zane C. Hodges

It would be difficult to find any single passage of Scripture more crucial and fundamental to daily Christian living than 1 John 1:5–10. For here, in a few brief verses, the "disciple whom Jesus loved" has laid down for believers the basic principles underlying a vital walk with God. It is always worthwhile, therefore, to examine these principles afresh so that their truths might be more effectively applied to daily life.

Verse 5

"This then is the message which we have heard of him, and declare unto you."[1] With these words, the apostle John embarked on his first specific exposition of truth in fulfillment of the expressed intention of his prologue (1 John 1:1–4). Moreover, he already stated there that the epistle is based on firsthand knowledge—"that which was from the beginning, which we have heard, which we have seen with our eyes, which we have looked upon, and our hands have handled, of the Word of life" (v. 1). It is therefore in keeping with this guarantee that what he now unfolded is "the message which we have heard of [from] him." In other words the apostle spoke of truth directly communicated to the apostolic circle by the same Savior whom he had heard, seen, and touched.

Verse 5 clearly perpetuates the first-second-third person relationships so plainly visible in verses 1–4. The "we," of course, both in verse 5 and in verses 1–4, can only be an apostolic "we" since the experiences claimed in verse 1 are such as were only enjoyed by those who had direct, personal contact with the Lord Jesus.[2] In particular the experience of touching Him is most fittingly mentioned since John was himself the one who reclined at the Last Supper in Jesus' bosom and leaned back on His breast to ask the identity of his Lord's betrayer (John 13:23–25). The "you," however, had not had such intimate experiences and therefore they relied on apostolic communication about them. The words "that which we have seen and heard declare we unto you, that ye also may have fellowship with us" (1 John 1:3) clearly establish the dependence of the readers on the message of the writer. The "him" of verse 5 is either the Father or the Son, who are mentioned in verse 3 without any effort really being made in verse 5 to distinguish them. Undoubtedly John thought of truth that had been disclosed by Christ, but his concept of the unity of Father and Son is too dynamic to allow the "him" to refer exclusively to the one or to the other.[3] Whatever John had heard from the Son, he had heard from the Father as well.[4] Thus "the message which we have heard of him, and declare unto you" is an apostolic communication to the epistle's readership, which has its source in the truth of God as unfolded by the Lord Jesus. This at once establishes its transcendent authority.

The precise content of the message is now stated: "That God is light, and in him is no darkness at all." It is, of course, entirely possible that this profound assertion about the nature and character of God was made in exactly this form by the Lord Himself. After all, only a fraction of His ministry is recorded in the Gospels (John 21:25), and John's insistence in this passage on the theme of hearing (1 John 1:1, 3, 5) would be appropriately carried out if verse 5 recorded a specific utterance of Christ. But in any case it is evident that the Lord's claim to be "the light of the world" (John 8:12; 9:5; 12:46) lies at the foundation of this concept. And since the Son is in His own person the unique revealer of the Father (John 1:18; 14:9–11), whatever He has disclosed about Himself becomes the basis of a predication about God. If the Son is light, it follows inevitably that God is light.

Moreover, the further observation that "in him is no darkness at all" is a consistent development of the strong antithesis between light and darkness that the fourth gospel portrays in the teaching of Jesus (John 3:19–20; 8:12; 12:35, 46). Indeed, it is so consistent a development that it is difficult to think it was not actually uttered by the Lord at some point in His ministry. Clearly John was imparting truth that was, at the very least, perfectly at home in the doctrine of his Master.

As has often been pointed out, the light-darkness motif was widely prevalent in the Hellenistic conceptual world of John's day.[5] Moreover, this motif was present in the thought patterns of the Jewish sectaries of Qumran.[6] But the apostle was not concerned with the analogies and parallels available in contemporary society but with the divine origin of this affirmation. It was "the message which we have heard [from] him." And for John the concepts of light and darkness are, above all, ethical concepts. The truth, which he associates with light, is not merely something to know but also something to do (cf. 1 John 1:6; John 3:21). By contrast, darkness is linked with the doing of evil deeds (John 3:19–20). Hence to affirm that God is light and in Him is no darkness at all is to affirm God's absolute holiness and His complete freedom from any taint of evil. It is, in short, a restatement of Jesus' own claim to sinlessness: "Which of you convinceth me of sin?" (John 8:46). And this truth has profound implications for all who claim a personal association with Him.

Verse 6

Here begins a series of three possible affirmations (cf. 1 John 1:8, 10) that, in view of the message just enunciated in verse 5, are false on the lips of those who make them. It is particularly striking and impressive that the writer continued the "we" of verse 5 and of the prologue itself. Taken at face value, the continuation of "we" demonstrates the intensely personal way in which the truth "we have heard from him" is applied by the apostolic writer to his own and his fellow apostles' experience. Of course he intended the readers to apply it to themselves as well—the message is something the apostles "declare unto you"—but there are no grounds for denying the applicability of the "we" statements to the circle that originally received the message.[7] Verse 6 cannot be divorced from verse 5.

Naturally the apostle did not affirm that he had made or could make the false statement of this verse. But he did not deny to himself the possibility. The form of the Greek conditional clause rendered "if we say" is one that expresses a contingency that is, at least theoretically, capable of realization. It is true that some forms of theology regard it as impossible that any Christian, much less an apostle, could ever make an assertion like this. But such theology finds no support in the straightforward statement of the text and indeed is guilty of an unrealistic view of human nature. But the apostle John was surely a realist, and as one of the disciples who had confidently affirmed unfailing loyalty to their

Lord on the eve of His passion (Mark 14:31), he had undoubtedly long since surrendered the facile notion that there were spiritual failures of which he was somehow quite incapable. As a matter of fact, when correctly understood, the false claim of this verse is one of the easiest for believers to make.

"If we say that we have fellowship with him, and walk in darkness." The Greek word for "fellowship" used here signified some form of mutual sharing or participation by two or more parties.[8] It is clear that in this context it is by no means a mere synonym for salvation because already John stated in verse 3 that the aim of the apostolic declaration to the readers is that "ye also may have fellowship with us." But John was perfectly clear in this epistle that his readership consisted of people already converted (2:12–14, 21, 27), yet the goal of the truth he set before them was "fellowship"—first with the apostles and, as a result of this, with the Father and the Son. "And truly our fellowship is with the Father, and with his Son Jesus Christ" (1:3). It follows therefore that for John fellowship must be something more than what his readers have automatically acquired as a result of their new birth. It is in fact something that is predicated on apostolic instruction— the things the apostles had seen and heard concerning the Word of life (v. 1) and were sharing now with their fellow believers (v. 3). Moreover, this connection of fellowship with apostolic teaching is a theme that may be traced back to the earliest days of the church. On the Day of Pentecost, the initial converts of that day are first said to have "continued steadfastly in the apostles' doctrine and [in] fellowship" (Acts 2:42). Thus John's thought here has its roots in primitive Christianity. Those who have come to faith in Christ need to be taught by the apostles of Christ so that they may have fellowship with them and with God Himself. It may be stated, then, as an axiom of Christian experience, that all true "fellowship" is predicated on apostolic doctrine. Today, of course, the Scriptures preserve this apostolic voice and continue to furnish the instruction on which such fellowship is founded.

What precisely is shared in the fellowship John spoke of here is not at this point defined. (It will become clearer in verse 7.) But the apostle was concerned, however, to show that this fellowship cannot occur for believers in the darkness. Inasmuch as "God is light, and in him is no darkness at all," it follows that darkness must be a sphere where God is not and where the sharing John spoke of is an impossibility.

"If we say that we have fellowship with him, and walk in darkness, we lie, and do not the truth." Should the claim be made—John said, "if we should make it!"—that a person moving in the realm of darkness is engaged in an experience of "sharing" with God, two things may be affirmed about that claim. First, it is false, "we lie," and second, it exposes a pattern of life inconsistent with divine revelation, "we . . . do not the truth." Thus darkness is revealed as a sphere where the light of God is inoperative in the life of him who walks there. He insists (whether sincerely or insincerely is not stated) that he is sharing with God, but this does not conform with reality and is consequently a lie. Moreover, the truth of God, which it is obviously the function of light to disclose, is not being actualized in the life. Hence, as to both words and deeds, the individual who makes this claim is devoid of the effective influence of the light on his personal experience. He is accordingly out of touch with Him who is the Light. But since negatives are best understood in the presence of positives (even in the physical world, darkness is simply the absence of light!), verse 6 is best comprehended by comparison with verse 7.

Verse 7

"But if we walk in the light, as he is in the light, we have fellowship one with another." This verse has often been misunderstood. It is not a statement about the way in which believers may have fellowship with each other.[9] It is transparently the converse of verse 6, where the subject is fellowship with God. Of course John had spoken in verse 3 of having fellowship with his readers (the we-you relationship), but he had also spoken there of the we-He relationship: "and truly our fellowship is with the Father, and with his Son Jesus Christ." Plainly verse 7 deals with this we-He relationship just as did the previous verse. The point is simple. "If we walk" where "he is" (in Greek the pronoun "he" is emphatic), then "we" and "he" both have something in common that is being shared. To put it crisply, believers share the light with Him and He shares the light with them. "We have fellowship one with another."

Thus the light becomes the foundation of a life, "walk," of sharing with God. Since "God is light" (v. 5) and since "he is in the light" (v. 7), if we do not share this with Him, our Christian experience will be devoid of real fellowship with the One who saved us. There should be no difficulty with this concept. A son may have in him the life of an earthly father because his father begat him, yet if he makes his home at a distance from his father they will not be able to have shared experiences. Similarly a Christian who lives at a moral distance from his heavenly Father loses the privilege of shared experience with God. Walking in the light brings Father and spiritual child into the same moral realm, and that realm itself becomes the foundational experience that they have in common. All other mutual experiences must be built on this.

But it must be noted that John did not say, if we walk *according to* the light, but if we walk *in* it. If conformity to the light were the issue, fellowship would be impossible for any except those who were perfectly sinless. For "God is light, and in him is no darkness at all." It follows, then, that where one is walking in relation to God is the paramount consideration. Another way of putting this is to say that when a believer walks in the light he exposes himself to God and to His truth. He allows the light to shine on his heart and life, and he does not shrink from it into the dark. The person who walks in darkness, on the other hand, has withdrawn himself from the presence of God and from the luminous reality of His holiness, as the apostles proclaimed it.

Because of this it becomes easy for a Christian to make the false claim of verse 6. When a believer is consciously doing evil, which is contrary to the light of divine truth apostolically communicated, he may undertake to hide from himself as well as from others the intolerable reality of the breach in his communion with God. The psychological defense he attempts to erect may be precisely that of denying that the breach exists. Yet at the same time he is not comfortable in God's presence. Indeed every Christian knows from experience how difficult it is to pray or read the Word of God when there is a consciousness that he is violating His revealed, specific will. He may claim fellowship, but he is hiding—walking—in the dark.

On the other hand, when the heart of a child of God is completely open to Him and to all His Word has revealed, he is then moving in the sphere of light. Apostolic truth—God's truth—thus illumines his life. This does not involve sinlessness, of course, but a willingness to see sin and to treat it for what it really is. John was clear, in fact, that walking in the light does not involve the total absence of failure from one's life. For, after declaring that "if we walk in the light, as he is in the light, we have fellowship one with another," he added a crucial concomitant reality.

"And the blood of Jesus Christ his Son cleanseth us from all sin." The verbal statements "have fellowship" and "cleanseth us" are the same tense and exist as coordinate fulfillments of the condition, "if we walk in the light."[10] That is, while the believer exposes himself openly to God and His truth, he experiences both a sharing with God and a cleansing by God. The latter makes the former both reasonable and right, for given the sinfulness of even the best of people—the apostles themselves, in fact—fellowship with a sinless God—in whom there is no darkness at all—could only occur if human unholiness were constantly under the efficacious influence of the blood of Christ. This has nothing to do with salvation, which is fully guaranteed at the moment of one's faith. Rather it has to do with the righteousness of God in permitting His far-from-perfect children to live in His presence and to share the light where He is. Nothing less than the blood of Christ could make this possible, and no Christian has ever enjoyed so much as a single moment of communion to which the Savior's sacrifice, in all its value, has not been contemporaneously applied.

Verse 8

"If we say that we have no sin, we deceive ourselves, and the truth is not in us." The second false assertion is now presented. And it is appropriate that it should follow at once John's claim that the blood of Jesus Christ is being applied to the believer's sin, even while he has fellowship with Him and with His Father. For ironically, while the assertion of verse 6 is most readily made by a person consciously out of fellowship, verse 8 is a tempting claim for the one who has hitherto been walking in the light. For if to walk in the light is to open one's heart to God for whatever He may show him about himself, when he for the moment sees nothing wrong he may foolishly believe that there is nothing wrong.[11] But John said that would be a mistake, a self-deception. The truth itself should point up this error, for who can contemplate the holiness of God who is light and the awfulness of the sacrifice made necessary by sin, without being overwhelmed by the desperate depths of human unholiness. If then, in the absence of conscious sin, one is able to deduce the absence of any sin, the Cross has not gripped him as it ought. When one feels that way, John said, be it ever so briefly, the truth is not in him—not that he has not believed the truth but rather that it is not interwoven into the fabric of his thoughts as it ought to be. It is not "in us" as a controlling force. For no one in whom God's truth is fully at home can say even for an instant, "I have no sin." To say that would be to make oneself for that same instant without need for the blood of Christ.

Verse 9

"If we confess our sins, he is faithful and just to forgive us our sins, and to cleanse us from all unrighteousness." If it is true, according to verse 8, that one may never at any time claim sinlessness without at the same time deluding oneself, it follows quite naturally that one should be ready to acknowledge one's sins whenever they appear. It is equally clear that this readiness to confess sin is an integral part of walking in the light. After all, light is the sphere where things appear ("for whatsoever doth make manifest is light," Eph. 5:13), while darkness is the realm in which reality is hidden. Indeed, the longer one walks exposed to God's character and God's Word, the more one sees by contrast the failures that mar one's earthly life. A newly converted believer will not have anywhere near the same sensitivity to sin as one who has walked for years in the presence of God, for the new Christian has just emerged blinking, as it were, from a lifetime of experience in the dark. But the longer a believer is in the light the more he becomes accustomed to it and the more plainly he sees the reality that it increasingly exposes to his gaze. Not that sin is one's major preoccupation there—God is—but God cannot be truly known apart from an extended, concurrent process of self-discovery. And it is this very self-discovery that forces a believer to confront his sin and to acknowledge it.

"If we confess our sins, he is faithful and just to forgive us our sins." Strangely, it has recently been denied that this verse could apply to Christians on the grounds that believers are already forgiven and need not ask for what they already have.[12] But this point of view directly contradicts the teaching of the Lord Jesus Christ. Indeed, the writer John himself was among the disciples to whom the Master taught His model prayer. And the Savior had prefaced that prayer with the words "whenever you pray"[13] and had instructed His followers, after their day by day petition for daily bread, to say: "And forgive us our sins; for we also forgive every one that is indebted to us" (Luke 11:4). John knew clearly, therefore, that one of the corollaries to that message that he heard and declared was his Lord's insistence on the need for daily forgiveness in the lives of His disciples.

Of course forgiveness, on the level at which John was discussing it, must be distinguished clearly from the doctrine of justification. Justification by faith imparts to the believing sinner a perfectly righteous standing before God at the moment he receives Christ (Rom. 3:21–26; 4:5), and nothing can be added to this or subtracted from it. But this legal and forensic issue is not the same as the question of fellowship with God within His family. Though the believer in Christ is promised that he "shall not come into judgment" (this is a better rendering than "condemnation" in John 5:24), it should be obvious that the question of family discipline is something different. The familiar illustration of the judge who paid a fine for his own son in court but was perfectly free to discipline that same son once they got home carries the point. Every sin of which the believer is guilty has been paid for by the Cross of Christ and thus he can never be summoned before the bar of eternal justice to answer for this, since the Savior has already atoned for it. But as a Father, God is free to set the terms on which His children shall commune with Him and His refusal to commune with the sinning child until confession has occurred is a divine prerogative. Hence in this context forgiveness relates to the restoration of broken communion within the household of God.

It is also true that there is a sense in which the believer enjoys a continuing and perfect forgiveness "in Christ" already, so that, for example, we read, *"In whom* we have redemption through his blood, the forgiveness of sins" (Eph. 1:7, italics added). But this is a part of a characteristically Pauline concept whereby he sees believers blessed "with all spiritual blessings in heavenly places in Christ" (1:3). In this sublime spiritual relationship, God "hath raised us up together, and made us sit together in heavenly places in Christ Jesus" (2:6), and there can be no question of sin there as a barrier between believers and Him. But John was not talking about one's standing in heavenly places, but about one's walk on earth. And down here sin is an undeniable reality, capable of erecting a true spiritual and psychological barrier between a believer and his heavenly Father. And the removal of sin's estrangement of the soul from God must still be called what the Christian consciousness has always called it—forgiveness.[14] That this is indeed the correct terminology is confirmed by the Lord's Prayer, the disciple's model whenever he prays.

The necessity of forgiveness, however, is coupled by John with the certainty of forgiveness. "He is faithful and just to forgive us our sins." In other words, when the believer acknowledges his sin to God, his heavenly Father is both *reliable* and *righteous* in extending His remission. And though a Christian immediately after confession sometimes may not feel forgiven, he must rely not on feelings but on facts. God can be counted on, John affirmed, to grant the forgiveness a believer seeks. Moreover, there is no unrighteousness in His doing so. For, as John will shortly point out, the heavenly Advocate with the Father is "Jesus Christ the righteous: and he is the propitiation for our sins: and not for ours only, but also for the sins of the whole world" (1 John 2:1–2). And if the propitiatory work of Christ is large enough in scope to cover even the sins of a world that never applies to Him for the benefits of His Cross, it is transparently sufficient for those who do. It is right that God should grant forgiveness whenever a child of God acknowledges his need of it.

But, of course, it is obvious in all this that one can only acknowledge what the light shows him. There can be no question of confessing unknown sins, since a person cannot confess what he does not know. And not surprisingly, John showed an awareness of this reality. And it must be observed that the word "our," printed in italics by the King James Version, is not present in the original Greek. The phrase should be read, "He is faithful and just to forgive us the sins," that is, the sins one confesses. But then John added, "and to cleanse us from all unrighteousness." The point is clear, for the contrast lies between *the* sins and *all* unrighteousness. In a word, when a Christian acknowledges the sins the light discloses, not only are these known faults forgiven, but all else that is not right in his life—however ignorant he may be about it—is at the same time thoroughly cleansed away. But in reality the provision does not differ greatly from that laid down in verse 7 as well. The honest, open walk in the presence of divine light is accompanied by a cleansing from all sin through the blood of Christ. It follows therefore that, as honest acknowledgment of failures takes place in that light, the same kind of cleansing from all unrighteousness must likewise take place. Everything hinges on one's integrity before God. If a believer is willing to keep himself exposed to what He is, (for He is light) even when this exposure compels him to acknowledge sin in his life, he will always have His perfect cleansing. The moment he begins to dissemble, to equivocate, to excuse his evil, that moment he lies and is not following the truth. The believer then is hiding—hiding in the dark.

Verse 10

"If we say that we have not sinned, we make him a liar, and his word is not in us." This is the third and final false assertion. John's train of thought runs smoothly; each of these false claims flows out of an immediately preceding truth that the claim contradicts. Thus verse 6, with its claim to fellowship with God by one who is actually walking in the dark, contradicts the reality of verse 5 that God is light, and in Him is no darkness at all. Thus also verse 8, with its claim to being without sin, clashes with the reality of verse 7 that even while one walks in the light one is not faultless, for the blood of Jesus Christ even then is cleansing one from all sin. So, as might be expected, the spurious assertion of verse 10 is the opposite of the truth of verse 9. If a Christian discovers sin in his life, he can confess it and thus agree with God concerning the true nature of what he has done. But there is another option. He can disagree with God! While God's Word tells him he has done wrong, he may seek to justify himself and rationalize his sin away. In short, he can say—on any given occasion of failure—not "I confess" but "I have not sinned."[15] But, as John wrote, if a believer says he has not sinned, he is contradicting God, making God a liar. And His word—which exposes sin—is not in the believer. For no person, true Christian though he may be, is genuinely under the influence of God's Word when in fact he is contradicting it. That dynamic indwelling of the Savior's words in His followers, of which He spoke elsewhere (cf. John 15:7), cannot exist unless those words can bend their consciences to the truth. And when they deny the sin Jesus' words so plainly disclose, it is evident that those words are not in them in any vital, transforming sense.

Conclusion

There is nothing complicated about John's concepts, though the depths of those concepts challenge a lifetime of careful thought. But in their essence they are simple. God is perfect light, perfect purity. To share anything with Him as Christians, we must at least share the light where He is. There is much else we can share with Him besides that, but nothing else without that! To share the light is to be in it, to be exposed to it, to refuse to hide in the dark from any reality it discloses. And if in fact it discloses a believer's sin, he must acknowledge that reality too, he must confess it, and then continued sharing of the light will go on. Christians are never perfect, even while they are in the light, but if they stay in that light they are perfectly clean! The blood of Jesus Christ provides for that. And God will always faithfully apply the value of that blood to the honest heart.

What then is the principle of fellowship with God? Succinctly stated, it is openness to God and full integrity in the light of His Word. Indeed the psalmist sensed it long ago and captured its essence in these lovely words: "Search me, O God, and know my heart: try me, and know my thoughts: and see if there be any wicked way in me, and lead me in the way everlasting" (Ps. 139:23–24).

Chapter Notes

Chapter 3—"Sinners" Who Are Forgiven or "Saints" Who Sin?

1. Benjamin Breckenridge Warfield, *Perfectionism,* 2 vols. (New York: Oxford University Press, 1931), 1:113–301.
2. Ibid., 1:115. The following quotations, expressing the "miserable-sinner" concept, are cited by Warfield, 1:118–19, 123.
3. Cited by Warfield, 1:128.
4. Neil Anderson, *Victory Over the Darkness* (Ventura, Calif.; Regal, 1990), 44–45.
5. Leon Morris, *The First and Second Epistles to the Thessalonians,* rev. ed. (Grand Rapids: Eerdmans, 1991), 155.
6. Peter T. O'Brien, *Colossians, Philemon,* Word Biblical Commentary (Waco, Tex.: Word, 1982), 190–91; Andrew T. Lincoln, *Ephesians,* Word Biblical Commentary (Dallas: Word, 1990), 287.
7. Lincoln, *Ephesians,* 285.
8. E. K. Simpson and F. F. Bruce, *Commentary on the Epistles to the Ephesians and the Colossians* (Grand Rapids: Eerdmans, 1957), 273. O'Brien similarly says that in addition to a reference to the new corporate humanity, the "new man" designates "the new nature which the Colossians had put on and which was continually being renewed" (*Colossians, Philemon,* 190).
9. Robert C. Tannehill, *Dying and Rising with Christ* (Berlin: Töpelmann, 1967), 52; A. Van Roon, *The Authenticity of Ephesians* (Leiden: Brill, 1974), 336–37.
10. John Calvin, *Institutes of the Christian Religion,* 3.3.11; cf. 3.12.1.
11. Ibid., 3.3.10.
12. Donald Guthrie, *The Pastoral Epistles* (London: Tyndale, 1957), 65 (italics his).
13. Karl Heinrich Rengstorf, s.v. "ἁμαρτωλός," in *Theological Dictionary of the New Testament;* George W. Knight, *The Pastoral Epistles* (Grand Rapids: Eerdmans, 1992), 101.
14. Knight, *The Pastoral Epistles,* 102.
15. Peter H. Davids, *The Epistle of James* (Grand Rapids: Eerdmans, 1982), 200.
16. "When Paul speaks of dying and rising with Christ, he is referring to Christ's death and resurrection as eschatological events. As such, they concern the old and new aeons. Through this death and resurrection the believers are freed from the old aeon and the new aeon is founded. . . . Because the existence of all within an aeon is

based upon and determined by the founding events, the whole of the aeon shares in these events" (Tannehill, *Dying and Rising with Christ,* 39). On the similar significance of dying and rising with Christ and stripping off the old man and putting on the new, see Tannehill, *Dying and Rising with Christ,* 52.

17. Ibid., 21.
18. Horatius Bonar, *God's Way of Holiness* (New York: Carter & Bros., 1865), 108 (italics his).
19. Robert Jewett, *Paul's Anthropological Terms* (Leiden: Brill, 1971), 313. John Laidlaw describes the heart as "the work-place for the personal appropriation and assimilation of every influence" (*The Bible Doctrine of Man* [Edinburgh: Clark, 1895], 122).
20. Andrew Tallon, "A Response to Fr. Dulles," in *Theology and Discovery: Essays in Honor of Karl Rahner,* ed. William J. Kelly (Milwaukee: Marquette University Press, 1980), 37.
21. Peter Kreeft, *Heaven: The Heart's Deepest Longing* (San Francisco: Ignatius, 1989), 45.
22. Jewett, *Paul's Anthropological Terms,* 322–23.
23. Calvin, *Institutes,* 2.3.6.
24. Franz Delitzsch, *A System of Biblical Psychology* (reprint, Grand Rapids: Baker, 1966), 416.
25. Johannes Pedersen, *Israel: Its Life and Culture,* 2 vols. (London: Oxford University Press, 1973), 1:166.
26. James D. B. Dunn, "Romans 7:14–25 in the Theology of Paul," *Theologische Zeitschrift* 31 (September–October 1975): 257–73.
27. For a brief sketch of this latter interpretation, see N. T. Wright, *The Climax of the Covenant* (Minneapolis: Fortress, 1992), 196–200.
28. C. E. B. Cranfield, *A Critical and Exegetical Commentary on the Epistle to the Romans,* 2 vols. International Critical Commentary, (Edinburgh: Clark, 1975), 1:358–59.
29. James D. B. Dunn, *Romans 1–8,* Word Biblical Commentary (Dallas: Word, 1988), 389.
30. Delitzsch, *Biblical Psychology,* 438. Delitzsch gives a helpful description of the interaction between the believing ego opposed to sin and the power of sin. Referring to the sin of unchastity, he says sin "is possible only when the might of temptation succeeds either in overmastering, or even in interesting, the Ego of the man. At times there are mingled in the range of man's thoughts impure thoughts which he acknowledges as not less thought by his Ego than the pure ones which it opposed to them in order to dislodge them. Sometimes temptation succeeds in drawing in the man's Ego into itself; but in the midst of the sinful act, the man draws it back from it, full of loathing for it. Sometimes, moreover, the Ego, in order to complete the sinful act unrestrainedly, is voluntarily absorbed into unconsciousness, and does not until after its completion return in horror to recollection of itself; and the spirit

with shame becomes conscious of its having been veiled by its
own responsibility."

31. J. Knox Chamblin, *Paul and the Self* (Grand Rapids: Baker, 1993),
    173–74.
32. Martin Luther, *Werke,* Erlangen ed., 2.197, cited by Warfield,
    Perfectionism, 1:116.
33. J. I. Packer, *Keep in Step with the Spirit* (Old Tappan, N.J.: Revell,
    1984), 123.
34. Fisher, *Marrow of Divinity,* cited by Bonar, *God's Way of Holiness,*
    72.

Chapter 4—Prayer and the Sovereignty of God

1. Robert L. Dabney, *Lectures in Systematic Theology* (1878; reprint,
   Grand Rapids: Zondervan, 1972), 715.
2. Charles Hodge, *Systematic Theology,* 3 vols. (reprint, Grand Rapids:
   Eerdmans, 1975), 3:692.
3. Charles Hodge, *Princeton Sermons* (1879; reprint, Edinburgh:
   Banner of Truth, 1979), 292.
4. John Calvin, *Institutes of the Christian Religion,* trans. Henry
   Beveredge, 2 vols. (Grand Rapids: Eerdmans, 1970), 3.20, 146.
5. Philip Schaff, *The Creeds of Christendom,* 2 vols. (Grand Rapids:
   Baker, 1966), 3:698.
6. Charles Hodge, *Systematic Theology,* 3:708.
7. Charles Hodge, *Princeton Sermons,* 291.
8. Charles Hodge, *Systematic Theology,* 3:708.
9. A. A. Hodge, *Evangelical Theology: A Course of Popular Lectures*
   (1890; reprint, Edinburgh: Banner of Truth, 1976), 85.
10. Dabney, *Lectures in Systematic Theology,* 716.
11. Charles Hodge, *Princeton Sermons,* 294.
12. Ibid., 295.
13. Calvin, *Institutes,* 3.20, 146–47.
14. Dabney, *Lectures in Systematic Theology,* 716.
15. Calvin, *Institutes,* 3.20, 147.
16. A. A. Hodge, *Evangelical Theology,* 91.
17. Charles Hodge, *Systematic Theology,* 3:709.
18. Calvin, *Institutes,* 3.20, 148.
19. Robert C. Sproul, "Does Prayer Change Things?" *Tenth* 6 (July
    1976): 53.
20. Ibid., 55.
21. Dabney, *Lectures in Systematic Theology,* 717.
22. Charles Hodge, *Systematic Theology,* 3:700.
23. Calvin, *Institutes,* 3.20, 147.
24. A. A. Hodge, *Evangelical Theology,* 85.
25. Dabney, *Lectures in Systematic Theology,* 719.
26. Ibid.
27. A. A. Hodge, *Evangelical Theology,* 88.

28. Francis Turretin, "Institutio Theologiae Elencticae," trans. George Musgrave Ginger, typewritten manuscript (Princeton, N.J.: Princeton Theological Seminary, n.d.), 175.
29. Ibid.
30. Sproul, "Does Prayer Change Things?" 58.
31. Dabney, *Lectures in Systematic Theology,* 718.
32. A. A. Hodge, *Evangelical Theology,* 93.
33. Turretin, "Institutio Theologiae Elencticae," 177.
34. Calvin, *Institutes,* 3.20, 147.

Chapter 5—The Meaning of Crossbearing

1. To define and evaluate each of these views fully would require another article the length of this one. Those who desire this may consult this writer's "Crossbearing in Mark 8" (Th.M. thesis, Dallas Theological Seminary, 1982), 4–23.
2. For example, "Mark undoubtedly means actual martyrdom" (John Knox, "The Gospel according to St. Luke," in *The Interpreter's Bible,* ed. George A. Buttrick, 12 vols. [New York: Abingdon], 8 [1952]: 170); and Manson's comment that to "take up his cross" meant "the voluntary acceptance of martyrdom at the hands of the Roman Empire" (T. W. Manson, *The Sayings of Jesus as Recorded in the Gospels According to St. Matthew and St. Luke Arranged with Introduction and Commentary* [Grand Rapids: Eerdmans, 1979], 131). Earnest Best cites some German works holding this view (*Following Jesus: Discipleship in the Gospel of Mark* [Sheffield: JSNT, 1981], 50, n. 67). On pages 38–39 he ably summarizes its major weaknesses.
3. Examples are Willoughby C. Allen, *A Critical and Exegetical Commentary on the Gospel According to St. Matthew,* 3d ed., International Critical Commentary (Edinburgh: T. & T. Clark, 1912), 111, 182; F. F. Bruce, *New Testament History* (Garden City, N.Y.: Doubleday, 1972), 187; C. E. B. Cranfield, *The Gospel according to Saint Mark,* Cambridge Greek Testament Commentary (Cambridge: University Press, 1979), 282; Donald R. Fletcher, "Condemned to Die: The Legion on Crossbearing: What Does It Mean?" *Interpretation* 18 (1964): 163–64; Norval Geldenhuys, *Commentary on the Gospel of Luke,* New International Commentary on the New Testament (Grand Rapids: Eerdmans, 1951), 398 (on Luke 14:27; however, on Luke 9:23 Geldenhuys supported the suffering view); William L. Lane, *The Gospel According to Mark,* New International Commentary on the New Testament (Grand Rapids: Eerdmans, 1974), 308; John Peter Lange, *The Gospel According to Matthew,* trans. Phillip Schaff, vol. 8 of *A Commentary on the Holy Scriptures* (reprint, Grand Rapids: Zondervan, 1978), 303; Gilmour S. MacLean, "The Gospel According to St. Luke," in *The Interpreter's Bible,* 8:1709; I.

Howard Marshall, *The Gospel of Luke: A Commentary on the Greek Text,* New International Greek Testament Commentary (Grand Rapids: Eerdmans, 1978), 372–73 (on 373 he also supports the self-denial view); Leon Morris, *The Cross in the New Testament* (Grand Rapids: Eerdmans, 1965), 26 (Morris supports several views); J. Oswald Sanders, *Bible Studies in Matthew's Gospel* (Grand Rapids: Zondervan, 1973), 62; R. V. G. Tasker, *The Gospel According to St. Matthew,* Tyndale New Testament Commentaries (Grand Rapids: Eerdmans, 1977), 109. Also see Johannes Schneider, "σταυρός," in *Theological Dictionary of the New Testament* 7 (1971): 578, item b.

4. Marshall, *The Gospel of Luke,* 373. However, Hengel has observed, "It is striking that the metaphorical terminology is limited to the Latin sphere, whereas in the Greek world the cross is never, so far as I can see, used in a metaphorical sense. Presumably the word was too offensive for it to be used as a metaphor by the Greeks" (Martin Hengel, *Crucifixion in the Ancient World and the Folly of the Cross* [Philadelphia: Fortress, 1977], 68). Thus an interpretation based on the saying as a metaphor seems unlikely.

5. Sanders, *Matthew's Gospel,* 62. Also see Schneider, "σταυρός," 7:579. Buttrick is poetic: "The cross is the plucking off of poor buds that one fine bud may come to flower; it is the pruning of the tree that there may be an abundant harvest" (Buttrick, "The Gospel According to St. Matthew," in *The Interpreter's Bible,* 7:375, see also 7:455); cf. David Hill, *The Gospel of Matthew,* New Century Bible Commentary (Grand Rapids: Eerdmans, 1981), 195; and Leon Morris, *The Gospel According to St. Luke,* Tyndale New Testament Commentaries (Grand Rapids: Eerdmans, 1974), 170.

6. Perhaps the best-known modern proponent of this view is Dietrich Bonhoeffer, who wrote, "the cross (for a disciple) means rejection and shame as well as suffering," and "if we refuse to take up our cross and submit to suffering and rejection at the hands of men, we forfeit our fellowship with Christ and have ceased to follow him." Indeed "the cross is triumph over suffering" (*The Cost of Discipleship,* trans. R. H. Fuller, rev. ed. [London: SCM, 1959], 77–81). Bultmann has suggested that σταυρός (cross) might have been "a traditional metaphor for suffering and sacrifice" (cited in Schneider, "σταυρός," 7 [1971]: 578, n. 51). Colin Brown says, "for Jesus the inevitable implications of being the Christ is suffering, death, and opposition of men. Inevitably, therefore, those who associate with him as the Christ are liable to the same facts" ("Cross," in *New International Dictionary of New Testament Theology,* 4 vols., 1 [1975]: 404). Lane presents an interesting theological speculation when he states "suffering with the Messiah is the condition of glorification with Him" (William L. Lane, *Mark,* 308). Hendriksen sees the disciples' cross as a "voluntary and decisive accepting of pain, shame and persecution" (William

Hendriksen, *Exposition of the Gospel According to Mark,* New Testament Commentary [Grand Rapids: Baker, 1975], 330). Other supporters of the suffering view are Albert Barnes, *Barnes' Notes on the New Testament* (Grand Rapids: Kregel, 1962), 51; John Calvin, *Institutes of the Christian Religion,* trans. Fred Lewis Battles, 2 vols. (Philadelphia: Westminster, 1960), 3.8.1–2 (1:765–67); Fletcher, "Condemned to Die," 159; Geldenhuys, *Luke,* 276; R. C. H. Lenski, *The Interpretation of St. Mark's Gospel* (Minneapolis: Augsburg Publishing House, 1961), 417; Morris, *The Cross,* 392–93; Burghard Siede, "Cross," *New International Dictionary of New Testament Theology,* 1:389–91; Ray Stedman, *The Servant Who Rules* (Waco, Tex.: Word, 1976), 215; Tertullian, "On Idolatry," in *The Anti-Nicene Fathers,* ed. Alexander Roberts and James Donaldson (Grand Rapids: Eerdmans), 3 (1976): 68. Martin Luther commented, "In a word, a Christian, just because he is a Christian, . . . must suffer either at the hands of men or from the devil himself, who plagues and terrifies him with tribulation, persecution, poverty, and sickness, or within the heart, with his poisonous darts" (cited in Ewald M. Plass, *What Luther Says: An Anthology,* 3 vols. [St. Louis: Concordia, 1959], 1:229).

7. Schneider, "σταυρός," 7:580.
8. Sherman E. Johnson, *A Commentary on the Gospel According to St. Mark,* Harper's New Testament Commentaries (New York: Harper & Brothers, 1960), 151.
9. Schneider, "σταυρός," 7:578.
10. Ibid., 578, n. 48.
11. Ibid., 578, n. 49.
12. Ibid., 579.
13. *The Midrash Rabbah* 56:3, vol. 1, *Genesis,* trans. H. Freedman and Maurice Simon, 10 vols. (Oxford: Oxford University Press, n.d.), 493. This translation is somewhat different from the one noted by Brandenburger: "Abraham took the wood for sacrifice and laid it on his son Isaac, like one who bears the cross on his shoulders" (Egon Brandenburger, "Cross," in *New International Dictionary of New Testament Theology* 1:403). Cf. Marshall, *The Gospel of Luke,* 374, and Gustaf Dalman, *Jesus-Jeshua Studies in the Gospels,* trans. Paul P. Levertoff (London: S.P.C.K., 1929), 191–92.
14. Bonhoeffer, *The Cost of Discipleship,* 76. Bonhoeffer's interpretation, however, is the suffering view.
15. Schneider, "σταυρός," 7:578, item c.
16. Marshal, *Gospel of Luke,* 373; and Brandenburger, "Cross," 1:403.
17. A. B. Bruce, *The Training of the Twelve* (reprint, Grand Rapids: Kregel, 1974), 183. However, Bruce's interpretation of crossbearing represents "troubles"; thus it is a minor variation of the suffering view.

18. Hans-Ruedi Weber, *The Cross: Tradition and Interpretation,* trans. Elke Jessett (Grand Rapids: Eerdmans, 1980), 123. Chrysostom, commenting on Matthew 16:24, said, "it will be impossible for thee even to be saved, unless thou thyself too be continually prepared for death" (Chrysostom, "Homily 55 on Matt. 16:24," in *Nicene and Post-Nicene Fathers,* ed. Philip Schaff [reprint, Grand Rapids: Eerdmans, 1978], 10:338). Morris comments that "salvation comes from faith . . . an attitude of wholehearted trust" as seen in the crossbearing invitation (*The Cross,* 102).

19. Morris, *The Cross,* 393.

20. J. Gwyn Griffiths, "The Disciple's Cross," *New Testament Studies* 16 (July 1970): 364.

21. Morris, *The Cross,* 393.

22. Matthew 16:21 and Mark 8:31 are quite forceful on the central issue of being submissive to the Father's will through the use of δεῖ, "it is necessary, one must, one has to" (William F. Arndt and F. Wilbur Gingrich, *A Greek-English Lexicon of the New Testament and Other Early Christian Literature,* 4th rev. ed. [Chicago: University of Chicago Press, 1957], 171). This term refers to a "necessity beyond human comprehension, grounded in the will of God" (Cranfield, *Mark,* 272). Cranfield suggests that δει" here probably refers to Scriptures such as Psalms 22; 118:10, 13, 18, 22; Isaiah 52:13–53:12; Daniel 7:21, 25; and Zechariah 13:7. However, Bennett seeks to refute this view and understands δεῖ as "a circumlocution which carries the weight of 'God has willed it'" (W. J. Bennett Jr., "The Son of Man Must . . . ," *Novum Testamentum* 17 [April 1975]: 128); he further links δεῖ with γέγραπται in Mark 9:12 as being synonymous circumlocutions for "God wills it," as part of a general "eschatological drama" (128–29). In either event the divine necessity is clear enough, and Jesus' concern is not that Peter was dissuading Him from suffering but that Peter was seeking to dissuade Him from obeying the Father's will.

23. "The blistering severity of Jesus' reply is evidence enough that what is at stake is a matter of quite central importance" (D. E. Nineham, *The Gospel of St. Mark,* Pelican New Testament Commentaries [New York: Penguin, 197], 225).

24. The question of whether crossbearing is soteriological is of great importance. The context in Mark seems to favor quite strongly a postsalvation situation, the view held by this author. For a helpful argument that the verb ἀκολουθέω does not connote salvation and that not every μάθητης is a believer, see David Rae Kelly, "The Relation between *Akoloutheo* and Discipleship in Luke's Gospel" (Th.M. thesis, Dallas Theological Seminary, May 1979). Donald R. DeBoer holds that in Mark "an equation of discipleship and salvation seems impossible" ("Salvation and Discipleship in Mark" [Th.M. thesis, Dallas Theological Seminary, July 1979], 28).

25. Heinrich Seesemann, "ὀπίσω," in *Theological Dictionary of the New Testament* 5 (1967): 291.
26. Arndt and Gingrich, *Greek-English Lexicon,* 30. However, the United Bible Societies text here uses ἀκολουθέω. Neither reading affects the interpretation of crossbearing. When it refers to individuals, it "is always the call to decisive and intimate discipleship of the earthly Jesus" (C. Blendinger, "Disciple," in *New International Dictionary of New Testament Theology,* 1: 482; cf. Gerhard Kittel, "ἀκολουθέω," in *Theological Dictionary of the New Testament* 1 [1964]: 210–15, es214). In contrast Lane sees this term as a reference to "the common commitment to Jesus which distinguishes all Christians from those who fail to recognize him as God's appointed Savior" (Lane, *Mark,* 307).
27. Arndt and Gingrich, *Greek-English Lexicon,* 80.
28. Such an attempt would ultimately be futile unless one were first regenerated. The verbs ἀπαρνησάσθω (deny) and ἀράτω (take up) are both aorist imperatives and probably are best understood as ingressive aorists.
29. Proponents of the submission view are practically nonexistent. One who comes close is Vincent Taylor, who sees "to take up your cross" as meaning "to accept the last consequences of obedience . . . the cross as an instrument of death" (*The Gospel According to St. Mark* [Grand Rapids: Baker, 1981], 381). He thus holds to a combination of the obedience and martyrdom views. It should be noted here that the submission view should not be understood to mean that the believer will not suffer for his faith in Christ. The Scriptures make this clear. Jesus was not advocating asceticism or saying that enduring pain, grief, suffering, or even death are the way to follow Him. One's cross is not essentially any of these. A disciple is one who has ceased rebelling against the rule of the King and who is actively and continually submitting himself to His rule.
    F. J. Taylor makes an almost unprecedented statement when, after describing crossbearing as an act of suffering, humility, and shame (he thus holds to the suffering view), he says, "to the Jew it was the public demonstration of servitude to the Roman overlord" ("Cross," in *A Theological Word Book of the Bible,* 57, n. 23). This observation supports the submission interpretation. The only obedience proponent found by this student is J. Dwight Pentecost. He writes, "An individual's cross is the revealed will of God for him" (*The Words and Works of Jesus Christ* [Grand Rapids: Zondervan, 1981], 196), and to take up one's cross is to "accept God's will" for his life (272).
    Pentecost stands alone (among scores of interpreters surveyed) in holding to the submission-to-God's-will view and in never mixing in even a little of the suffering or self-denial views. Some would

add Lane to this list, for on Mark 8:34 he urges "a sustained willingness to say 'No' to oneself in order to be able to say 'Yes' to God" (Lane, *Mark,* 307). This certainly sounds like the submission view of crossbearing, and it would be if Lane were describing crossbearing, but he is not. The quotation above is a description of "the central thought in self-denial." On the next page Lane describes crossbearing as a "commitment" that "permitted no turning back, and if necessary, a willingness to submit to the cross in pursuance of the will of God" (308). Thus Lane's interpretation of crossbearing is potential martyrdom or the commitment necessary to fulfill denying self.

30. Morris, *The Cross,* 293.
31. G. Campbell Morgan, *The Bible and the Cross* (New York: Revell, 1909), 93.
32. John Murray, *Redemption, Accomplished and Applied* (Grand Rapids: Eerdmans, 1955), 19. For a discussion of the righteousness of Christ being composed of passive obedience and active obedience see Charles Hodge, *Systematic Theology,* 3 vols. (reprint, Grand Rapids: Eerdmans, 1979), 142–43.
33. Murray, "Atonement," in *Encyclopedia of Christianity* 1:467.
34. Schneider, "σταυρός," 7:575.
35. Many writers seek to understand this event in terms of similar pagan or even Jewish analogies. For an excellent refutation of these interpretations see Hengel, *The Atonement,* trans. John Bowden (Philadelphia: Fortress, 1981).
36. Brooke Foss Westcott, *The Epistle to the Hebrews* (1892; reprint, Grand Rapids: Eerdmans, n.d.), 128. F. F. Bruce comments: "We know the sense in which the words are true of us; we learn to be obedient because of the unpleasant consequences which follow disobedience. It was not so with Him: He set out from the start on the path of obedience to God, and learned by the sufferings which came His way in consequence just what obedience to God involved in practice in the conditions of human life on earth" (*The Epistle to the Hebrews,* New International Commentary on the New Testament [Grand Rapids: Eerdmans, 1964], 103).
37. Calvin, *Institutes,* 3.8.2 (1:766–67).
38. Hengel, *Crucifixion,* 22–23. For a full listing of classical sources consulted see Green, "Crossbearing in Mark 8," 62–65.
39. Hengel, *Crucifixion,* 23.
40. Schneider, "σταυρός," 7:573.
41. Hengel, *Crucifixion,* 76.
42. Plutarch *Moralia* 554B.
43. Chariton, cited by Hengel, *Crucifixion,* 82 (italics added).
44. Hengel, *Crucifixion,* 82.
45. The *crux* was the foremost of the Roman *summa supplicia* (supreme penalties). The other two were *crematio* (burning) and *decollatio*

(decapitation); cf. Hengel, *Crucifixion,* 23. There was also death by the beasts as well as other forms, often depending on the local situation.

46. F. F. Bruce, *New Testament History* , 201.
47. Hengel, *Crucifixion,* 83. Hengel also gives a specific listing of crimes punished by crucifixion: "desertion to the enemy, the betraying of secrets, incitement to rebellion, murder, prophecy about the welfare of rulers *(de salute dominorum),* nocturnal impiety *(sacra impia nocturnal),* magic *(ars magica),* serious cases of falsification of wills, etc."
48. Ibid., 88. In general the crucifixion of a Roman citizen was prohibited. Though a few exceptions occurred, they always were met with public indignation (D. G. Burke, "Cross," in *International Standard Bible Encyclopedia,* 1 [1979]: 828). For a stirring statement of a Roman citizen's attitude on crucifixion consider Cicero: "Even if we are threatened with death, we may die free men. But the executioner, the veiling of the head, and the very word 'cross' should be far removed not only from the person of a Roman citizen but from his thoughts, his eyes, and ears. For it is not only the actual occurrence of these things or the endurance of them, but liability to them, the expectation, nay, the mere mention of them, that is unworthy of a Roman citizen and a free man" (Cicero *In Defense of Rabirius* 5.16, trans. H. Grose Hodge, in Cicero *The Speeches,* Loeb Classical Library [New York: Putnam's Sons, 1927]).
49. Tacitus *The Annals* 14.42–45. See also Seneca the Elder *Controversiae* 7.6, which illustrates the submission-rebellion theme present in crucifixion.
50. Hengel, *Crucifixion,* 49.
51. Schneider, "σταυρός," 7:573
52. E. Benz, "Der gekreuzigte Gerechte bie Plato, im NT v. in d. Alten Kirche," *AA Mainz* (1950): 1055, cited by Schneider, "σταυρός," 7:574, n. 21.
53. Brandenburger, "Cross," 1:392.
54. Ibid.
55. Hengel, *Crucifixion,* 87.
56. Schneider, "σταυρός," 7:547.
57. Ibid., 573. For an example of this see Dio *Roman History* 54.3.7. Sometimes the tablet was carried by a herald who preceded the offender.
58. For a detailed description of an actual crucified man see J. H. Charlesworth, "Jesus and Jehohanan: An Archaeological Note on Crucifixion," *Expository Times* 74 (February 1973): 147–50; and N. Haas, "Anthropological Observations on the Skeletal Remains from Giv'at Hamiutar," *Israel Exploration Journal* 20 (1970): 38–59.
59. Most encyclopedias list the types of crosses employed. Hengel has

an important observation: "In view of the evidence from antiquity, it is incomprehensible that some scholars could have stated recently that crucifixion was 'by nature a bloodless form of execution'" (Hengel, *Crucifixion*, 31). For a description of the medical cause of death, see H. L. Drumwright, "Crucifixion," in *Zondervan Pictorial Encyclopedia of the Bible* 1:1041.

60. See Hengel, *Crucifixion*, 84. Also see 1 Corinthians 1:23 and Galatians 5:11.

61. Hengel, *Crucifixion*, 84 (citation of conclusion recorded by Y. Yadin).

62. Brandenburger, "Cross," 1:403.

63. Fletcher states that "crossbearing was not a Jewish metaphor" ("Condemned to Die," 162). Dalmon notes that "the figurative application of this expression is in rabbinic literature without example" (*Jesus-Jeshua Studies*, 191). However, a rabbinic example does exist (the Abrahamic-parallel view).

64. Harold W. Hoehner, *Chronological Aspects of the Life of Christ* (Grand Rapids: Zondervan, 1977), 143. The revolt at Sepphoris has been made well known largely through Barclay's commentary on Luke 9:23–27. He incorrectly says that Jesus was 11 years old when this happened; actually He was one year old (Barclay, *The Gospel of Luke* [Philadelphia: Westminster, 1956], 122).

65. *Student Map Manual and Historical Geography of the Bible Lands*, map 13-5. Four miles is a straight line distance on a "line of communication" shown on this map. The distance is also given as seven miles, apparently from a reference in *The Macmillan Bible Atlas* (New York: Macmillan, 1968), 142.

66. See Josephus *The Antiquities of the Jews* 17.10.5–10 and *The Jewish War*, 2.4.1–2. Varus was in Syria from 6 B.C. to 4 B.C. and died in A.D. 9 in Germany.

67. Hengel, *Crucifixion*, 85.

68. J. J. Blinzier, *Der Prozess Jesu* (1960): 269, cited by Schneider, "σταυρός," 7:574, n. 22.

69. See Matthew 27:48 and Luke 23:36, which record one of the soldiers offering Jesus the drink.

Chapter 6—Encountering God at Bethel

1. The critical analysis of this passage is rather complex. Long says that J is partially preserved in verses 10, 13, 15, 16, and 19 but that it is now overlaid and dominated by E in verses 11, 12, 17, 18, and 20–22 (Burke O. Long, *The Problem of Etiological Narrative in the Old Testament* [Berlin: Topelmann, 1968], 60). Von Rad's combination is different. He argues that verses 16 and 17 are parallel, as are 19a and 22a, and he then takes verses 13–16 and 19 as J and verses 10–12, and 17–22 (except 19) as E (Gerhard von Rad, *Genesis* [Philadelphia: Westminster, 1961], 278). According to von Rad only J contains the etymological formula

on the name. Even if a case could be made convincingly for these sources and if there was agreement on the divisions, one would still be left with the difficulties and tensions in the final, fixed form of the text. All the ideas in the story were apparently understood as a unified tradition of the founding of Bethel. Moreover, the literary design of the account bolsters its unity. The problem of the parallel passage in Genesis 35 could then also be understood as a stylistic device of confirmation and recapitulation.

2. The author is indebted to Fokkelman's discussion of the basic ideas about the literary features of this passage (J. P. Fokkelman, *Narrative Art in Genesis* (Assen: Van Gorcum, 1975], 65–81.

3. Michael Fishbane, *Text and Texture* (New York: Schocken, 1979), 53–54.

4. C. Houtman, "Jacob at Mahanaim: Some Remarks on Genesis 32:2–3," *Vetus Testamentum* 28 (1978): 39. See also Fokkelman, *Narrative Art,* 198. Fishbane adds that מַלְאָךְ is a theme word in chapter 32, referring to both the angels of God and the messengers sent to Esau (*Text and Texture,* 54).

5. Westermann develops the idea of these liturgical acts that belong to Jacob exclusively (Claus Westermann, *The Promises to the Fathers,* trans. David E. Green [Philadelphia: Fortress, 1980,] 90).

6. Ibid., 85.

7. Derek Kidner, *Genesis* (Chicago: InterVarsity, 1967), 155.

8. The effect of this gracious revelation in Genesis 28 appears to have had just such an effect. In 29:1 the text says, "And Jacob picked up his feet and went." In other words, with this assurance from God, Jacob had a new gait in his steps.

9. The verb פָּגַע adds to the note of casualness. It means "to encounter, meet." Fokkelman translates it "he struck upon" a place (*Narrative Art,* 48).

10. It is unlikely that a stone large enough to be a pillar should be a pillow. The word signifies what is at the head. It is used in 1 Samuel 26:7 in the same way: Saul lay sleeping within the trench, with his spear stuck in the ground "at his head."

11. Fokkelman, *Narrative Art,* 51–52. The King James Version, of course, uses "behold" in all three place, as does the *New American Standard Bible.* The *New International Version* has not reflected the impact of הִנֵּה by translating the verses, "He had a dream in which he saw a stairway resting on the earth, with its top reaching to heaven, and the angels of God were ascending and descending on it. There above it stood the Lord."

12. It is interesting to note that the next chapter uses הִנֵּה in a similar way. It first introduces the setting, "there is a well in the field" (29:2); then the participants, "and oh, there are three flocks of sheep lying by it" (29:2); and then the focus of the story, "and look, Rachel his daughter is coming with the sheep" (29:6). By the repetition of this pattern the narrative shows a direct

correspondence between the sections, the second being the beginning of the outworking of the first.

13. Some of these are a temple tower with a pathway winding around it, a tower with a stairlike entrance, and a staircase leading into a palace; see C. Houtman, "What Did Jacob See in His Dream at Bethel?" *Vetus Testamentum* 27 (1977): 337–52; A. Henderson, "On Jacob's Vision at Bethel," *Expository Times* 4 (1982): 151; C. A. Keller, "Über einige alttestamentlichen Heiligtumslegenden I," *Zeitschrift für die alttestamentliche Wissenschaft* 67 (1955): 141–68.

14. The connection between סֻלָּם and *simmiltu* involves a metathesis; see Sabatino Moscati, *An Introduction to the Comparative Grammar of the Semitic Languages* (Wiesbaden: Harrassowitz, 1964), 63.

15. The view was first presented by Landsberger, "Lexikalisches Archiv," *Zeitschrift für Assyriologie und vorderasiatische Archäologie* 41 (1933): 230; it is discussed briefly in Harold R. Cohen, *Biblical Hapax Legomena in the Light of Akkadian and Ugaritic* (Missoula, Mont.: Scholars, 1978), 34. For the relevant texts see O. R. Gurney, "The Myth of Nergal and Ereshkigal," *Anatolian Studies* 10 (1960): 105–31; and "Nergal and Ereshkigal— Additions," in *Ancient Near Eastern Texts Relating to the Old Testament,* ed. James B. Pritchard, 3d ed. (Princeton, N.J.: Princeton University Press, 1969): 507–12.

16. J. G. Griffiths, "The Celestial Ladder and the Gate of Heaven (Gen. 28:12, 17)," *Expository Times* 76 (1964/65): 229–30; and "The Celestial Ladder and the Gate of Heaven in Egyptian Ritual," *Expository Times* 78 (1966/67): 54–55.

17. A. R. Millard, "The Celestial Ladder and the Gate of Heaven (Gen. 28:12, 17)," *Expository Times* 78 (1966/67): 86–87.

18. If there is an implied connection to the ziggurat here, then this passage forms an antithesis to the story of the tower of Babel in Genesis, which also has a Mesopotamian background. Comparing the two passages one could say that if there is communication between heaven and earth it is initiated in heaven (Gen. 28) and not on earth (Gen. 11).

19. Christ compared Himself to the stairway in John 1:51: "and the angels of God ascending and descending on the Son of Man." He is the Mediator between heaven and earth: He is the Way to God.

20. S. R. Driver, *The Book of Genesis* (London: Methuen, 1904), 265.

21. The prepositional phrase can be translated "over it" or "beside it" or "beside him." The use in Genesis 18:1 suggests "beside him," but the context here suggests "over it" because God's realm is in the heavens and because Jacob anointed the top of the stone.

22. The purpose of the *casus pendens* is to throw the independent nominative to the beginning for emphasis.

23. Fokkelman observes what he calls a sound fusion, a melting of consonants in the transition: כְּעֵפֶר הָאָרֶץ is followed by וּפָרַצְתָּ; the letters פ-ר-צ out of the prepositional phrase become the verb. He says, "The levels of sound and meaning have become integrated: they point to each other, they explain each other, they pervade each other" (*Narrative Art*, 59).

24. One clear example of this is Genesis 31:24, which records how God warned Laban in a dream not to harm Jacob (see also v. 29).

25. George Bush, *Notes on Genesis*, 2 vols. (New York: Ivision and Phinney, 1860), 2:109.

26. C. F. Graesser, "Standing Stones in Ancient Palestine," *Biblical Archaeologist* 35 (1972): 34–63.

27. The shrine later became the place of corrupt, idolatrous worship (2 Kings 12, 28–29). Hosea alluded to this passage but altered the name by a wordplay from בֵּית־אֵל to בֵּית־אָוֶן, "house of vanity" (i.e., idols, Hos. 4:15). Amos 5:5 states that "Bethel shall come to nothing" (i.e., be destroyed), but it expresses this with יִהְיֶה לְאָוֶן.

28. Von Rad, *Genesis*, 286.

29. Some biblical passages may suggest "Bethel" could be used as a divine epithet. Jeremiah 48:13 says that "Moab shall be ashamed of Chemosh, as the house of Israel was ashamed of Bethel, their confidence." Zechariah 7:2 could be interpreted to read "Bethel-shar-ezer," a personal name, instead of "the house of the god Sharezer" (see J. Philip Hyatt, "A Neo-Babylonian Parallel to Bethel-šar-eṣer, Zech. 7:2," *Journal of Biblical Literature* 56 [1937]: 387–94; and "The Deity Bethel and the Old Testament," *Journal of the American Oriental Society* 59 [1939]: 81–98). Support for the theophoric element "Bethel" in names comes from Babylonian names like *bit-ili-šēzib* and *bit-ili-šar-uṣur,* as well as some attested in Elephantine: *Bethel-natan, Bethel-nûrî,* and *Anat-bethel.* (See Otto Eissfeldt, "Der Gott Bethel," *Andover Review* [1930]: 20 [reprinted in *Kleine Schriften* I]; Rudolph Kittel, "Der Gott Bet' el," *Journal of Biblical Literature* 44 [1925]: 123–53; Wolf Wilhelm Grafen Baudissin, "El Bet-el [Genesis 31:13; 35:7]," *Beihefte zur Zeitschrift für die alttestamentliche Wissenschaft* 41 [1925]: 1–11; and W. F. Albright, *Archaeology and the Religion of Israel* [Baltimore: Johns Hopkins University Press, 1942], 169–75). In addition, see the list of thirty-two names with this element from Elephantine in Bezalel Porten, *Archives from Elephantine* (Berkeley, Calif.: University of California Press, 1968), 328.

30. Long, *Etiological Narrative*, 60.

31. Many translations begin the apodasis with "then the Lord will become my God," which is equally possible. If God actually promised to be his God in the words of the Abrahamic promises (as in Gen. 17:7), then it would not be something Jacob would be promising to do.

Chapter 7—Reexamining Biblical Worship

1. Robert Webber, *Worship—Old and New* (Grand Rapids: Zondervan, 1982), 11.
2. Ibid., 20.
3. John Calvin, cited by James F. White, "Where the Reformation Was Wrong on Worship," *Christian Century,* October 27, 1982, 1077.
4. Langdon Gilkey, *How the Church Can Minister to the World Without Losing Itself* (New York: Harper & Row, 1964), 108.
5. Leslie B. Flynn, *Worship: Together We Celebrate* (Wheaton, Ill.: Victor, 1983).
6. Justin Martyr, "The First Apology of Justin the Martyr," *Early Christian Fathers,* ed. Cyril Richardson (Philadelphia: Westminster, 1953), 287.
7. Wilfred Funk, *Word Origins and Their Romantic Stories* (New York, Bell, 1960), 257.

Chapter 10—Christlikeness in Ephesians 4:13

1. A. T. Robertson, *Word Pictures in the New Testament,* 6 vols. (Nashville: Broadman, 1931), 4:537.
2. R. C. H. Lenski, *The Interpretation of St. Paul's Epistles to the Galatians, to the Ephesians, and to the Philippians* (Minneapolis: Augsburg, 1961), 533.
3. Markus Barth, *Ephesians: Translation and Commentary on Chapters 4–6,* Anchor Bible (Garden City, N.Y.: Doubleday, 1960), 485.
4. Ibid., 484–96.
5. J. Armitage Robinson, *St. Paul's Epistle to the Ephesians* (London: Macmillan, 1939), 139–40.
6. S. D. F. Salmond, "The Epistle to the Ephesians," in *The Expositor's Greek Testament,* 5 vols. (Grand Rapids: Eerdmans, 1956), 3:332.
7. D. M. Lloyd-Jones, *Christian Unity: An Exposition of Ephesians 4:1 to 16* (Grand Rapids: Baker, 1980), 210.
8. F. F. Bruce, *The Epistle to the Ephesians* (London: Pickering & Inglis, 1961), 87.
9. Lenski, *St. Paul's Epistles,* 535.

Chapter 11—The Christian Life According to Colossians

1. F. F. Bruce, "Colossians," in *International Standard Bible Encyclopedia,* 1 [1979]: 733.
2. Walter Bauer, William F. Arndt, and F. Wilbur Gingrich, *A Greek-English Lexicon of the New Testament and Other Early Christian Literature,* 2d ed., rev. F. Wilbur Gingrich and Frederick W. Danker (Chicago: University of Chicago Press, 1979), 657.
3. "Early Christianity took over from rabbinic Judaism the idea of

transmitting and safeguarding a tradition (the verbs 'receive,' 'accept,' παραλαμβάνω, and 'transmit,' παραδίδωμι, correspond to the rabbinic terms qibbēl and māsar)" (P. O'Brien, *Colossians and Philemon*, Word Biblical Commentary [Dallas: Word, 1982], 105).

4. C. J. Ellicott, *The Epistles of St. Paul*, 2 vols. (Andover, Mass.: Draper, 1884), 2:160.
5. Bauer, Arndt, and Gingrich, *Greek-English Lexicon*, 776.
6. Eduard Lohse, *Colossians and Philemon* (Philadelphia: Fortress, 1971), 94.
7. O'Brien, *Colossians and Philemon*, 109.
8. This is not to advocate that the Colossian heresy was Merkabah mysticism but to provide an example only for comparative purposes to demonstrate the delinquency of syncretism. For a list of opinions on the nature of the heresy see J. J. Gunther, *St. Paul's Opponents and Their Background: A Study of Apocalyptic and Jewish Sectarian Teachings* (Leiden: Brill, 1973), 3–4.
9. Keith Crim, ed., *The Perennial Dictionary of World Religions* (New York: Harper & Row, 1989), 477.
10. Ibid.
11. Ibid.
12. For a discussion of various views see H. Wayne House, "Heresies in the Colossian Church," *Bibliotheca Sacra* 149 (January–March 1992): 45–59.
13. O'Brien, *Colossians and Philemon*, xxxiii–xxxvi.
14. Ἐμβατεύω was employed as a technical term in mystery religions (Bauer, Arndt, and Gingrich, *Greek-English Lexicon*, 253).
15. Herbert Preisker, ἐμβατεύω, in *Theological Dictionary of the New Testament*, 2:536. Reinecker and Rogers suggest, "Perhaps the meaning here is the entering into heavenly spheres as a sort of superspiritual experience" (Fritz Rienecker and Cleon L. Rogers, Jr., *A Linguistic Key to the Greek New Testament* [Grand Rapids: Zondervan, 1980], 576).
16. Ibid.
17. James H. Moulton and George Milligan, *The Vocabulary of the Greek New Testament Illustrated from the Papyri and Other Non-literary Sources* (Grand Rapids: Eerdmans, 1930), 206.
18. O'Brien, *Colossians and Philemon*, 110.
19. Ibid.
20. Παράδοσι is used of "the tradition preserved by the scribes and Pharisees"; cf. Matthew 15:2; and Mark 7:5 (Bauer, Arndt, and Gingrich, *Greek-English Lexicon*, 615).
21. Lohse, *Colossians and Philemon*, 96.
22. Ibid.
23. See Scholem's comments on the origin of Gnosticism from Jewish roots (Gershom C. Scholem, *Jewish Gnosticism, Merkabah*

Mysticism, and Talmudic Tradition [New York: Jewish Theological Seminary of America, 1965], 1–8).
24. O'Brien, *Colossians and Philemon,* 51–52.
25. Ibid., 111.
26. Ibid.
27. Lohse, *Colossians and Philemon,* 100.
28. Bullinger defines the use of root repetition of this sort as "paregmenon" (E. W. Bullinger, *Figures of Speech in the Bible* [1898; reprint, Grand Rapids: Baker, 1968], 304).
29. Πεπληρωμένοι is a "divine passive," that is, no agent is stated; rather the agent of the action is implied and understood to be God.
30. Merrill F. Unger, *The New Unger's Bible Dictionary* (Chicago: Moody, 1988), 238.
31. A. T. Lincoln, *Ephesians,* Word Biblical Commentary (Dallas: Word, 1990), 136.
32. Lohse, *Colossians and Philemon,* 103.
33. O'Brien, *Colossians and Philemon,* 124.
34. Ibid.
35. Lohse, *Colossians and Philemon,* 112.
36. O'Brien, *Colossians and Philemon,* 165.
37. Bauer, Arndt, and Gingrich, *Greek-English Lexicon,* 501.
38. Lohse, *Colossians and Philemon,* 137.
39. O'Brien, *Colossians and Philemon,* 179.
40. Lohse, *Colossians and Philemon,* 140.
41. Bauer, Arndt, and Gingrich, *Greek-English Lexicon,* 101.
42. Buist M. Fanning, *Verbal Aspect in New Testament Greek* (Oxford: Clarendon, 1990), 363.
43. O'Brien, *Colossians and Philemon,* 186.
44. Ibid., 192.
45. Lohse, *Colossians and Philemon,* 146.
46. The phrase τοῦ Χριστοῦ may be a subjective genitive, implying that Christ is the One who brings peace to believers.
47. O'Brien, *Colossians and Philemon,* 215.
48. Lincoln, *Ephesians,* 398–99.
49. Ibid.
50. Ibid., 341.

Chapter 12—Christian Apparel in Colossians 3:5–17

1. P. T. Forsyth, *Lectures on the Church and the Sacraments* (New York: Longmans, Green, 1917), 61.
2. C. F. D. Moule, *The Epistles of Paul the Apostle to the Colossians and to Philemon* (Cambridge: University Press, 1957), 114.
3. F. F. Bruce, *Commentary on the Epistles to the Ephesians and the Colossians* (Grand Rapids: Eerdmans, 1957), 267.
4. This is the sense of the word in its other two occurrences in the New Testament (Rom. 4:19; Heb. 11:12), but the physical body is in view in both places.

5. Considerable discussion has taken place over the sense of τὰ μέλη (your members), the most unusual view being that the noun is a vocative (cf. Charles Masson, *L'Epitre de Saint Paul aux Colossiens* [Neuchatel: Delachaux et Nestle, 1950], 142) and that it refers to the members of the body of Christ, that is, believers. It seems that, by natural extension of meaning, the apostle moved from its usual sense of the bodily members to the products of the body when it becomes the instrument of the sin principle within (cf. Rom. 6:19; 7:23; cf. Bruce, *Commentary,* 267–68).

6. H. C. G. Moule, *The Epistles of Paul the Apostle to the Colossians and Philemon* (Cambridge: University Press, 1894), 121.

7. C. F. D. Moule, *The Epistles of Paul,* 117.

8. Ibid.

9. It is not sufficiently realized that the present prohibition, that is, the present imperative and μή, is not always to be translated by the use of the word "stop." Surely the sense of 3 John 11, in the light of the context, is not "stop following evil." The prohibition rather refers to the resistance of action not yet going on but which might conceivably begin and continue! The habit is forbidden. Even more certain is it that μὴ χωλύετε in 1 Corinthians 14:39 is not to be rendered, "stop forbidding to speak in tongues." The Corinthians were in no danger on that score. But in the light of the Pauline exaltation of prophecy at the expense of tongues, they might now be tempted to hinder the exercise of the gift, to hinder the habit. Robertson and Plummer are correct in suggesting this rendering, "Do not, in consequence of what I have said, attempt to hinder . . ." (Archibald Robertson and Alfred Plummer, A *Critical and Exegetical Commentary on the First Epistle of St. Paul to the Corinthians,* International Critical Commentary [Edinburgh: Clark, 1914], 328): The more recent grammars have frequently omitted discussion of this rare but well established usage (cf. 1 Tim. 4:14; 5:22).

10. Forsyth, *The Person and Place of Jesus Christ* (Boston: Pilgrim, 1909), 4.

11. Bruce, *Commentary,* 272.

12. Bauer has *"ausziehen"* (Walter Bauer, *Griechisch-Deutsches Wörterbuch,* col. 165). The middle may add the sense of "to strip off from oneself" as if the believer was hopelessly entangled in the clutches of the old man before he came to Christ (G. Abbott-Smith, *A Manual Greek Lexicon of the New Testament* [Edinburgh: Clark, 1937], 46).

13. W. R. Nicholson, *Oneness with Christ* (Grand Rapids: Kregel, 1903), 228.

14. C. F. D. Moule, *The Epistles of Paul,* 119.

15. Christ is called the last Adam because if He had failed, there would have been no other. He, of course, is the Second Man, because there are other men, believers, who share His destiny. As

usual, Paul's terminology in its most minute details is instructive (cf. 1 Cor. 15:45–47).
16. It is difficult to be sure about the gender of the ἐν πᾶσιν (in all). The preceding neuter argues for the neuter here. But the parallel in Galatians 3:28 argues for the masculine. Perhaps it is simply an emphatic way of saying that Christ is everything (cf. 1 Cor. 15:28). The decision is difficult, but with no sense of dogmatism this writer prefers the masculine.
17. John Baillie, *The Sense of the Presence of God* (New York: Scribners, 1962), 237.
18. C. F. D. Moule, *The Epistles of Paul*, 124. If there existed evidence of σύνδσμος in the sense of "the girdle" as an article of clothing, the sense would be that love holds the other graces in their place. The word does refer to a ligament of the body in 2:19 and a ligament is such a bond, but as an article of clothing the word has not been found.
19. J. B. Lightfoot, *Saint Paul's Epistles to the Colossians and to Philemon* (1875; reprint, Grand Rapids: Zondervan, 1959), 221. Bauer has *"Schiedsrichter sein,"* to be an arbitrator (*Griechisch-Deutsches Wörterbuch,* col. 290). The word occurs in a compound in 2:18 and there is rendered "beguile of reward" (KJV).
20. Bruce refers to Tertullian's description of a Christian agapē as evidence for the practice of teaching through psalms and hymns in the meetings of the churches (*Commentary,* 284; Tertullian, *Apology,* 39).
21. Lightfoot, *Saint Paul's Epistles,* 222.
22. George Goodman, *I Live; Yet Not I,* 84–85.

Chapter 13—Sarah As a Model for Christian Wives (1 Peter 3:5–6)

1. Wayne Grudem, *1 Peter,* Tyndale New Testament Commentaries (Grand Rapids: Eerdmans, 1988), 141.
2. Ernest Best, *1 Peter,* New Century Bible (London: Oliphants, 1971), 126.
3. J. Ramsey Michaels, *1 Peter,* Word Biblical Commentary (Waco, Tex.: Word, 1988), 163–64.
4. Edward Gordon Selwyn, *The First Epistle of St. Peter* (London: Macmillan, 1946), 185.
5. The present active participle indicates a consistent quality.
6. D. Edmond Hiebert, *First Peter* (Chicago: Moody, 1984), 189.
7. Peter H. Davids, *The First Epistle of Peter,* New International Commentary on the New Testament (Grand Rapids: Eerdmans, 1990), 120.
8. Grudem, *1 Peter,* 141.
9. Michaels, *1 Peter,* 164.
10. Grudem, *1 Peter,* 141.
11. *Megilla* 15a.
12. *Baba Meṣa* 87a.

13. *JW* is often used to introduce a concrete example (Walter Bauer, William F. Arndt, and F. Wilbur Gingrich, *A Greek-English Lexicon of the New Testament and Other Early Christian Literature*, 2d ed., rev. F. Wilbur Gingrich and Frederick W. Danker [Chicago: University of Chicago Press, 1973], 906).

14. Ibid., 845.

15. Michaels, *1 Peter*, 165.

16. Francis W. Beare, *The First Epistle of Peter* (Oxford: Blackwell, 1947), 130.

17. Michaels, *1 Peter*, 164.

18. Dorothy I. Sly, "1 Peter 3:6b in Light of Philo and Josephus," *Journal of Biblical Literature* 110 (Spring 1991): 129.

19. Robert Johnstone, *The First Epistle of Peter* (1888; reprint, Minneapolis: James Family, 1978), 205.

20. Curtis Vaughn and Thomas D. Lea, *1, 2, Peter, Jude,* Bible Study Commentary (Grand Rapids: Zondervan, 1988), 76; J. W. C. Wand, ed., *The General Epistles of St. Peter and St. Jude* (London: Methuen, 1934), 91; and Hiebert, *1 Peter,* 190.

21. Hiebert, *1 Peter,* 191.

22. Charles Bigg, *A Critical and Exegetical Commentary on the Epistles of St. Peter and St. Jude,* International Critical Commentary (Edinburgh: Clark, 1902), 154.

23. Davids, *The First Epistle of Peter,* 121.

24. Michaels, *1 Peter,* 167.

25. Susan T. Foh, *Women and the Word of God* (Phillipsburg, N.J.: Presbyterian and Reformed, 1979), 185.

26. Mary A. Kassian, *Women, Creation and the Fall* (Westchester, Ill.: Crossway, 1990), 70.

27. Ibid., 73.

28. Beare contends, "The writer can hardly be thinking of anything else than the intimidation that might be attempted by a husband displeased with his wife's new faith" (*The First Epistle of Peter,* 131). Kelly suggests Peter may be thinking of the husband's rough treatment of his wife (*A Commentary on the Epistle of Peter and Jude,* 132).

29. Wand, *St. Peter and St. Jude,* 91; and Bo Reicke, *The Epistles of James, Peter, and Jude,* Anchor Bible (Garden City, N.Y.: Doubleday, 1964), 102.

30. Bigg, *A Critical and Exegetical Commentary,* 154; and Hiebert, *1 Peter,* 191.

31. Michaels, *1 Peter,* 167.

32. Grudem, *1 Peter,* 141.

33. Mark Kiley, "Like Sara: The Tale of Terror behind 1 Peter 3:6," *Journal of Biblical Literature* 106 (December 1987): 692 (italics his).

Chapter 14—Living in the Light of Christ's Return (1 Peter 4:7–11)

1. James Macknight, *A New Literal Translation from the Original Greek of All the Apostolic Epistles* (1821; reprint, Grand Rapids: Baker, 1969), 5:491. So also Jay E. Adams, *Trust And Obey: A Practical Commentary on First Peter* (Phillipsburg, N.J.: Presbyterian & Reformed, 1978), 129–30; Guy N. Woods, *A Commentary on the New Testament Epistles of Peter, John, and Jude* (Nashville: Gospel Advocate, 1954), 111–12.
2. John T. Demarest, *A Translation and Exposition of the First Epistle of the Apostle Peter* (New York: John Moffet, 1851), 224–26.
3. William R. Newell, "The End of All Things Is at Hand," *Bibliotheca Sacra* 109 (July–September 1952): 249.
4. Nathaniel Marshman Williams, "Commentary on the Epistles of Peter," in *An American Commentary on the New Testament* (reprint, Philadelphia: American Baptist, n.d.), 61.
5. John Henry Newman, *Parochial and Plain Sermons* (1896), 241, cited by F. F. Bruce, *The Epistles of John* (Old Tappan, N.J.: Revell, 1970), 65.
6. Bruce, *The Epistles of John*, 65.
7. Charles R. Erdman, *The General Epistles* (1919; reprint, Philadelphia: Westminister, n.d.), 78.
8. C. E. B. Cranfield, *I & II Peter and Jude*, Torch Bible Commentaries (London: SCM, 1960), 113.
9. William F. Arndt and F. Wilbur Gingrich, *A Greek-English Lexicon of the New Testament and Other Early Christian Literature* (Chicago: University of Chicago Press, 1957), 540.
10. F. B. Meyer, *"Tried by Fire": Expositions of the First Epistle of Peter* (London: Morgan & Scott, n.d.), 161.
11. Cranfield, *I & II Peter and Jude*, 57.
12. R. C. H. Lenski, *The Interpretation of the Epistles of St. Peter, St. John and St. Jude* (Minneapolis: Augsburg, 1961), 198.
13. W. E. Vine, *An Expository Dictionary of New Testament Words* (1940; reprint [4 vols. in 1], Westwood, N.J.: Revell., 1966), 4:32.
14. James Moffatt, *The General Epistles, James, Peter, and Judas*. Moffatt New Testament Commentary (London: Hodder & Stoughton, 1947), 153.
15. Robert Young, *The Holy Bible Consisting of the Old and New Covenants Translated according to the Letter and Idioms of the Original Languages* (London: Pickering & Inglis, n.d.).
16. Lenski, *St. Peter, St. John and St. Jude*, 200.
17. Demarest, *Translation and Exposition*, 231.
18. Meyer, *"Tried by Fire,"* 171.
19. Ernest Best, *1 Peter*, New Century Bible (London: Oliphants, 1971), 161.
20. Robert Johnstone, *The First Epistle of Peter: Revised Text, with Introduction and Commentary* (1888; reprint, Minneapolis: James Family, 1978), 351.

Chapter 15—Growth in the Christian Life (2 Peter 1:5–11)

1. J. W. C. Wand, *The General Epistles of St. Peter and St. Jude,* Westminster Commentaries (London: Methuen, 1934), 153.
2. W. Bauder, "σπουδή," in *New International Dictionary of New Testament Theology,* 4 vols., 3:1168–69.
3. James Hope Moulton and George Milligan, *The Vocabulary of the Greek Testament* (London: Hodder and Stoughton, 1952), 492.
4. G. F. C. Fronmueller, "The Second Epistle General of Peter," in *Lange's Commentary on Holy Scripture,* trans. with additions by J. Isidor Mombert (reprint, Grand Rapids: Zondervan, n.d.), 13.
5. Michael Green, *The Second Epistle General of Peter and the General Epistle of Jude,* Tyndale New Testament Commentaries (Downers Grove, Ill.: InterVarsity, 1968), 67.
6. "At the time of the NT the word ἀρετή had so many meanings that it gave rise to misunderstandings" (Otto Beuernfeind, "ἀρετή," in *The Theological Dictionary of the New Testament* 1 [19]: 457).
7. Translations in English versions are as follows: (1) "virtue"—KJV, RSV, NEB, Darby, New Berkeley, Lattey; (2) "excellence"—Rotherham; (3) "moral excellence"—NASB; (4) "worthiness"—R. Young; (5) "goodness"—NIV, 20th Century New Testament, Goodspeed, Jerusalem Bible; (6) "noble character"—Weymouth, Williams; (7) "manliness"—Montgomery; (8) "resolution"—Moffatt; (9) "moral courage"—Kleist and Lilly.
8. Marvin R. Vincent, *Word Studies in the New Testament* (reprint, Grand Rapids: Eerdmans, 1946), 1:679.
9. Albert E. Barnett, "The Second Epistle of Peter," in *The Interpreter's Bible,* ed. George Arthur Buttrick, 12 vols. (New York: Abingdon, 1957), 12:176.
10. Ibid.
11. Green, *Peter and Jude,* 69.
12. Henry Alford, *The Greek Testament,* rev. Everett F. Harrison (reprint [4 vols. in 2], Chicago: Moody, 1958), 4:392.
13. Joseph Bryant Rotherham, *The Emphasized New Testament* (reprint, Grand Rapids: Kregel, 1959).
14. Robert H. Mounce, *A Living Hope: A Commentary on 1 and 2 Peter* (Grand Rapids: Eerdmans, 1982), 110.
15. Nathaniel Marshman Williams, "Commentary on the Epistles of Peter," in *An American Commentary on the New Testament,* ed. Alvah Hovey (1888; reprint, Minneapolis: Klock and Klock, 1978), 381.
16. John Lillie, *Lectures on the First and Second Epistles of Peter* (reprint, Minneapolis: Klock and Klock, 1978), 381.
17. Ray Summers, "2 Peter," in *The Broadman Bible Commentary,* ed. Clifton J. Allen, 12 vols. (Nashville: Broadman, 1972), 12:177.
18. J. R. Lumby, "The Second Epistle General of Peter," in *The Speaker's Commentary,* ed. Frederic Charles Cook, 13 vols. (London: John Murray, 1981), 13:243.

19. Green, *Peter and Jude,* 73–74.
20. Stephen W. Paine, "The Second Epistle of Peter," in *The Wycliffe Bible Commentary,* ed. Charles F. Pfeiffer and Everett F. Harrison (Chicago: Moody, 1962), 1458.
21. H. E. Dana and Julius R. Mantey, *A Manual Grammar of the Greek New Testament* (New York: Macmillan, 1967), 266–67.
22. Green, *Peter and Jude,* 75.
23. Ibid. Green notes that Aristides' *Apology* "becomes a very early witness to the antiquity of this Epistle" (75, n. 1).
24. Mounce, *A Living Hope,* 113.
25. Williams, "Commentary on the Epistles of Peter," 87.

Chapter 16—Fellowship and Confession in 1 John 1:5–10

1. The text commented upon in this article is that of the King James Version.
2. This interpretation has been denied by C. H. Dodd, *The Johannine Epistles* (New York: Harper, 1946), 9–16. His arguments are effectively rebutted by J. R. W. Stott, *The Epistles of John: An Introduction and Commentary* (Grand Rapids: Eerdmans, 1964), 26–34
3. In fact John's pronouns so easily glide back and forth between references to the Father and the Son that it is clear that precise distinctions are out of harmony with his thought. Compare especially 2:28–3:2.
4. Compare, for example, John 14:9–10, 24; 17:8, 14.
5. Cf. Dodd's succinct survey in *The Johannine Epistles,* 18–19.
6. For example in "The Manual of Discipline" there are phrases like "the children of light" and "the children of darkness, "on paths of light he sees but darkness," "the true light of life," and "the spirits of light and darkness." Cf. Theodor H. Gaster, *The Dead Sea Scriptures: An English Translation with Introduction and Notes,* rev. and enlarged ed. (Garden City, N.Y.: Anchor, 1964), 46, 49–51.
7. This, however has nevertheless been done. In *Love Is Now* (Grand Rapids: 1970), Peter E. Gillquist writes, "John in this section writes with a style called the 'editorial we.' By saying 'we' instead of 'you,' he can readily identify with his readers without sounding as though he is preaching at them" (62). But this is inaccurate and misleading. An "editorial we" is not a "we" used in place of a "you," but a "we" used for an "I." The fact is that the kind of "we" Gillquist wants here has no recognized place in Greek grammar and is without analogy in the New Testament.
8. See Friedrich Hauck "χοινός, κ.τ.λ.," in *Theological Dictionary of the New Testament* 3 (1965): 797–98.
9. Despite the prevalence of the "Christian fellowship" view among modern commentators, R. E. O. White, siding with Augustine and Calvin, is surely right when he says, "Nevertheless it is essential to the coherence of the passage, and to the meaning of the next

phrase, that the idea of fellowship with God who is light remain the fundamental one. John has already emphasized his desire to promote fellowship among Christians, and stressed that this is a common fellowship with the Father: doubtless this motive shapes his language here. To be out of fellowship with God, through sin, is to be out of fellowship with each other, and *vice versa*" (*Open Letter to Evangelicals: A Devotional and Homiletic Commentary on the First Epistle of John* [Grand Rapids: Eerdmans, 1964], 235–36) (italics his).

10. This is certainly the most natural way to read the text with the verbs ἔχομεν and χαθαρίζει forming a compound apodosis for the conditional sentence. The other option, to place a major mark of punctuation after μετ᾽ ἀλλήλων, destroys the rhythm of the passage. (This option is not even offered in the punctuation apparatus of the United Bible Societies edition of the Greek text.)

11. The interpretation that to "have no sin" is a reference to the sin nature cannot be harmonized with John's usage elsewhere of the phrase ἔχειν ἁμαρτίαν. Cf. John 15:22, 24; 19:11. The view given in the text accords fully with these other uses, as well as fitting the immediate context better.

12. Gillquist, *Love Is Now*, 64.

13. The Greek phrase is ὅταν ποοσεύχησθε (Luke 11:2). Of the use of ὅταν with the present subjunction, Arndt and Gingrich point out, "Preferable of (regularly) repeated action *whenever, as often as, every time that* . . ." (William F. Arndt and F. Wilbur Gingrich, *A Greek-English Lexicon of the New Testament and Other Early Christian Literature* [Chicago: University of Chicago Press, 1957], 592 [italics theirs]).

14. Estrangement between the offender and the offended is the lowest common denominator in unforgiven sin, whether on a human or a divine level. Punishment may or may not be involved. On an earthly level when one person extends forgiveness to another, the personal barrier between them is removed and "fellowship" can begin again. In personal relationships the remission of penalty is usually not involved—unless the estrangement itself is regarded as a penalty. Within the family of God the experience of forgiveness may be understood in precisely these terms. Indeed "forgiveness" as extended to a sinning saint may not at all undo the necessary consequences of his failure (cf. the case of David in 2 Sam. 12:13–14), but harmonious relationships with God are always renewed thereby (cf. Ps. 51).

15. The perfect tense of the verb here (ἡμαστήχαμεν) is no objection to this interpretation. The perfect tense is used in reference to specific cases of sin in 2 Corinthians 12:21; 13:2; and James 5:15. The thought of a total denial of sin, as though the person had never done any at all, is not germane to the context and is most certainly not implied merely by the use of a perfect tense.

Rightly Divided

Readings in Biblical Hermeneutics

Roy B. Zuck, gen. ed.

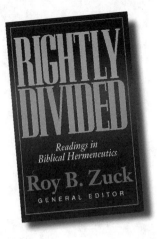

Everyone who studies and teaches the Bible has a responsibility to accurately interpret and communicate God's message. Pastors, Bible teachers, and anyone who studies the Scriptures will appreciate the helpful guidance of this new collection of contemporary and classic scholarship.

Rightly Divided brings together the insights of twenty-one experienced Bible scholars in the field of hermeneutics, providing a basic overview of hermeneutics and addressing specific issues of interpretation. Included are chapters by:

- Darrell L. Bock—"Evangelicals and the Use of the Old Testament in the New"
- G. B. Caird—"Ambiguity in the Bible"
- Norman Geisler—"The Relation of Purpose and Meaning in Interpreting Scripture"
- Walter C. Kaiser, Jr.—"Issues in Contemporary Hermeneutics"
- I. Howard Marshall—"The Holy Spirit and the Interpretation of Scripture"
- J. Robertson McQuilkin—"Identifying the Audience God Intended"
- Bernard Ramm—"The Devotional and Practical Use of the Bible"
- Roy B. Zuck—"The What and Why of Bible Interpretation"

"This compilation of twenty-two chapters introduces readers to a number of issues. I hope this anthology will supplement standard introductory works on hermeneutics by gathering in one volume a variety of helps."

— Roy B. Zuck
Senior Professor of Bible Exposition Emeritus
Dallas Theological Seminary

Available from your local bookseller or

kregel
PUBLICATIONS